TK
7825
.M264
1983

Mandl, Matthew.

Electronics handbook

1903

DATE			
JY 6'84			
FE 1'85			
OC 31 '86			

Electronics Handbook

Electronics Handbook

Matthew Mandl

RESTON PUBLISHING COMPANY, INC.
A Prentice-Hall Company
Reston, Virginia

Library of Congress Cataloging in Publication Data

Mandl, Matthew.
 Electronics handbook.

 Includes index.
 1. Electronics — Handbooks, manuals, etc.
2. Electronic circuits — Handbooks, manuals, etc.
I. Title.
TK7825.M264 1983   621.381   83-3414
ISBN 0-8359-1603-0

©1983 by Reston Publishing Company, Inc.
A Prentice-Hall Company
Reston, Virginia 22090

Printed in the United States of America

Contents

3   Signal Modification, Routing, and Control   101

4   Integrated Circuits   123

8   Transmission Principles   218

9   Fundamental Principles of Instrumentation   239

10 Graphic Symbols of Basic Components 270

11 Complete System Block Diagrams 287

12   Letter Symbols, Acronyms, and Definitions   309

Index   355

Preface

Data Reference Book of Electronics contains a broad coverage of electronic topics ranging from basic concepts to radio, television, communications, and digital circuitry. It is intended as a reference text for all students, technicians, and engineers who need to update their knowledge of the basics of topics unfamiliar or far afield from those in which the reader is actively engaged. Sufficient cross-references are given throughout the text so that associated topics may be consulted when referencing a particular areas. Numerous illustrations and circuit drawings are included to expedite comprehension of operational details.

Chapter 1 is devoted to basic equations most commonly used in electronics. Samples of applications are given in addition to the explanations. Chapter 2 describes and illustrates numerous circuits commonly used in all aspects of electronics, including a variety of amplifiers, detectors, rectifiers, and relaxation oscillators, as well as radio-frequency types. Circuit descriptions are continued in Chapter 3 and involve signal modification, signal routing, and signal control types. Chapter 4 details the factors involving fabrication of integrated circuits, their general characteristics, and the special circuits used in switching and gating.

The various digital-system codes are outlined in Chapter 5 and include tables giving representative comparisons and applications. Digital-circuit logic gates and switches are covered in Chapter 6 and include the basic principles of symbolic logic. Chapter 7 lists more than two dozen tables, including decibel ratios, conversions, measurements, dielectric constants, mathematical symbols, color codes, and similar material.

Chapter 8 describes the fundamental principles of communications. Included are discussions on amplitude modulation, frequency modulation, the combination of AM and FM used in television, as well as pulse code modulation. Chapter 9 is devoted to the fundamental principles of instrumentation, including analog and digital meters as well as those reading decibels and volume units.

Graphic symbols of basic components, plus a description of them, are given in Chapter 10. Included are diodes, silicon-controlled rectifiers, transistors, and the basic symbols used for resistors, capacitors, inductors, switches, and similar components. Chapter 11 illustrates and explains the formation of complete systems, using block diagrams. Included are communications systems (radio, television, etc.), and computers, computerized games, and similar items.

A special feature of this text is Chapter 12, which contains tables listing comprehensive letter abbreviations and definitions of commonly used words and phrases in all branches of electronics. Thus, the reader has ready access to the meaning of letter symbols such as ATC, BIFET, H-MOS, PIA, VCO, and numerous others. Similarly, complete definitions are listed for words such as baud, biquinary, mnemonic, siemens, varactor, and others.

MATTHEW MANDL

Electronics Handbook

1 Basic Equations In Electronics

1-1. OHM'S LAW

The basic equations relating values of current, voltage, and resistance are known as *Ohm's law*. Use of these equations permits the solving of an unknown quantity by utilizing the known values of two other quantities. The basic equation, $I = E/R$, states that the quantity of current in a circuit is equal to the values of electromotive force divided by resistance. The equation $P = EI$ states that the power is equal to the values of electromotive force multiplied by current. The unit value of electromotive force (E) is the volt (V); for current (I) it is the ampere (A); and for resistance (R) it is the ohm (Ω). Multiple or fractional values may be encountered as well as basic unit values. Thus, if $E = 5$ V and $I = 2$ A, the power (P) $= 2 \times 5 = 10$ W. Had the voltage been 5 kilovolts (5 kV), the power would have been 10 kW. Similarly, if E is 0.2 μV and I is 100 mA, the power is $0.2 \times 10^{-6} \times 100 \times 10^{-3} = 0.02$ μW.

The four quantities (E, I, R, and P) can be rearranged to find any unknown quantity. Thus, the various relationships can be shown in a wheel arrangement as shown in Figure 1–1(A) for dc or ac (with no phase shifting) or as in (B) for ac exclusively. Thus, voltage can be found by the following:

$$E = IR \quad \text{or} \quad \frac{P}{I} \quad \text{or} \quad \sqrt{PR} \tag{1-1}$$

1

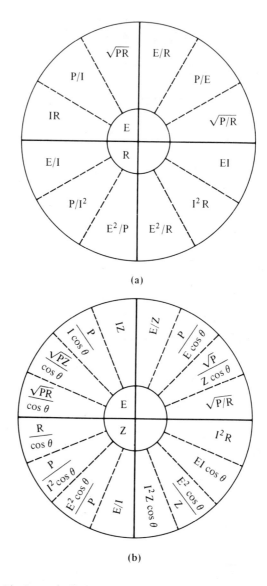

(a)

(b)

Figure 1–1 Ohm's Law Wheels

Hence, if current has a value of 2 A and resistance 300 Ω, the voltage is 600. Had the current been 5 mA and the resistance 20 kΩ, the voltage would be 100 (0.005 × 20,000). If the power is 60 W and the current is 2 A, the voltage is 30 (60/2). As another example, if the power is 2 W and the resistance 8 Ω, the voltage is 4, since $2 \times 8 = 16$, of which the square root is 4.

Knowing the values of voltage, resistance, and power, we can solve for current using the following equations:

$$I = \frac{E}{R} \quad \text{or} \quad \frac{P}{E} \quad \text{or} \quad \sqrt{\frac{P}{R}} \tag{1-2}$$

Thus, if the voltage is 260 and the resistance is 13,000 Ω, the current is 0.02 A. Similarly, if the power is 75 W and voltage is 5, the current is 15 A. For solving resistance values the following equations apply:

$$R = \frac{E}{I} \quad \text{or} \quad \frac{E^2}{P} \quad \text{or} \quad \frac{P}{I^2} \tag{1-3}$$

As in previous examples, simple calculations solve for the unknown. Thus, if a circuit has 60 V applied and the power dissipated in a resistor is 2 W, the resistance is 1800 Ω, since $60 \times 60 = 3600$ and when the latter is divided by 2 we obtain the resistance.

For dc or ac power (assuming no phase shift between voltage and current) the following equations are useful:

$$P = EI \quad \text{or} \quad I^2R \quad \text{or} \quad \frac{E^2}{R} \tag{1-4}$$

From the foregoing it is indicated that a voltage of 30 multiplied by a current of 0.06 A gives a wattage dissipation of 1.8. Similarly, a current of 0.07 A and a resistance of 2 kΩ would indicate a power dissipation of 9.8 W. For ac the power expressed as EI is also termed the *apparent power* because any phase difference between current and voltage could decrease the power value found by multiplying voltage by current. As shown in Figure 1–1(B), the cosine of the angle must be considered for solving true power, since $P = EI \cos \theta$ (see also Sec. 1–17). When the true power is divided by the apparent power, we solve for the power factor:

$$\text{Power factor} = \frac{\text{true power}}{\text{apparent power}} \tag{1-5}$$

Thus, if we have 2.5 V and 2 A, the apparent power is 2.5 × 2 = 5 W. If the phase angle between voltage and current is 45°, however, the cosine is 0.707 and hence the true power is 2.5 × 2 × 0.707 = 3.5 W. Thus, the power factor (cosine) is 3.5/5 = 0.707.

Thus, when a value of cosine is involved, the true power is always less than the apparent power because of the phase difference between voltage and current. With no phase angle the power factor is 1 (cosine of 0°). With a 90° phase angle the cosine is 0 and hence the product of voltage, current, and 0 is 0. Current can also be related to the quantity of electrons. The charge unit is called the *coulomb* and its symbol is Q. The coulomb is equal to 6.28 × 10^{18} electrons. The rate of flow of a single coulomb in 1 second represents 1 A of current:

$$I = \frac{Q}{t} \qquad\qquad (1\text{–}6)$$

where I is the current in amperes
Q is the quantity of electrons in coulombs
t is the time in seconds

From Eq. 1–6 it is obvious that a current of 105 Q of electron flow past a point in a circuit in 15 seconds = 105/15 = 7 A.

As with the basic Ohm's law, the symbols of current, time, and coulombs can be rearranged as needed:

$$Q = It \qquad\qquad (1\text{–}7)$$

1–2. SERIES AND PARALLEL RESISTANCE

When resistors are placed in series, the total resistance is the sum of individual resistances:

$$R_{\text{total}} = R_1 + R_2 + R_3 + \cdots + R_n \qquad\qquad (1\text{–}8)$$

Thus, if a circuit has three series resistors and the values are 2.5 Ω, 750 Ω, and 2 kΩ, the total resistance by simple addition is 2752.5 Ω. When resistors are in *parallel* the total resistance is always less than the smallest value resistance. To solve for total resistance when *two* parallel resistors are involved, the following equation can be used:

$$\frac{R_1 \cdot R_2}{R_1 + R_2} \qquad (1-9)$$

Thus, for two parallel resistors having values of 2 and 8 Ω, respectively, the total resistance would be 1.6 Ω. When more than two resistors are in parallel the following equation applies:

$$R_{total} = \frac{1}{(1/R_1) + (1/R_2) + (1/R_3) + \cdots + (1/R_n)} \qquad (1-10)$$

Equation 1-10 does, of course, also apply to two resistors. In our previous example of 2 and 8 Ω we obtain 1.6 Ω total. Similarly:

$$\frac{1}{(1/2) + (1/8)} = \frac{1}{(4/8) + (1/8)} = \frac{1}{5/8} = 1.6 \ \Omega$$

1-3. SERIES AND PARALLEL INDUCTORS

When inductors are wired *in series* the total inductance is the sum of all the inductors. If the individual coils are separated sufficiently so that their fields do not interact, the total inductance of series string can be expressed as

$$L_T(\text{in series}) = L_1 + L_g + L_3 + \cdots + L_n \qquad (1-11)$$

When inductors are *in parallel* the total inductance is always less than the smallest-value inductor. Thus, the reciprocal formula is used for finding total inductance, in similar fashion to the equation for solving for total resistance in parallel resistors:

$$L_T(\text{in parallel}) = \frac{1}{(1/L_1) + (1/L_2) + (1/L_3) + \cdots + (1/L_n)} \qquad (1-12)$$

When inductors are coupled sufficiently close so that the magnetic lines of the individual inductors interact with each other, the total inductance for series and parallel inductors is influenced by *mutual inductance* (*M*). The latter also applies to the coupling of primary and secondary windings in transformers. Mutual inductance of 1 henry (H) occurs when alternating current having a value of 1 A in the primary induces 1 V of ac in the secondary. When all magnetic lines of the primary cut the secondary winding (as is the case in a closely wound transformer) the mutual inductance in equation form is

$$M = \sqrt{L_1 L_2} \qquad (1\text{-}13)$$

When inductors are coupled loosely and all the lines of force of each inductor do not interact, the *coefficient of coupling* (k) becomes a factor and hence the following equation applies:

$$k = \frac{M}{\sqrt{L_1 L_2}} \qquad (1\text{-}14)$$

The coefficient of coupling indicates the *percentage* of coil interaction. Thus, if only one-fifth of the lines of force of one inductor interrupts another inductor, the coefficient of coupling is 20%. The equation for finding the mutual inductance when the coefficient of coupling is involved is

$$M = k \sqrt{L_1 L_2} \qquad (1\text{-}15)$$

For series inductors the mutual inductance is additive if each inductor is wound in the same direction so that the magnetic fields aid each other. Such wiring is termed *series aiding* and the equation for total inductance then becomes

$$L_T(\text{series aiding}) = L_1 + L_2 + 2M \qquad (1\text{-}16)$$

If coupled inductors are wound in opposite directions so that the magnetic fields of one coil oppose that of the other, the following equation applies:

$$L_T(\text{series opposing}) = L_1 + L_2 - 2M \qquad (1\text{-}17)$$

1-4. SERIES AND PARALLEL CAPACITORS

When capacitors are placed in *parallel* the total capacitance *increases*; hence, the following equation applies:

$$C_T(\text{parallel}) = C_1 + C_2 + C_3 + \cdots + C_n \qquad (1\text{--}18)$$

Thus, if three capacitors are in a circuit and their respective values are 0.05, 2.00, and 0.003 μF, the total capacitance is 2.053 μF. When capacitors are placed in series, however, total capacitance is less than the lowest capacitance in the circuit and hence the reciprocal equation is used:

$$C_t(\text{series}) = \frac{1}{(1/C_1) + (1/C_2) + (1/C_3) + \cdots + (1/C_n)} \qquad (1\text{--}19)$$

When only two capacitors are in series the following equation can be used:

$$\frac{C_1 \cdot C_2}{C_1 + C_2} \qquad (1\text{--}20)$$

Thus, if two capacitors are in series and the values are 6 and 12 μF, Eq. 1–20 gives us

$$\frac{6 \cdot 12}{6 + 12} = \frac{72}{18} = 4 \ \mu\text{F}$$

Equation 1–19 can, of course, also be used, with the same result:

$$\frac{1}{(1/6) + (1/12)} = \frac{1}{(2/12) + (1/12)} = \frac{1}{3/12} = \frac{12}{3} = 4$$

1-5. REACTANCE AND IMPEDANCE

The opposition offered by an inductor to the flow of ac is termed reactance (symbol X) as opposed to the resistance offered by a resistor. Where resistance consumes power, however, reactance does not because a pure inductor creates an out-of-phase condition with voltage leading current. Thus, when voltage is at its peak the current flow is at the zero point of the sine wave; hence, the energy is returned to the generator or other source. The amount of reactance offered by an inductance is related to the amount of inductance in henrys and the rate of change of the alternating current. Inductive reactance is usually identified by the symbol X_L and the following equation applies:

$$X_L = 2\pi f L \quad (\text{or } 6.28 \times f \times L) \tag{1-21}$$

or

$$X_L = \omega L \quad (\text{since } 6.28f = \omega)$$

where X_L is the inductive reactance in ohms
f is the frequency in hertz
L is the inductance in henrys

Reactance is expressed in ohms just as with resistance. Knowing the value of reactance and frequency, Eq. 1–21 can be used to solve for inductance:

$$L = \frac{X_L}{6.28f} \tag{1-22}$$

Similarly, if the inductive reactance and inductance values are known, we can solve for the frequency:

$$f = \frac{X_L}{6.28L} \tag{1-23}$$

Compared to an inductor, the capacitor has an opposite reactive characteristic. At any instant when the voltage is leading in an inductor, it lags in the capacitor, when both L and C are in the same circuit. Similarly, for a current lead in the capacitor at any instant, there is a corresponding current lag in the inductor, creating a 90° difference in phase relationships (assuming that resistance is absent). Thus, capacitive reactance (symbol X_C) can be calculated by the following equation:

$$X_C = \frac{1}{2\pi f C} = \frac{1}{\omega C} = \frac{1}{6.28 \times f \times C} \tag{1-24}$$

where X_C is the capacitive reactance in ohms
f is the frequency in hertz
C is the capacitance in farads

As was the case with the inductors, we can rearrange Eq. 1–24 to solve for either capacitance or for frequency if two known values are available:

$$C = \frac{1}{6.28fX_C} \tag{1–25}$$

$$f = \frac{1}{6.28CX_C} \tag{1–26}$$

Inductive and capacitive reactances can be related to ac voltage and current values as was the case for E, I, and R with dc. Thus, the following equations apply:

$$X_L = \frac{E}{I} \tag{1–27}$$

$$I = \frac{E}{X_L} \tag{1–28}$$

$$E = IX_L \tag{1–29}$$

$$X_C = \frac{E}{I} \tag{1–30}$$

$$I = \frac{E}{X_C} \tag{1–31}$$

$$E = IX_C \tag{1–32}$$

When both reactance and resistance are present in a circuit, the combination of the two forms an opposition termed *impedance*, symbol Z. The relationships of resistance, reactance, and impedance in a series circuit are trigonometric, as shown in Figure 1–2(A) and as indicated by the following equation:

$$Z = \sqrt{R^2 + X^2} \tag{1–33}$$

Equation 1–33 shows the basic equation applicable to the reactance of either inductance or capacitance. When both the latter are in a circuit with resistance, however, the total reactance is either predominantly ca-

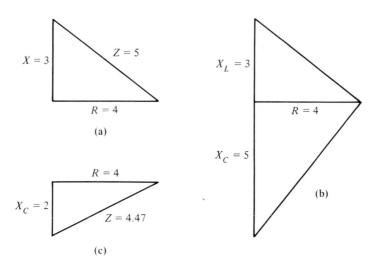

Figure 1–2 Trigonometric Aspects of R, X, and Z

pacitive or inductive, depending on the amplitude of each, as shown in Figure 1–2(B) and (C). Thus, if the reactance of the inductor is 20 kΩ and that of a capacitor is 50 kΩ, the total reactance is 30 kΩ and is primarily X_C. If the capacitive reactance is 3000 Ω and inductive reactance is 15,000 Ω, the total reactance is 12,000 Ω of X_L. The standard equation for a circuit having resistance, inductive reactance, and capacitive reactance indicates the subtraction of X_C from X_L. Obviously, if X_C predominates, the two reactance values are interchanged in the following equation:

$$Z = \sqrt{R^2 + (X_L - X_C)^2} \tag{1–34}$$

In a series circuit the same current flows through each component but the voltage drops across components vary as resistance or reactance varies. Total voltage is, therefore, a vector quantity and may be found by the following equation:

$$E_T = \sqrt{E_T^2 + E_X^2} \tag{1–35}$$

In finding the E_X value, the voltage value across inductive reactance is subtracted from the quantity of voltage across the capacitive reactance if the latter voltage is higher.

The relationships among Z, E, and I are indicated in the following equations:

$$Z = \frac{E}{I} \tag{1-36}$$

$$I = \frac{E}{Z} \tag{1-37}$$

$$E = IZ \tag{1-38}$$

For parallel resistance and reactance Eq. 1–34 no longer applies. Values of voltages and currents can be used to solve for impedance, as shown in Eq. 1–36. In a parallel circuit the voltage has a constant value across the resistors, inductors, and capacitors. Current values through these components differ, however. Hence, the following equation must be used to solve for total current as an initial step toward finding impedance:

$$I_T = \sqrt{I_R^2 + (I_{X_L} - I_{X_C})^2} \tag{1-39}$$

Having found total current, impedance can be calculated by E/I_T, as shown in Eq. 1–36. Advantage can be taken of trigonometric functions for solving unknown values. Since the quotient of the side opposite divided by the side adjacent is the tangent θ, the quotient of X/R is also the tan θ. Once the tan is known, trigonometric-ratio tables or scientific calculations will give the phase angle, cosine, and other values. Because the cosine of an angle is the ratio of the side adjacent to the hypotenuse (R/Z), the value of the side adjacent (R) can be divided by the cosine value to find the hypotenuse (Z). As an example, if $X = 1560 \ \Omega$ and $R = 2080 \ \Omega$ the following calculations apply:

$$\tan \theta = \frac{1560}{2080} = 0.75$$

$$\theta = 36.87°$$

$$\cos \theta = 0.8$$

$$Z = \frac{2080}{0.8} = 2600 \ \Omega$$

Additional equations involving impedance (Z) are illustrated in

Figure 1–1(B). The equation derivations for Z, R, and X are given in Table 1–1. Additional factors related to trigonometry are given in Sec. 1–15.

TABLE 1–1. Z, R, and X Equation Derivations

$BC^2 = AB^2 + AC^2$

$AB^2 = BC^2 - AC^2$

$AC^2 = BC^2 - AB^2$

$c = \sqrt{a^2 + b^2}$ $\qquad Z = \sqrt{R^2 + X^2}$

$a = \sqrt{c^2 - b^2}$ $\qquad R = \sqrt{Z^2 - X^2}$

$b = \sqrt{c^2 - a^2}$ $\qquad X = \sqrt{Z^2 - R^2}$

If $R = 3\,\Omega$, $X = 4\,\Omega$, and $Z = 5\,\Omega$, the **calculations that apply are:**

$Z = \sqrt{3^2 + 4^2} = \sqrt{9 + 16} = \sqrt{25} = 5$

$R = \sqrt{5^2 - 4^2} = \sqrt{25 - 16} = \sqrt{9} = 3$

$X = \sqrt{5^2 - 3^2} = \sqrt{25 - 9} = \sqrt{16} = 4$

1–6. RESONANCE, BANDWIDTH, AND Q

In an electronic circuit when the ohmic value of capacitive reactance equals the inductive reactance, the opposing factors of the two reactances cancel, leaving only resistance. Signal voltages and currents are thus in phase and since $(X_L - X_C) = 0$ in Eq. 1–34, resistance is the only dominant factor and the condition known as *resonance* prevails. Resonant circuits are widely used in various branches of electronics for the selection of signals having specific frequencies while rejecting other signals with frequencies above or below the resonant-circuit selection span. Tuning circuits in communications and other electronic systems permit adjustment of the inductance/capacitance ratio (L/C) by variable capacitors or inductors, or by circuitry that changes specific reactance values (see Sec. 2–32). For finding the resonant frequency when L and C values are known, the following equation applies:

$$f_r = \frac{1}{6.28 \sqrt{LC}} \tag{1–40}$$

This ability of a resonant circuit to select a given signal or group of signals within the resonant bandpass is termed *selectivity* (Q). The latter indicates the degree by which a resonant circuit accepts signals around the desired frequencies while rejecting signals of unwanted frequencies. The degree of selectivity is related to the amount of resistance in a circuit. Resistance may also be present in the inductor and for this reason the selectivity (Q) is referenced to the ratio of inductive reactance to resistance. The respective equations for series and parallel circuits are:

$$(\text{Series})Q = \frac{X_L}{R} \quad (\text{Parallel})Q = \frac{R}{X_L} \qquad (1\text{-}41)$$

In Figure 1–3 the resonant series circuit current (I_s) is plotted against frequency (f) to produce the selectivity curve shown. The sharpness of the slope indicates a high degree of selectivity and a conventional reference are points f_1 and f_2. The latter are the frequencies at which the amplitude of the high- and low-frequency slopes are 0.707 of the peak amplitude of the curve. These points are also termed *half-power frequencies*. The amplitude of these points f_1 or f_2 is $1/\sqrt{2}$ of its value at the resonant frequency point (f_r). The bandwidth of a circuit is considered as the distance between the two half-power frequencies:

$$\text{Bandwidth} = f_2 - f_1 \qquad (1\text{-}42)$$

Since Q is related to resistance and inductance values, either of the half-power frequencies can be found as well as bandwidth, as indicated by the following equations:

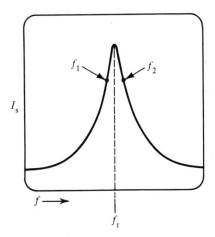

Figure 1–3 Selectivity Curve

$$f_2 = f_r + \frac{R}{4 \pi L} \tag{1-43}$$

$$f_1 = f_r - \frac{R}{4 \pi L} \tag{1-44}$$

$$\text{Bandwith} = f_2 - f_1 = \frac{R}{2 \pi L} \tag{1-45}$$

$$Q = \frac{f_r}{f_2 - f_1} \tag{1-46}$$

$$f_r = Q(f_2 - f_1) \tag{1-47}$$

1-7. DECIBELS

Decibel ratings are *comparisons* of amplitudes and not of unit measurements. Thus, the decibel (dB) represents a unit indicating the *difference* in amplitude levels. The decibel can relate to one power level as compared to another, one voltage level as compared to another, or one current level as compared to another. Decibel ratings relate to the manner in which the human ear responds to sounds having different intensities. The ear has a logarithmic response and hence is more receptive to low-intensity sound-level changes than to high-intensity changes. When the change in sound level is barely noticeable to the average ear it is approximately 1 decibel.

The unit *bel* (named after Alexander Graham Bell) is too large a unit and is not used. Instead, one-tenth of a bel (the decibel) is commonly used. The equation for finding the decibel in *power* is:

$$\text{dB} = 10 \log \frac{P_1}{P_2} \tag{1-48}$$

The larger power value is divided by the smaller to obtain the ratio. A doubling of power is equal to 3 dB:

$$10 \log \frac{2}{1} = 10 \times 0.30 = 3$$

A 3-dB rating is obtained when we compare an audio amplifier having a 30-W output with another having a 60-W output. Since the decibel rating is not a measurement of power, the same 3-dB rating is obtained if we compare a 100-W unit with one of 200 W. When the decibel rating relates to a higher value, the decibel value may be preceded by a plus sign, although the sign could be omitted to indicate a plus quantity. When the comparison relates to a lower value, a minus decibel figure is indicated. Thus, a change of power from 10 W to 20 W = 3 dB, and a change of power from 20 W to 10 W = −3 dB (see Table 7–1). The 3-dB difference for a doubling or halving power is a convenient reference, as is the fact that when power is increased 10 times, it represents 10 dB:

$$10 \log \frac{10}{1} = 10 \times 1.0 = 10 \text{ dB}$$

When comparisons are made involving several decibel levels, the unit values are additive. If, for instance, amplifier A has a rating of 25 W and amplifier B a rating of 50 W, the decibel difference is 3. Comparing amplifier B to amplifier C having a rating of 100 W again gives us a value of 3 dB. When, however, we compare amplifier A to amplifier C (25 W to 100 W) we obtain 3 dB + 3 dB = 6 dB. Similarly, the power increase of 10 times for a reading of 10 dB is related to a power increase of 100 times, which equals 20 dB. Thus, increasing the power difference of 10 dB tenfold, we obtain an additional 10-dB increase: 10 dB + 10 dB = 20 dB. Similarly, of course, a multiple 3-dB increase gives us a total sum value:

$$3 \text{ dB} + 3 \text{ dB} + 3 \text{ dB} = 9 \text{ dB}$$

The decibel equations relating to amplitude levels of voltage and current are as follows:

$$20 \log \frac{E_1}{E_2} \qquad\qquad (1\text{–}49)$$

$$20 \log \frac{I_1}{I_2} \qquad\qquad (1\text{–}50)$$

The term "20 log" in Eqs. 1–49 and 1–50 instead of 10 log is necessary because if voltage (or current) is doubled in a circuit, the power quadruples. This is evident by the following examples, where the current value is doubled and the power changes from 120 W to 480 W:

$$P = I^2R = 2^2 \times 30 = 120 \text{ W}$$

and

$$P = I^2R = 4^2 \times 30 = 480 \text{ W}$$

On occasion, specific levels are used for reference to simplify designations of changes in power, current, and voltage. A common reference is 0.006 W (6 mW) across a resistance of 500 Ω. Analog-type multimeters often have a decibel scale included on the dial as discussed in Chap. 9 and illustrated in Figure 9–6.

1–8. NEPERS

The decibel rating system is commonly used in the United States, whereas in Europe the *neper* has been widely used to express amplitude relationships similar to those of the decibel system. The neper system uses the natural logarithm base ϵ (2.7182...). A neper is the $\log_\epsilon$ of the scalar ratio of two *voltages* or two *currents* and the appropriate equations are:

$$n = \log_\epsilon \frac{I_1}{I_2} \tag{1–51}$$

$$n = \log_\epsilon \frac{E_1}{E_2} \tag{1–52}$$

As an example, if a change is made to increase a 2-A circuit current to 4 A, $n = \log_\epsilon 4/2 = \log_\epsilon 2 = 0.69314$. The same neper quantity is obtained for two voltages having a ratio of 2. There is a constant relationship between decibels and nepers and 1 dB = 0.1151 neper, or 1 neper = 8.686 dB. Thus, for the 0.69314 neper obtained above, multiplication by 8.686 yields 6 dB, the correct amount for a doubling of either voltage or current.

With the power ratio related to the square of the voltage and circulating current, the number of nepers by which these voltage and current differ is found by

$$n = \frac{1}{2} \log_\epsilon \frac{P_1}{P_2} \qquad (1-53)$$

Thus, if there were a power change from 3 W to 12 W, Eq. 1–53 yields $1/2 \log_\epsilon (12/3) = 1/2 \log_\epsilon 4 = 0.69314$. Again multiplying the latter by 8.686 produces the same 6 dB as in the earlier example in this section, showing the related voltage ratio that produces this neper and decibel quantity. (As an alternative for finding the decibel value in the foregoing example, the quantity 0.69314 could be divided by 0.1151 to produce the 6 dB.)

1–9. TIME CONSTANTS

When a voltage is applied to either a capacitor or inductor a specific interval of time is required for electric energy amplitudes to reach maximum values. The time required for a specific value of voltage or current to reach 63% of its maximum value is known as the *time constant*. The symbol for the time constant is the lowercase Greek letter tau (τ). For a capacitor in series with a resistor, a minimum of electric pressure is needed initially to create a significant amount of current flow. As electrons move to one side of the capacitor and away from the other, increased voltage (electric pressure) is needed. This characteristic is illustrated in Figure 1–4, which shows exponential curves representative of capacitor charge voltage and capacitor charge current. As the capacitor charges it acquires a voltage having a polarity that opposes the supply potential. The time necessary for the voltage across a capacitor to reach 63% of its maximum value is given by the equation

$$\tau = RC \qquad (1-54)$$

where C is the capacity in farads
  τ is the time constant in seconds
  R is the resistance value in ohms

Equation 1–54 can be rearranged to solve for capacitance or for resistance:

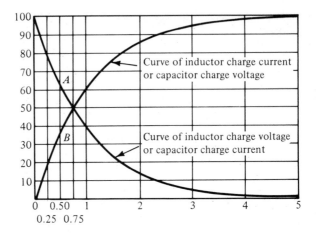

Figure 1–4 *RC* and *L/R* Time Constant Curves

$$C = \frac{\tau}{R} \qquad\qquad (1\text{–}55)$$

$$R = \frac{\tau}{C} \qquad\qquad (1\text{–}56)$$

With a series inductor and resistor the application of a voltage causes current to be built up in each successive turn, producing a counter voltage that delays current buildup as shown in Figure 1–4. The time required for the current through the inductor to reach a value that is 63% of its maximum value represents the related time constant as shown by the following equation:

$$\tau = \frac{L}{R} \qquad\qquad (1\text{–}57)$$

where L is the inductance in henrys

  τ is the time constant in seconds

  R is the resistance value in ohms

As with the capacitor time constant, Eq. 1–57 can be rearranged as shown below to solve for L and R:

$$L = \tau \times R \qquad\qquad (1\text{–}58)$$

$$R = \frac{L}{\tau} \qquad (1\text{-}59)$$

Representative time-constant values are given in Table 7–4. This table, however, does not give intermediate time constants (such as 0.22, 0.063, etc.). In such tables, the voltage and current percentages are taken to the nearest two-digit value of the exponential function. A time constant of 0.7, for instance, would show the percentage of inductive charge voltage as 49.66 instead of 50. Thus, when intermediate values or greater accuracy is required, it is necessary to utilize equations based on exponential functions. The equations necessitate the use of tables for such functions for determining values of ϵ^{-x} or the use of a calculator that is scientifically oriented and will give values of ϵ. For equations involving RC circuits, the X value is always t/RC, where t is the time in seconds, R the value of the resistances in ohms, and C the capacitance in farads. For equations involving L/R circuits, the X value is always $t(R/L)$, with the inductance in henrys.

The various equations related to the time constants involving instantaneous values follow. These include the instantaneous voltage across a capacitor, e_C, the instantaneous voltage across the resistor, e_R (in series with a capacitor), the instantaneous current through the resistor, i_R (in series with a capacitor), the current through the inductor i_L, the voltage across the inductor e_L, and the voltage across the resistor (in series with an inductor).

$$e_C = E(1 - \epsilon^{-t/RC}) \qquad (1\text{-}60)$$

$$e_R = E\epsilon^{-t/RC} \qquad (1\text{-}61)$$

$$i_R = \frac{E}{R}\epsilon^{-t/RC} \qquad (1\text{-}62)$$

$$i_L = \frac{E}{R}(1 - \epsilon^{-tR/L}) \qquad (1\text{-}63)$$

$$e_L = E\epsilon^{-tR/L} \qquad (1\text{-}64)$$

$$e_R = E(1 - \epsilon^{-tR/L}) \qquad (1\text{-}65)$$

1–10. TRANSFORMER TURNS RATIO

The relationship of voltages and currents in a transformer primary and secondary winding are related to the number of turns of wire within each transformer section. The basic turns-ratio relationships may be expressed as

$$\frac{E_{sec}}{E_{pri}} = \frac{N_{sec}}{N_{pri}} \qquad (1\text{--}66)$$

where E_{sec} is the voltage across the secondary
E_{pri} is the voltage across the primary
N_{sec} is the number of coil turns in the secondary
N_{pri} is the number of coil turns in the primary

Equation 1–66 can be rearranged for finding individual primary and secondary voltages:

$$E_p N_s = N_p E_s \qquad (1\text{--}67)$$

$$E_p = \frac{N_p E_s}{N_s} \qquad (1\text{--}68)$$

$$E_s = \frac{E_p N_s}{N_p} \qquad (1\text{--}69)$$

When the ratio of turns between the primary and secondary is known, the secondary voltage (E_s) can be found:

$$E_s = \text{turns ratio} \times E_p \qquad (1\text{--}70)$$

There is an inverse relationship between the voltage and current in a transformer, since a current availability step-down effect occurs when a voltage step-up prevails for a given power transfer from primary to secondary. Hence, the following relationships apply:

$$\frac{I_p}{I_s} = \frac{N_s}{N_p} \qquad (1\text{--}71)$$

Equations similar in form to Eqs. 1–67 through 1–69 are also readily derived:

$$I_p N_p = N_s I_s \tag{1-72}$$

$$I_p = \frac{N_s I_s}{N_p} \tag{1-73}$$

$$I_s = \frac{I_p N_p}{N_s} \tag{1-74}$$

In a transformer, the ratio of the impedance of the secondary (Z_s) to the impedance at the primary (Z_p) varies as the square of the transformer turns ratio:

$$\frac{Z_s}{Z_p} = \frac{N_s^2}{N_p^2} \tag{1-75}$$

The turns ratio is instrumental in establishing an impedance match between two circuits coupled by the transformer as shown by the following equation:

$$\text{Turns ratio} = \sqrt{\frac{Z_1}{Z_2}} \tag{1-76}$$

By using Eq. 1–76 we can step down the ohmic value of an impedance of one circuit to equal that of a lower impedance of another circuit, or the impedance of a circuit can be stepped up to match the higher impedance of the circuit to which the first is coupled.

1–11. POLAR AND *j* NOTATIONS

Notations involving the polar forms and the *j* operators are widely used in electronics for expressing and identifying signal phases and types of amplitudes. When a vector quantity is identified by indicating the amplitude and phase angle (with the horizontal axis representing resistance), the expression is known as *polar notation*. Thus, if the impedance is 150 Ω and the phase angle is 36.8°, we can express this in polar form as

$$Z = 150 \,\underline{/36.8°}$$

The notation using the j operator designates j values as reactance quantities and numbers only resistive values. The j operator is identical to the operator i used to identify *imaginary* numbers in conventional mathematics. The use of j in electronics avoids confusion with the i symbol for instantaneous current values. The j-operator system is also known as *rectangular notation* as well as *complex algebra*. It designates a vector quantity by an ordinate of real quantity and an ordinate of the j quantity, as $Z = 330 + j400\Omega$. In rectangular notation the operator designation relates to the characteristics of -1. Multiplication of any positive number by -1 results in a negative sum. Multiplication of a negative number by -1 produces a positive sum. Hence, -1 can be considered as an *operator* that reverses the sign of the number by which it is multiplied (without altering the amplitude of such a number).

The basic principle of the j operator is illustrated in Figure 1–5. The vector arm (A) has a fixed length. Assume that the magnitude is 30 units and the latter is multiplied by the -1 operator. A counterclock-wise 180° rotation would occur, reaching the position identified as B. Another multiplication by -1 produces another 180° change and the original position is reached. Thus, when the vector arm amplitude is multiplied twice by -1 it creates a 360° rotation. To facilitate calculations involving alternating current, the operator must produce a counter-clockwise rotation of 90° instead of 180°. In theory this special operator must be one that produces -1 when multiplied by itself. The unit value of the required operator cannot, however, be ascertained by taking the square root of -1 since there is no real root for a minus number. Thus, that number representing $\sqrt{-1}$ is designated the *imaginary number* with the symbol j.

In rectangular notation resistance values are plotted along the X axis of a graph and reactance values along the Y axis, as was shown in Figure 1–2. An inductive reactance value is designated as $+j$ and a capacitive reactance by $-j$. Polar-form notation can be changed to rectangular notation by

$$Z = Z \cos \theta + jZ \sin \theta \qquad (1\text{–}77)$$

As a typical example, the conversion of $Z = 400 \underline{/43°}$ yields

$$Z = 400 \times 0.731 + j400 \times 0.682$$
$$= 292.4 + j272.8 \ \Omega$$

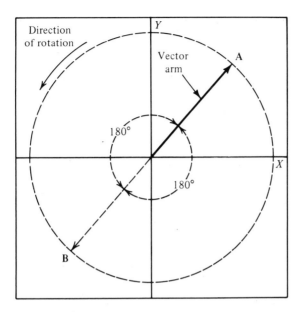

Figure 1–5   Vector Rotation for Multiplication by -1

Equation 1–77 is also useful for ascertaining the rectangular-form amplitudes of voltage or current from polar notation. The equation is expressed as

$$E_T = E_T \cos \theta + jE_T \sin \theta \qquad (1\text{--}78)$$

1–12. ADMITTANCE AND SUSCEPTANCE

Conductance has for its symbol G and it is the reciprocal of resistance. The reciprocal of reactance is *susceptance*, for which the symbol is B. On occasion, inductive susceptance may use the symbol B_L and capacitive susceptance as B_C. The reciprocal of impedance is *admittance*, having the symbol Y. Instead of expressing these values in ohms (Ω) they are designated as siemens (S) in the SI system (see Table 7–22). In the older mks and cgs systems the reciprocal function was given in *mho* (*ohm* spelled backward). These values can be related for finding unknown quantities as shown by the following equations:

$$G = \frac{1}{R} \tag{1-79}$$

$$Y = \frac{1}{Z} \tag{1-80}$$

$$B = \frac{1}{X} \tag{1-81}$$

$$Y = \frac{1}{R - jX} \tag{1-82}$$

$$Y = G - jB_L \tag{1-83}$$

$$Y = G + jB_C \tag{1-84}$$

$$B_L = \frac{X_L}{Z^2} \tag{1-85}$$

$$B_C = \frac{X_C}{Z^2} \tag{1-86}$$

1-13. EFFECTIVE, AVERAGE, AND PEAK AC VALUES

In alternating-current designations, the term *effective value* of either voltage or current indicates the magnitude level equivalent to the dc value. Thus, an electric light bulb used in an ac line of 120 V produces as much light as it would when used on a 120-V dc line. The effective value is ascertained by sampling numerous instantaneous values, squaring them, obtaining the sum of the squared values, and then finding the average value. The square root of the latter produces the effective value. It is for this reason that the latter is also referred to as the *root-mean-square* (rms) value. The following equations permit solving for effective values when peak values are known, or vice versa. The 0.707 in the equations equals one-half of the square root of 2 ($\sqrt{2} = 1.414$).

$$E_{\text{effective}} = 0.707 \times E_{\text{peak}} \tag{1-87}$$

$$E_{\text{peak}} = \frac{1}{0.707} = 1.414 \times E_{\text{eff}} \tag{1-88}$$

Although the peak amplitude of one alternation of alternating current or voltage has a very short duration, the value is important in calculating other values. By dividing successive alternations of the sine wave into a number of ordinates and averaging them, the *average value* is obtained. The appropriate equations for solving either average or peak values are:

$$E_{\text{average}} = 0.637 \times E_{\text{peak}} \tag{1-89}$$

$$E_{\text{peak}} = 1.57 \times E_{\text{average}} \tag{1-90}$$

1-14. TRANSMISSION-LINE EQUATIONS

Basic transmission lines are shown in Figure 1-6. Part (A) shows a two-wire line with insulating spacers separating the conductors. Often a plastic insulating material is utilized, as shown in (B), typically a 300-Ω tele-

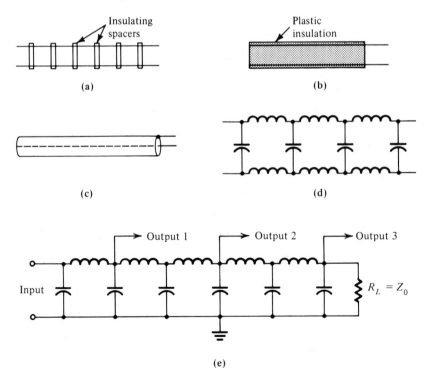

Figure 1-6   Line Factors

vision system twin lead. The coaxial cable is shown in part (C), where an inner conductor is held in place by a plastic insulation or by washer-like spacers. Essentially all three lines illustrated are two-wire lines. (The coaxial cable uses the outer shield as one of the conductors.) As shown in part (D) a transmission line can be represented as series inductors and shunt capacitors having specific values per unit length. Some resistive components are present in the conductors themselves, although for larger-diameter conductors the ohmic value is negligible per unit length. The line's impedance is termed *characteristic impedance* (symbol Z_0). The term *iterative impedance* is sometimes used instead of "characteristic impedance" because of the repetitive Z for successive unit lengths. Another term also in use is *surge impedance*. Since all these terms refer to the identical characteristic, the same symbol (Z_0) is used. Since, for any additional series inductance there is a corresponding shunt capacitance, the characteristic impedance remains substantially constant regardless of line length. When spacers are used such as in Figure 1–6(A), the line is considered to have air as its insulation and Z_0 is calculated as

$$Z_0 = 276 \log \frac{2_b}{a} \tag{1–91}$$

where Z_0 is the characteristic impedance

      a is the radius of each conductor

      b is the center-to-center conductor spacing

In Eq. 1–91 the a/b ratio can represent millimeters, feet, inches, or other units and the Z_0 will still be the same.

As an example of the application of Eq. 1–91, assume that a two-wire line had a spacing of 3 cm between wires and that each conductor had a diameter of 0.04 cm. The characteristic impedance would then be

$$Z_0 = 276 \log \frac{2 \times 3}{0.04}$$

$$= 276 \log \frac{6}{0.04}$$

$$= 276 \times 2.1761$$

$$= 600.6 \ \Omega$$

If the values of inductance and capacitance are measured over a given line length, the same L/C ratio prevails. For any additional length selected the increased *series* inductance is offset by the added *shunt* capacitance. Hence, Z_0 can be calculated by the following equation:

$$Z_0 = \sqrt{\frac{L}{C}} \tag{1-92}$$

As an example, if a transmission line (with air dielectric) has, for a given unit length, an inductance of 0.24 mH and a capacitance of 0.001 μF, the Z_0 is

$$Z_0 = \sqrt{\frac{0.25^{-3}}{0.001^{-6}}}$$

$$= \sqrt{250{,}000}$$

$$= 500 \ \Omega$$

For a coaxial cable having air as the dielectric the characteristic impedance is found by the following equation:

$$Z_0 = 138 \log\frac{b}{a} \tag{1-93}$$

where a is the outside diameter of the inner conductor
b is the inside diameter of the outer conductor

When the dielectric material of the coaxial cable is not air, Eq. 1-93 must be multiplied by

$$\frac{1}{\sqrt{k}} \tag{1-94}$$

In Eq. 1-94 the symbol k is the *dielectric constant* of the material referenced in relation to air considered to have a k of 1, with all other materials having a higher value. Table 7-13 lists k values for some typical materials. The k value, however, may vary with temperature, applied voltage, signal frequency, and other circuit factors. Hence, the k values must be considered as approximate.

As shown in Figure 1–6(E), a section of transmission line can be used for time delay of signals. One or more taps can be used at selected intervals along the line for obtaining various time-delay signal outputs. Regardless of line length, the end of the line is terminated in a load resistor (R_L) having an ohmic value equal to the characteristic impedance (Z_0). When the line is terminated in a resistance of this value all the energy reaching the end of the line is absorbed and none is reflected back. If the terminating resistance is omitted (open line) or if the line is shorted, the radio-frequency (RF) energy reaching the end of the line will be reflected back and create standing waves along the line. This comes about because signals now travel in two directions along the line, resulting in phase differences. At sections where voltages are in phase high amplitudes prevail, whereas sections having out-of-phase conditions have low- or zero-voltage amplitudes. When standing waves occur along the line, no energy is consumed by the line since all the energy is reflected back into the generator. Sections of the line now have voltage peaks or current peaks (called *loops*), while other sections will have voltage or current low points (called *nodes*). The distance between two loops (or the distance between two nodes) is equivalent to a half-wavelength of the frequency of the RF signal causing the standing waves. The distance between two loops can thus be measured and the value utilized in Eq. 1–95 for RF measurement purposes. Utilizing the distance in meters (d) the following equation applies:

$$f = \frac{300,000}{2d} \tag{1-95}$$

where f is the frequency in kilohertz
d is the distance in meters

In Eq. 1–95 the 300,000 is related to the travel of light and electromagnetic waves through space during which each has a velocity of 299,792.5 kilometers per second (km/s) or 186,282 miles per second (mps). (The kilometer designation is rounded off to 300,000.)

For the delay line shown in Figure 1–6(E), no standing waves occur to distort the signal. The time in seconds for signal energy to travel a given length of line is found by

$$t = \sqrt{LC} \tag{1-96}$$

As an example, assume that a line has a total inductance of 0.25 mH and a total capacitance of 0.001 μF. The delay in seconds for this length of line (using Eq. 1–96) is

$$t = \sqrt{(0.25^{-3})(0.001^{-6})}$$
$$= \sqrt{2.5^{-13}}$$
$$= 0.5 \ \mu s$$

1–15. TRIGONOMETRIC RELATIONSHIPS

Trigonometry is widely used in electronics for calculations involving phase angles in alternating current, reactance and impedance relationships, and so on. In summarizing the fundamental concepts of this branch of mathematics it must be emphasized that the basic terms relate to the right-angle triangle as shown in Figure 1–7. Using the angle (θ) as a reference, the sides of the triangle are designated the *side adjacent* to the angle, the *side opposite*, and the *hypotenuse*, as shown in Figure 1–7(A). These sides are used in electronics to reference amplitudes of impedance (Z), resistance (R), inductive reactance (X_L), and capacitive reactance (X_C), as shown in Figure 1–7(B) and (C) (see also Sec. 1–5).

Various relationships are utilized for calculation purposes, including the solving of an unknown length by utilizing the length of one of

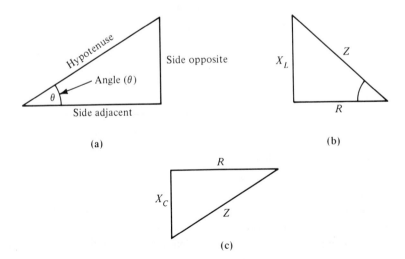

Figure 1–7 Trigonometric Terms

the sides plus the phase angle. Ratios of the sides produce values designated as *sine, cosine, tangent, cosecant, secant,* and *cotangent.* These terms relate to the angle (θ) and hence the angle symbol is often used with the abbreviation as: *sin θ, cos θ, tan θ, cosec θ, sec θ,* and *cot θ.* The derivations of the ratios of sides are given in Table 1–2.

TABLE 1–2. Basic Trigonometric Factors

$$\frac{\text{Opposite}}{\text{Hypotenuse}} = \sin \theta \text{ (sine of the angle)}$$

$$\frac{\text{Opposite}}{\text{Adjacent}} = \tan \theta \text{ (tangent of the angle)}$$

$$\frac{\text{Adjacent}}{\text{Hypotenuse}} = \cos \theta \text{ (cosine of an angle)}$$

$$\frac{\text{Adjacent}}{\text{Opposite}} = \text{cotangent } \theta \left(\frac{1}{\tan \theta}\right)$$

$$\frac{\text{Hypotenuse}}{\text{Adjacent}} = \text{secant } \theta \left(\frac{1}{\cos \theta}\right)$$

$$\frac{\text{Hypotenuse}}{\text{Opposite}} = \text{cosecant } \theta \left(\frac{1}{\sin \theta}\right)$$

$$\sin^2\theta + \cos^2\theta = 1$$

$$\tan \theta = \frac{\sin \theta}{\cos \theta}$$

$$\cot \theta = \frac{\cos \theta}{\sin \theta}$$

$$\sec^2\theta = \frac{1}{\cos^2\theta} = 1 + \tan^2\theta$$

$$\text{cosec}^2\theta = \frac{1}{\sin^2\theta} = 1 + \text{cotan}^2\theta$$

The length of a side of a right-angle triangle can be solved utilizing the known angle and the length of one of the sides by the combinations shown in Table 1–3.

Tables listing the values of various ratios are published in mathematics texts and are accurate to the number of places shown. Extensions beyond the numbers shown are rounded off. A typical example is the partial listing shown in Table 1–4.

TABLE 1-3. Relationships of Triangle Lengths

Hypotenuse Length	Opposite-Side Length	Adjacent-Side Length
Opposite × cosecent	Hypotenuse × sine	Hypotenuse × cosine
Opposite/sine	Hypotenuse/cosecent	Hypotenuse/secent
Adjacent × secent	Adjacent × tangent	Opposite × cotangent
Adjacent/cosine	Adjacent/cotangent	Opposite/tangent

TABLE 1-4. Trigonometric Ratios

Degrees	Sin	Cos	Tan
0	0.0000	1.0000	0.0000
1	0.0175	0.9998	0.0175
2	0.0349	0.9994	0.0349
3	0.0523	0.9986	0.0524
4	0.0698	0.9976	0.0699
5	0.0872	0.9962	0.0875
6	0.1045	0.9945	0.1051
7	0.1219	0.9925	0.1228
8	0.1392	0.9903	0.1405
9	0.1564	0.9877	0.1584
10	0.1736	0.9848	0.1763
11	0.1908	0.9816	0.1944
12	0.2079	0.9781	0.2126

In Table 1-4 the sin, cos, and tan values have been rounded off to four places. Thus, in many instances the true value involves more numbers. For example, at 2° the cos is given as 0.9994, but a scientific calculator may display 0.99939. Also, the scientific calculators can give enumerable intermediate values between whole numbers that, in table form, would be quite lengthy. For Table 1-4, for instance, the sin value for 1.35° would have to be extrapolated, but a scientific calculator displays 0.023559 in a fraction of a second. Similarly 1.7 yields a sin of 0.029666, and so on.

The scientific calculators also provide for the finding of inverse trigonometric functions. Thus, if the tangent is given as 0.72655, it can be entered on the keyboard and the tan^{-1} key depressed to display the angle (36° in this instance). Similarly, if a cosine value of 0.92719 is entered and the $\cos^{-1}$ key depressed, we get the angle of 22°. In such scientific calculators the degree/radian switch can be used for converting to either mode as needed (see also Sec. 1–16). As an example, to solve for (tan $\pi/5$) we enter $\pi/5$ and with the switch at Rad depressing the tangent key produces 0.72656 (using 3.1416 as the representative pi). Other basic equations derived from the trigonometric functions include the impedance equations given in Sec. 1–5.

1–16. RADIANS AND ANGULAR VELOCITY

A pure sine wave of alternating current or voltage has trigonometric characteristics as shown in Figure 1–8. Although many of the signals utilized in electronics are not pure sine waves the latter are usually used to illustrate and discuss the relationships involved. Figure 1–8(A) shows a circle illustrating the relationship between the radius and the circumference. When the length of the radius is successively measured along the circumference, it always fits 2π or approximately 6.28 times. The length of a single radius along the circumference creates an angle for its arc of 57.3°. This angle is termed a *radian*.

As shown in Figure 1–8(B), a pure sine wave consists of two alternations, each of opposite polarity. Each alternation has the same *duration* as the other, has an identical *incline* and *decline*, and has the same *amplitude*, although of opposite polarity. There is an interrelationship between the radius and the velocity factor of the sine wave shown in Figure 1–8(B). If the circle shown in (A) is assumed to rotate *clockwise* through 360° but the radius were made to rotate *counterclockwise* through 360°, the radius line arrowhead would trace out the waveform of a complete sine wave. For a movement of the radius arm from the horizontal position shown in (A) to a vertical position involves an angular change of 90° as shown in (B). In the vertical position it also represents the peak amplitude of the sine-wave signal. Because the movement of the radius arm illustrates the continuous changing of the angle as well as representing instantaneous amplitudes, the radius arm movement represents the *velocity* of the sine wave. Thus, the expression 2π mentioned above, when multiplied by the frequency of the sine wave, produces what is termed the *angular velocity*, the symbol for which is ω (lowercase Greek letter omega). Since 2π radians represents 360°, and since each ra-

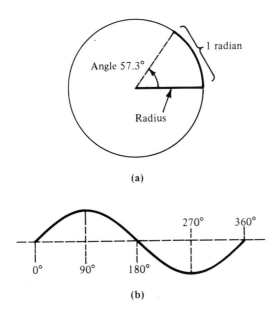

(a)

(b)

Figure 1-8 Radians and Angular Velocity

dian has an angle for its arc of 57.3°, the circumference equals 2π × radius $= 2\pi$ × arc of 1 rad. Thus, the following relationships prevail:

Circumference $= 2\pi$ times radius $= 2\pi$ times arc of 1 radian
$360° = 2\pi$ radians
1 radian $= 57.3°$ (57° 17′ 44.8″ approx.)
$180° = \pi$ radian
$90° = \frac{1}{2}\pi$ radian
$1° = 0.01745$ radian

For the factors discussed in this section, the term *vector* is often used, with the radius referred to as a *vector arm*. For specific discussions of vectors and phasors, see Sec. 1–17.

1-17. VECTORS, PHASORS, AND SCALARS

A vector quantity has both magnitude and direction and essentially is represented as a straight-line segment having motion in a particular direction. The latter is based on a specific reference system to which the word *vector* thus applies. For the vector, its length is proportional to magnitude and in electronics thus has reference to voltage or current. Although the term *phasor* is sometimes used as being synonymous with vector, there are essential differences between the two. In a phasor diagram the angle represents a *timing* difference, not a *directional* one. In this respect the phasor differs from the vector, although both are normally represented on a phasor diagram. Another term, *scalar*, is defined as a quantity of mass, length, time, temperature, and so on, exactly specified numerically on an appropriate scale.

On occasion reference is made to a *vector product*. For the latter there is a magnitude proportional to the product of the magnitude of two related vectors as illustrated in Figure 1–9(A). Another term for vector product is *cross product*. A *scalar product* is the product of the lengths of two related vectors, multiplied by the cosine of the angle between the two. The scalar product has also been termed *dot product* or *inner product*. A representative scalar product application occurs when solving for true power when the voltage and current are out of phase, as shown in Figure 1–9(B) (see Sec. 1–1).

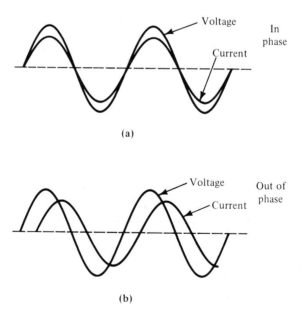

Figure 1–9   Vector and Scalar Product Factors

1–18. TRANSISTOR PARAMETER EQUATIONS

Parameter equations for transistors must take into consideration the type of circuit involved, such as common emitter, common base, common source, and so on, as described in Chap. 2 and illustrated in Figures 2–1 through 2–3. For the grounded-base circuit the ratio of a change in collector current (I_c) to a change in emitter current (I_e) is termed the *alpha* (α) and represents the forward-current transfer ratio of a circuit. The equation is

$$\alpha = \frac{dI_c}{dI_e} \qquad (1\text{–}97)$$

Current gain in a grounded-emitter circuit is termed *beta* and the symbol is β. The equation is the ratio of collector current to the base current:

$$\beta = \frac{dI_c}{dI_b} \qquad (1\text{–}98)$$

Field-effect transistors have a transconductance rating usually obtained with the gate bias at 0. The transconductance has for its symbol g_m. When the ohmic value of the load resistance (R_L) and the g_m are known, signal gain is calculated by the following equation:

$$\text{Gain} = g_m \times R_L \qquad (1\text{–}99)$$

The characteristics of a transistor circuit, including the operational parameters, are symbolized by letter combinations (see Tables 12–2 and 12–3). The lowercase letter *h* (for hybrid) combines constant-voltage and constant-current procedures. In circuit analysis a common practice is to designate the input and output lines as shown in Figure 1–10(A). Here E_1 and I_1 represent the input-signal voltage and current values, while E_2 and I_2 indicate the output voltage and current values. The transistor circuit is represented by a square or rectangle and this concept is often referred to as a *black box*. The latter implies unknown quantities and characteristics within the circuit that can be ascertained by applying specific voltages while also shorting certain terminals as required.

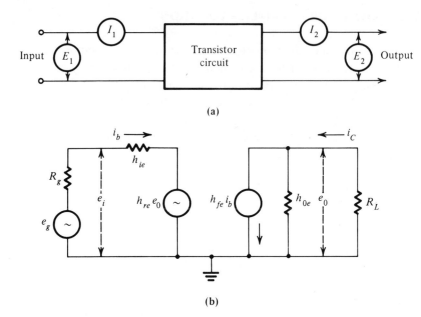

Figure 1–10 Transistor Circuit Symbol Designations

For the h parameters the following equations apply in relation to Figure 1–10(A). The input impedance parameter, with output terminals 3 and 4 shorted (and $E_2 = 0$), is designated as h_{ie} for common emitter, h_{ib} for common base, and h_{ic} for common collector. The input impedance equation is

$$h_i = \frac{E_1}{I_1} \qquad (1\text{–}100)$$

The reverse-transfer voltage ratio, with input terminals 1 and 2 open and $I_1 = 0$, is

$$h_r = \frac{E_1}{E_2} \qquad (1\text{–}101)$$

The forward-transfer current ratio, with output terminals 3 and 4 shorted and $E_2 = 0$, is

$$h_f = \frac{I_2}{I_1} \qquad\qquad (1\text{--}102)$$

The output admittance, with input terminals 1 and 2 open and I_1 at 0, is

$$h_o = \frac{I_2}{E_2} \qquad\qquad (1\text{--}103)$$

In Figure 1–10(B) is shown the equivalent circuit for the grounded-emitter amplifier. The h symbols with letter subscripts are utilized with the base current indicates as i_b, collector current i_c, and input voltage e_g (which also develops across resistor R_6). Consequently, the actual voltage appearing between base and emitter is notated as e_1. The output voltage across the load resistor is designated as e_o. The output admittance is given as h_{oe} and the reverse-voltage transfer voltage symbol is h_{re} for the emitter circuit. The forward-current transfer ratio is given as h_{fe} in reference to the emitter, and corresponds to β given in Eq. 1–98. The forward-current transfer ratio, with $e_o = 0$ in equation form, is

$$h_{fe} = \frac{i_c}{i_b} \qquad\qquad (1\text{--}104)$$

Some manufacturers use A_i for signal-current gain to symbolize current amplification. The equation is

$$A_i = \frac{i_c}{i_b} = \frac{h_{fe}}{1 + h_{oe}R_L} \qquad\qquad (1\text{--}105)$$

Equation 1–105, as with others, can be altered for circuits other than the common-emitter type. The equation remains the same except for a change from e in the second subscript letter to suit the particular circuit involved (see Tables 12–2 and 12–3).

Admittance factors were covered in Sec. 1–12, where it was pointed out that admittance (Y) is the reciprocal of impedance (Z). The Y parameters are useful for investigating the operational characteristics of field-effect transistors. As with the h parameters, the Y parameters also have subscripts identifying the circuit type. Thus, Y_{is} is the input admittance for the common-source circuit, Y_{ig} is for the common gate, and so on. Similarly, Y_{od} is the common-drain output admittance, and Y_{fg} is a common-gate forward-transfer admittance. The basic admittance equations that follow omit the second subscript, which can be added to accommodate the circuit configuration utilized.

Again referring to the black-box concept of Figure 1–10(A) the input admittance parameter with output terminals 3 and 4 shorted ($E_2 = 0$) in equation form is

$$Y_i = \frac{I_1}{E_1} \tag{1–106}$$

The reverse-transfer admittance is obtained with input terminals 1 and 2 shorted and $E_1 = 0$:

$$Y_r = \frac{I_1}{E_2} \tag{1–107}$$

The forward-transfer admittance with the output terminals shorted and $E_2 = 0$ has the equation

$$Y_f = \frac{I_2}{E_1} \tag{1–108}$$

The equation for the output admittance with the input terminals shorted and $E_1 = 0$ is

$$Y_o = \frac{I_2}{E_2} \tag{1–109}$$

Input and output current equations for source-follower circuitry are:

$$I_g = Y_{is}E_g + Y_{rs}E_d \tag{1–110}$$
$$I_d = Y_{fs}E_g + Y_{os}E_d \tag{1–111}$$

For common-gate or common-drain circuits, the second subscripts in Eqs. 1–110 and 1–111 are changed accordingly. As an example, for a common-gate circuit the equations become

$$I_s = Y_{ig}E_s + Y_{rg}E_d \qquad (1\text{–}112)$$

$$I_d = Y_{fg}E_s + Y_{og}E_d \qquad (1\text{–}113)$$

2 Circuit Descriptions

2-1. INTRODUCTION

Various basic circuits widely used in electronics are described in this chapter. A schematic of each circuit is included and the purpose of the circuit is given. Next, a description of the general operational principles follows, with emphasis on essential factors.

Circuits in this chapter include amplifiers, oscillators, demodulators, and others relating to various branches of electronics. Auxiliary circuits such as pads, attenuators, feedback, integration, differentiation, and other signal modification and routing types are covered in Chap. 3. Circuits forming logic gates and switches are discussed in Chap. 6. System applications of circuitry are described in Chaps. 8 and 11.

For quick localization of a particular circuit, refer to the index at the back of the book for the page number that starts the discussion.

2-2. COMMON-EMITTER CIRCUITS

A common-emitter circuit is a widely used audio or RF amplifier type. Its primary purpose is to increase the amplitude of the input signal. A typical circuit using a *pnp* transistor is shown in Figure 2–1(A). Here the emitter is grounded and the input signal is applied across the base and ground terminals as shown. The output signal is obtained from the collector (as against ground) and there is a 180° phase reversal between the input and output signals as shown. Component values and transistor

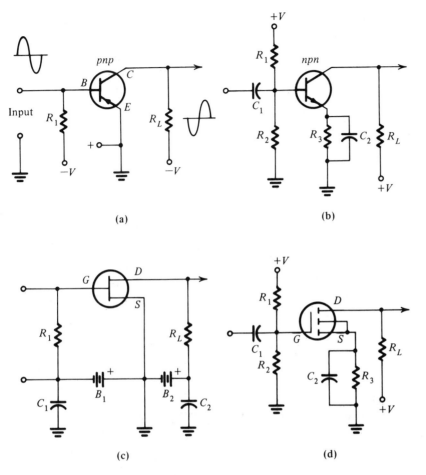

Figure 2–1   Common-Emitter and Source Circuits

types depend on the circuit requirements and characteristics needed. The *pnp* bipolar junction transistor has three terminals: base, emitter, and collector, designated as B, E, and C.

A circuit such as this can be designed to operate in any desired amplifier classification. For Class A operation the bias between the base and emitter terminals of a *pnp* transistor should be such that the base is negative with respect to the emitter to form *forward* bias. The voltage between collector and emitter should be reverse bias and consequently (for the *pnp* transistor) the collector is made negative with respect to the emitter. Resistor R_1 is in series with the bias potential and the input signal adds to and subtracts from the bias voltage. In turn, the degree of conduction through the emitter–collector changes and hence the voltage drop across the load resistor R_L varies accordingly. When the forward bias between base and emitter undergoes a positive change the total negative bias potential is reduced and the current through R_L declines, thus reproducing an amplified replica of the input signal with a 180° phase change.

The circuit shown in Figure 2–1(A) is a basic type and a more practical version is illustrated in (B). Here, an *npn* transistor is used and it illustrates the changes necessary in bias polarities. Now, for forward bias the base should be positive with respect to the emitter, and for reverse bias the collector potential is also positive. A voltage divider consisting of R_1 and R_2 is utilized to establish the proper bias at the base terminal. A stabilizing circuit composed of R_3 and C_2 is usually utilized to compensate for the transistor's thermal changes that may alter conduction levels. If transistor conduction increases slightly because of thermal effects, current through R_3 rises and the voltage drop across this resistor also rises. This voltage increase establishes a countereffect on the bias and the bias reduction would tend to decrease emitter–collector current flow to compensate for the unwanted increase. Capacitor C_2 has a bypass effect for the signals and minimizes voltage variations across R_3 for such signals. Essentially, capacitor C_2 places the emitter *at signal ground* and the circuit thus conforms to the common-emitter designation. Hence, another term for this circuit is *grounded emitter*.

For the circuit shown in Figure 2–1(B), capacitor C_1 isolates the dc at the base terminal from the input system. The signal-current gain for the grounded-emitter circuit relates the ratio of current available at the output to the current circulating at the input, with a collector voltage held constant. The signal-current gain is also commonly referred to as the *forward-current transfer ratio* and is expressed by Eq. 1–102.

2–3. COMMON-SOURCE CIRCUITS

When a field-effect transistor (FET) is utilized to form a circuit equivalent to the common-emitter type, it is designated as a *common-source* or *grounded-source* circuit. The primary purpose for such a circuit is signal amplification, as was the case for the common-emitter type. A typical representation is shown in Figure 2–1(C), where an *n*-channel-type FET is used having elements consisting of the gate (G), source (S), and drain (D). For a *p*-channel FET, the only circuit changes would be a reversal of bias polarities. For the circuit shown at (C), batteries B_1 and B_2 are illustrated to indicate the relative bias relationships at the input and output sections. The signal input developed across R_1 and capacitor C_1 bypasses the bottom of this resistor to ground. Similarly, capacitor C_2 places the bottom of the load resistor R_L at signal ground.

The bias potentials between the input and output of an FET differ from those of the bipolar transistor. Basically, the latter is a signal-current amplifier that has an amplified current change in the output section that represents similar changes of the signal current at the input. For an FET, however, a *signal voltage* applied across the input terminal controls the amplified signal-current changes in the output system. The two types of FET units consist of the *junction* type (JFET) and the *metal-oxide semiconductor* type (MOSFET). The MOSFET is also referred to as the *insulated-gate field-effect transistor* (IGFET). Both types are fabricated for either the *n*-channel or the *p*-channel characteristic (see Figure 4–2). For the circuit shown in Figure 2–1(C) the JFET unit is utilized. For this circuit there is a decrease in channel conduction when the applied potential is negative at the gate, since it depletes the channel of carriers within the FET. For the *p*-channel type, positive gate voltage decreases conduction. Thus, the JFET is normally in a conductive state between source and drain even without a gate-to-source voltage (V_{gs}). Thus, the channel can conduct current in either direction (drain to source or source to drain). In typical Class A operation, reverse bias is applied to the unit in contrast to the forward bias applied to the bipolar junction transistor.

In comparison to the JFET, the MOSFET has its gate structure within the transistor insulated from the channel by a dielectric such as silicon dioxide. Hence, the gate input impedance is extremely high. Forward bias can be used to enhance the channel current (increase current flow) or reverse bias to deplete (decrease) it. Hence, MOSFETs can be designated as *enhancement* or *depletion* types. For the depletion types there is drain-current flow without bias at the input. When bias is applied, drain current decreases to the value required for signal-handling (dynamic) operation. The terminal-enhancement MOSFET is utilized in the circuit shown in Figure 2–1(D). Bias is established by the voltage divider consisting of R_1 and R_2. The input signal is coupled by capacitor C_1 and alternately adds to or subtracts from the established bias. The resultant change in drain-source current is felt across R_L and forms the amplified output signal. Resistor R_3 and capacitor C_2 have the same function as those in Figure 2–1(B); they stabilize the effects of thermal changes within the transistor.

2–4. COMMON-BASE CIRCUITS

Common-base circuits are illustrated in Figure 2–2(A) and (B). Since the base elements are grounded, another term for this circuitry is *grounded base*. The purpose of the grounded-base circuit is to amplify the input signal to the degree established by circuit characteristics. Because the base terminal is grounded, there is a minimum of undesired coupling between output and input sections and hence this circuit is superior in this respect to the grounded-emitter circuit. As shown in Figure 2–2(A), the input signal is applied between emitter and base and the amplified version is obtained from across the load resistor (R_L) on the collector side. There is no phase reversal between the input and output signals as is the case for the grounded-emitter circuit.

For the circuit shown in Figure 2–2(A) a *pnp* transistor is used. The equivalent circuit using an *npn* transistor is illustrated in (B). The voltage-divider arrangement, consisting of R_1 and R_2, could also have been used for the circuit in (A). Operational characteristics for the two circuits are similar. Signal-current gain represents the division of the output-signal current by the value of the input-signal current (see Eq. 1–97). Because the ratio of the current available at the output to that current circulating in the input determines current gain, the full term is *forward-current transfer ratio*.

2–5. COMMON-GATE CIRCUITS

The JFET equivalent circuit of the common-base junction bipolar transistor type is shown in Figure 2–2(C). Here the *p*-channel JFET is used and the circuit is termed a *common-gate* or *grounded-gate* type. Operation is similar to that shown in Figure 2–2(A) and (B) because isolation between input and output is again achieved and there is no phase reversal between input and output signals. Another version showing the MOSFET is illustrated in Figure 2–2(D). The element termed "SUB" is an additional gate terminal connecting to the foundation solid-state substrate during the fabrication process. Sometimes G_1 and G_2 designations

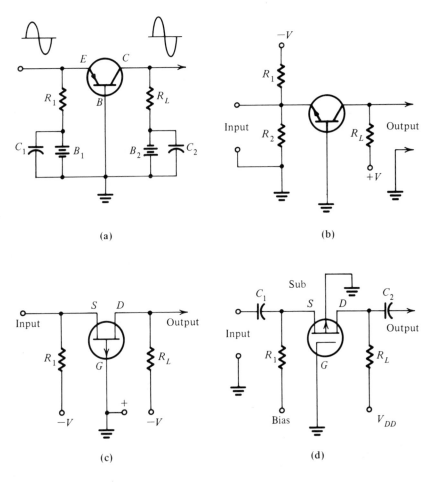

(a)

(b)

(c)

(d)

Figure 2–2   Common-Base and Gate Circuits

are utilized. The designation V_{DD} is often employed in reference to the applied FET drain potential (see Table 12–3). As with other circuits of this type, the input signal is applied between the source and ground and the amplified resultant obtained across the drain-circuit load resistor R_L.

2–6. EMITTER-FOLLOWER CIRCUITS

The emitter-follower circuit is also known as the *grounded-collector* circuit. Such a circuit is used for impedance step-down purposes because the input impedance is substantially higher than the output impedance.

Hence, such a circuit is useful as a substitution for a step-down trans-former for signal-routing purposes. The basic circuit is shown in Figure 2–3(A). Here capacitor C_1 places the collector terminal at signal ground. The input signal has the same phase as the output signal. The term *fol-lower* is derived from the fact that the output signal phase *follows* that of the input. With such a circuit there is unity *signal-voltage* gain or a gain loss, although some *signal-current* amplification is possible. A more prac-tical version is illustrated in (B), where the input coupling capacitor C_1 is shown as well as voltage-divider resistors R_1 and R_2. Since the voltage drop across R_2 is positive at the base, the required forward bias is pres-ent between it and the negative-polarity emitter. Capacitor C_3 couples the output signal to subsequent circuits. The latter, in shunt with R_3, affects total output impedance.

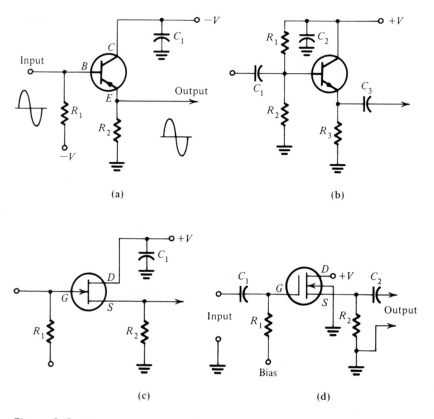

Figure 2–3 Emitter and Source-Follower Circuits

2-7. SOURCE-FOLLOWER CIRCUITS

A JFET source-follower circuit is shown in Figure 2–3(C). Here the drain element is placed at signal ground by capacitor C_1 and the output signal is obtained from across resistor R_2. Because the phase of the output signal *follows* in phase that of the input signal, the term *source follower* applies. Since the drain is at *signal ground,* the term *grounded-drain* circuit also applies. The subsequent circuits following resistor R_2 contribute to the total impedance at the output. Since the input impedance is high, a step-down impedance occurs between input and output. A more practical version is illustrated at (D), where a terminal depletion IGFET is illustrated. Capacitor C_1 provides for dc isolation between the gate element and prior circuitry. Bias is supplied via resistor R_1 and the output follower signal appears across R_2 and is coupled to subsequent circuitry by C_2. For MOSFET units, the input impedance is so high that the impedance can be considered virtually equal to the value of R_1. The output impedance is substantially lower because of R_2 and the associated shunting circuitry coupled by C_2.

2-8. COUPLED LOW-SIGNAL AMPLIFIERS

Two low-signal amplifiers commonly coupled by a capacitor (C_4) are shown in Figure 2–4(A). The purpose for such circuitry is to build up the signal amplitude by successive amplifier stages until the desired level is achieved. The input signal is applied between the coupling capacitor C_1 and ground and hence appears across the base and emitter of transistor Q_1 [see also Figure 2–1(B)]. Capacitor C_2 of the thermal stabilizing network that includes R_2 places the bottom of the emitter at signal ground.

The output signal develops across resistor R_4, but not across R_5, since the latter is shunted by the low reactance of C_3. Capacitor C_4 couples the signal to the base input of Q_2 and across resistor R_7. Since resistors and a capacitor are involved in the coupling system, this method is sometimes referred to as *R-C* coupling. Such coupling is widely used and generally more inexpensive and simple than inductor or transformer couplings. On rare occasions, resistor R_4 may be replaced by an inductor, or the coupling can consist of a transformer between Q_1 and Q_2, as shown in Figure 2–4(B). The purpose for a transformer coupling is for impedance step-down or step-up as required. By a step-up of the signal voltage some signal gain is realized across the transformer between the primary

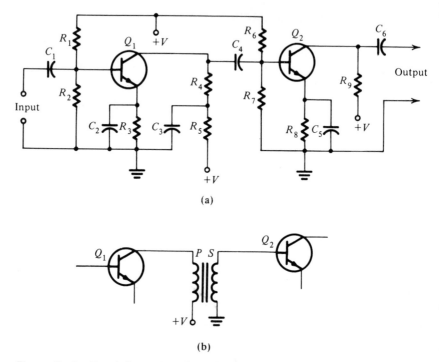

Figure 2–4 Coupled Low-Signal Amplifiers

(P) and secondary (S). Note that the transformer eliminates the resistors R_4 and R_7 as well as coupling capacitor C_4. The disadvantages of the transformer are its variation of inductive reactance for various signal frequencies as well as in the distributed capacitances between coil turns that creates variations in capacitive reactance. These undesired changes contribute to an uneven frequency response in audio or video systems.

Capacitor C_3 and resistor R_5 are referred to as a *decoupling network.* Resistor R_5 is also utilized to set the proper voltage for the collector system. The decoupling circuit isolates signal voltages between amplifier stages by preventing their distribution throughout the system by virtue of a common power supply. The decoupling network of C_3 and R_5 also extends the signal-frequency response of the amplifier by providing low-frequency compensation. The capacitor has a low-reactance shunting effect that increases for higher-frequency signals and hence minimizes common coupling in the power supply. At the same time, capacitor C_3 places the bottom of R_4 at signal ground as shown in Figure 2–4(A). The base-compensating factor arises because the network effectively increases or decreases the collector load resistance of Q_1. For *higher signal frequencies* C_3 has a very low reactance and R_5 is substantially shunted and consequently virtually all signal voltages appear only across resistor R_4. Similarly, coupling capacitor C_4 also has a low reactance for the higher signal frequencies. Thus, most of the high-frequency signal energy is coupled to the input of Q_2. For *lower-frequency signals*, the reactance of C_4 rises and the amplitude of the signals applied to the next stage declines. Hence, the lower-frequency signals are attenuated. The decoupling network compensates for the diminished low-frequency signals because the latter causes the reactance of C_3 to increase. Consequently, C_3 has less of a shunting effect across R_5 and hence a portion of the signal components develop across both R_4 and R_5 in series. In effect, the total load-resistance value has been raised and thus the signal voltage drop across the total load also rises. Hence, low-frequency signal amplitudes are decreased to compensate for their attenuation caused by coupling capacitor C_4.

In practical systems the ohmic value of R_5 is selected to be approximately one-fifth the ohmic value of R_4 and about 10 times the reactance of C_3 for the lowest-frequency signal handled by the amplifiers.

2-9. VIDEO AMPLIFIERS

In a television receiver or transmitter it is necessary to increase the amplitude of video signals obtained from the detector or generator. The amplifiers used for this purpose are similar to audio amplifiers except that the signal frequency response range must be increased considerably to accommodate the picture signals, which have a span from 30 Hz to 4 MHz. A typical two-stage system for a black-and-white receiver is shown in Figure 2–5. Here, special components have been added to extend the signal-frequency range necessary. One of these units is the shunt inductor L_5 which parallels capacitances of both the transistors and those formed within the circuitry. The latter consist of capacitances from the wiring to ground, and from metallic components to ground. The inductance of L_5 in parallel with circuit capacitances form a low-Q broadly resonant circuit for the upper-frequency signals. Since a parallel L-C combination has a high impedance for signals at resonance, the shunting effects for high-frequency signals are minimized. In addition, a narrow group of signals each side of resonance also encounters sufficient impedance to prevent signal attenuation. An inductor such as L_5 is termed a

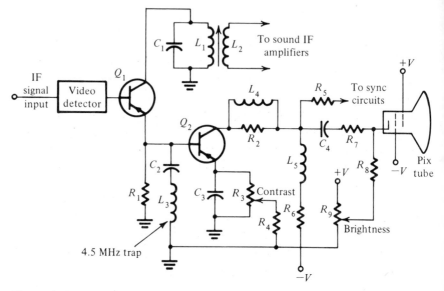

Figure 2–5 Television Video Amplifier

peaking coil, and for Figure 2–5 this coil is in series with R_6, to which the collector potential is applied.

Another peaking coil, L_4, is in the collector line of Q_2 and isolates shunt capacitances of the two amplifiers. A shunting resistor R_2 loads the coil R_4 to minimize transient oscillations that may cause oscillations or ringing. This inductor, in series with any circuit capacitances, will have a low-impedance bandpass for higher-frequency signals. Inductor L_3 has a function different from the other inductors: it forms a 4.5-MHz series-resonant circuit with capacitor C_2. Because of the low impedance of a se-ries-resonant circuit, 4.5-MHz signals are shunted and hence are not ap-plied to the Q_2 input, where they would eventually cause interference patterns on the picture screen.

Both the demodulated picture and sound intermediate-frequency (IF) signals are applied to the base input of Q_1. In addition, a 4.5-MHz signal is produced in the video detector and this is a lower-frequency version of the sound IF signal generated in the tuner. Transistor Q_1 feeds the demodulated signals to the base of Q_2 for amplification and applica-tion to the picture tube. Sound signals are trapped out as shown. The 4.5-MHz sound IF signal present in the emitter–collector circuitry of Q_1 is applied to a parallel-resonant circuit tuned to this signal. A transformer is created by the coupling of L_1 to L_2 as shown. Thus, the resonant circuit composed of C_1 and L_1 tend to reject all signals except the 4.5-MHz one to which it is tuned.

Resistor R_3 in the emitter of Q_2 alters the bias potential when the movable arm is adjusted. Thus, the gain of this transistor is set by the viewer to the level desired. Resistor R_4 prevents the emitter from being placed at direct ground when the variable arm of R_4 is at the top of R_3. Brilliancy is regulated by adjusting R_9. As the picture-tube cathode is made more positive with respect to the control grid, the latter becomes more negative and hence repels more of the electrons coming from the cathode structure. Consequently, beam intensity is decreased, as is the brightness level. For a less positive picture-tube cathode, control grid bias is reduced, more current flows, and brilliancy increases.

2–10. CHROMA AMPLIFIERS

In color television receivers several amplifiers are used to increase the amplitude of the three signals representing red, blue, and green. Typical circuitry is shown in Figure 2–6 and the combination of the three colors produced at the output of the amplifiers is applied to the cathodes of the picture tube as shown. The color signals are combined with the black–white luminance signal to produce the various shades of colors appearing on the screen.

The signals obtained from the color detector circuitry are applied to the base inputs of the three transistors utilizing the common-emitter circuitry. Resistors establish the proper voltages for the forward- and reverse-bias values needed. Thus circuit function is similar to the grounded-emitter system described in Sec. 2–2. Two color-gain controls are utilized, R_{13} and R_{14}. There is no specific gain control for the green signals, since its relative value in comparison to the red and blue signals can be established by adjustment of R_{13} and R_{14}. If, for instance, the amplitude of the signals representing green is too high in comparison to the red and blue signal gain, the gain of the red and blue signals is increased by R_{13} and R_{14} so that, in effect, the amplitude of the green is lowered to balance the three. The inductor identified as RFC is a radio-frequency choke coil that provides a high reactance for the signals and thus prevents their leakage to the power supply. The low resistance for dc has a negligible loading effect on the feed lines. Spark gaps (SG) are used in each circuit, as shown, for discharging any buildup of high voltage in

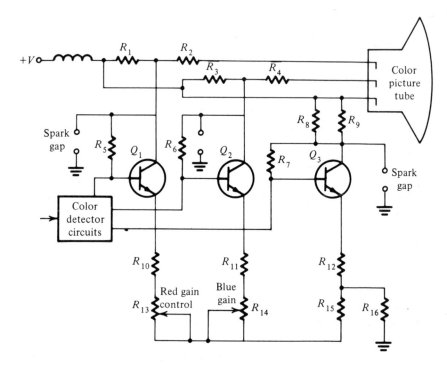

Figure 2–6   Chroma-Signal Amplifiers

circuit components. When the potential builds up beyond a specific value it causes an arc-over and thus is discharged.

2–11. SINGLE-ENDED AUDIO AMPLIFIERS

The purpose of a power amplifier is to develop sufficient signal energy for application to a loudspeaker, recording head, or other similar transducer. Usually, the power amplifier is preceded by several low-signal amplifiers. Where the original sound source is picked up by low-sensitive transducers such as dynamic microphones and magnetic phono cartridges, special low-signal amplifiers (termed *preamplifiers*) are also utilized. A typical single-ended audio power amplifier is shown in Figure 2–7. Here, the input signal from the previous low-signal amplifier stages is impressed across resistor R_1. The latter is a variable type and forms the volume-level control for the output amplifier. Capacitor C_1 couples the signal energy across resistor R_3 and hence across the base and emitter

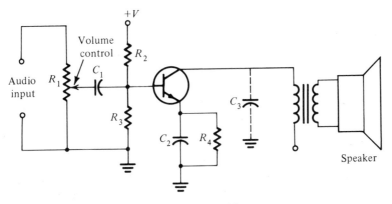

Figure 2–7 Single-Ended Audio Power Amplifier

terminals of the transistor. The addition of resistor R_2 to the input circuit forms a voltage divider for establishing the forward bias to the base terminal as shown.

The circuit shown in Figure 2–7 functions in similar fashion to the low-signal amplifiers described earlier in this chapter. Resistor R_4 and capacitor C_2 form the thermal stability circuitry described in Sec. 2–2. For the circuit shown, an output transformer is used, although for most modern audio systems, dual transistors coupled directly to the speaker or other transducer are utilized. The transformer provides an impedance match between the voice coil impedance (or other transducer) and the impedance of the recommended load resistance value for the transistor. The turns ratio between the primary and secondary of the transformer determines the impedance-matching factor: (Z_1/Z_2) (see also Sec. 1–10).

Transformers are more costly than other components and, in addition, have several disadvantages over other coupling methods. Unless a transformer is of superior design, it has significant distributed capacitances between turns of wire and layers of wire and hence exhibits a low capacitive reactance for higher-frequency signals and consequently tends to attenuate them. Also, any dc resistance in the wire of the transformer windings consumes some audio power and represents a signal loss. Since the primary and secondary windings are inductors, their inductive reactance also varies for changes of signal frequency and consequently contributes to an uneven frequency response. To improve transformers requires costly design changes consisting of larger cores, which permits the use of fewer turns of the winding for less dc resistance. Because an increase in the core area of the transformer increases permeability, fewer turns are required for obtaining the same inductance values that would prevail for the smaller-core transformer using additional wire. The circulating magnetic fields also create other losses, including eddy currents. Any thermal buildup in the core and windings causes energy losses.

2–12. PHASE INVERSION

Amplifiers utilizing the phase-inversion principle are needed to form push-pull circuits. The latter provide for increased power output, a reduction of harmonic distortion, and a more even frequency response. As with the transformer factors discussed in Sec. 2–11, the use of phase-splitting transformers not only increases the cost over R-C coupling, but also adds bulk, uneven frequency responses, and produces other losses as described in Sec. 2–11. For comparison purposes a typical transformer-coupled phase inverter and push-pull circuit is shown in Figure 2–8(A) and an R-C type in (B).

The purpose for phase inversion is to furnish signals of opposite phase to the input terminals of push-pull amplifiers (either audio or RF types). For the circuit shown at (A), transformer T_1 has a split secondary winding; hence, the signal applied to the primary of T_1 appears across each half of the secondary as an out-of-phase pair, as shown. Because there is a phase inversion between the input signals at the base terminals of a common-emitter amplifier and the signals appearing at the collector circuitry, the amplified versions of the signals appear across the primary of T_2 again inverted as shown. The negative-polarity signal across one-half of the output transformer primary winding combines with the positive-going signal and the other half of the winding to produce a combined resultant at the secondary of T_2. Thus, although there are dual signals produced by the two transistors, the center-tapped primary of T_2 performs an additive function and thus combines the individual amplitudes of the two signals into one signal of approximately double the original amplitude.

Resistor R_1 from the common-emitter terminals to ground requires no bypass capacitor when the transistors have similar characteristics and are fairly evenly matched. Since a symmetrical circuit is present, the increase in emitter–collector current for Q_1 flowing through R_1 is offset by the decrease in emitter–collector current for Q_2 flowing through R_1; hence, no signal voltage appears across the latter.

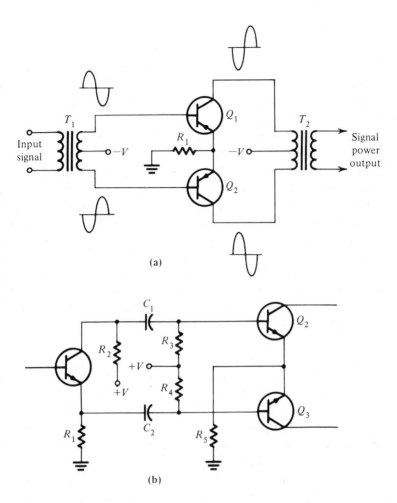

(a)

(b)

Figure 2–8 Phase-Inversion Circuitry

A transistor circuit wherein signals are obtained from both the collector and emitter resistors can serve as a phase inverter, as shown in Figure 2–8(B). Both R_1 and R_2 have the same ohmic value and thus the signal voltage that develops across each has the same amplitude. These signals, however, are 180° out of phase with each other since current flow is up through one resistor and down the other. The two signals are coupled to the base elements of Q_2 and Q_3 and the push-pull output circuitry has the identical function to that at (A).

2–13. COMPLEMENTARY-SYMMETRY AMPLIFIERS

A widely used audio amplifier, the *complementary-symmetry* type, is shown in Figure 2–9. Although two transistors are utilized to provide a single output, the system is not the push-pull type. Transistor Q_1 applies a signal to the base terminal of Q_2 as well as Q_3. Unlike push-pull, however, the signals appearing at Q_2 and Q_3 have the same phase. Note, however, that Q_2 is an *npn* transistor and Q_3 is a *pnp* type. The voltage-divider network R_5 and R_6 apply a positive potential to the base of Q_2 and a negative voltage at Q_3. When a positive alternation of an input signal appears at the base terminals of the output transistors the *npn* transistor Q_2 undergoes an increase in its forward bias, hence a conduction increase. For Q_3, however, the positive input signal decreases the forward bias; hence this transistor has a decrease in conduction between emitter and collector. Thus, for a given input signal, there is an opposite effect on conduction. For a negative-polarity input signal conduction decreases for Q_2 but increases for Q_3. The consequence is that equivalent push-pull symmetry is achieved with the complementing transistor output (*npn* and *pnp*). Thus, there is no need for a phase-inversion circuit and the low im-

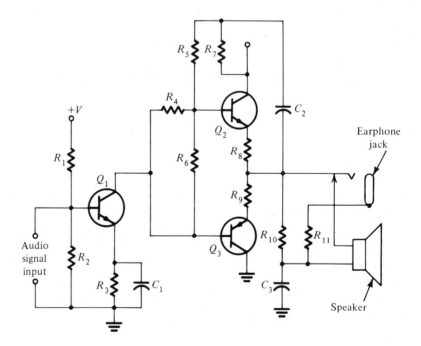

Figure 2–9   Complementary-Symmetry Audio Amplifier

pedance of the output circuitry of transistors permits application of signal power to the loudspeaker without intervening transformers.

When the speaker is in operation, resistor R_{11} presents an open-circuit condition. When the earphone jack is plugged in, the speaker is disengaged and resistor R_{11} is placed in series with the earphones to minimize overload. This is standard practice, and the values of resistor R_{11} may range up to 330 Ω. Often, the bottom speaker lead is placed directly to ground instead of using capacitor C_3. When in use, however, C_3 usually has a value of over 200 μF and thus has a sufficiently low reactance for most of the audio signals to provide for a signal-grounding effect. Additional resistors or capacitors are sometimes utilized to achieve a greater circuit symmetry for Q_2 and Q_3 since Q_3 has a grounded collector and hence Q_2 is above ground by comparison.

2–14. RF AND IF AMPLIFIERS

Audio amplifiers are operated as Class A for many low-signal types and Class A or B for some power types. Amplifiers designed for radio-frequency signals may utilize any type of operation, such as A, B, or C. The characteristics of these types are defined in Table 12–3. Radio-frequency amplifiers in receivers are usually employed in tuners. For transmitting purposes, successive RF stages are utilized (see Chap. 8). In receivers of all types the superheterodyne principle is employed almost exclusively, as described in Chap. 11. Thus, the stages following the tuner are intermediate-frequency (IF) amplifiers since they increase the signal amplitude of the intermediate signal produced by the heterodyning process in the tuner.

The basic circuits for RF and IF amplifiers are shown in Figure 2–10. An n-channel enhancement MOSFET is utilized in part (A). Note that the bias voltage for the gate (G) as well as the voltage for the drain (D) are shunt fed; that is, the feed lines parallel the resonant circuits rather than having the power applied in series with the resonant circuit as shown for the amplifier in (B). For the MOSFET circuit in (A) a series radio-frequency choke (RFC) is present in the V_{DD} line and helps to confine the signal energy to the amplifier circuits. The higher reactance of the RFC provides an isolation factor and minimizes common signal coupling by the power supply for various circuits fed by it.

Inductor L_3 in series with capacitor C_3 constitute a series-resonant circuit acting as a feedback loop for neutralization purposes. The variable capacitor C_3 permits adjustment of the proper feedback signal amplitude to minimize oscillatory tendencies. The term *neutralization* is a carryover from vacuum-tube electronics but is also applicable to solid-state circuitry. For the latter, however, a more appropriate term is *unilateralization* and it has been widely used. A unilateral circuit essentially refers to one having only a single-direction path for the signal handled. Thus, unilateralization is a process wherein the external feedback system cancels both reactive and resistive coupling between input and output sections of a transistor. Neutralization, however, is deemed to cancel only resistive coupling between input and output circuitry.

As shown at (A), the input RF signal is applied across L_1 that forms the primary of a transformer with L_2 as the secondary. The latter, however, is shunted by tuning capacitor C_2 and forms a parallel-resonant circuit having a high impedance for the desired signal. The signal is applied to the gate circuit by capacitor C_1, which also isolates the dc bias from the grounding effect of L_2. The amplified signal appears across the output resonant circuit consisting of C_5 and L_5. Capacitor C_4 prevents the shorting of the dc drain potential by inductor L_5. The signal output is obtained from the transformer secondary L_6. When such a circuit must be tuned for various signal frequencies, the tuning capacitors C_2 and C_5 are usually ganged; that is, both rotor sections are on a common shaft. The ganging is depicted on a schematic by an interconnecting dashed line as shown in Figure 2–10(A).

The basic intermediate-frequency amplifier shown in Figure 2–10(B) is tuned to only a single frequency and hence dispenses with the variable capacitors shown in (A). For precise adjustments to resonance, variable core transformers are utilized as shown. Again, the signal is impressed across the transformer, the inductors of which form resonant circuits with shunting capacitors. Bias voltages related to incoming signal amplitude are obtained from the detector and applied to resistor R_1 for automatic volume control (AVC) purposes. The latter system maintains a fairly constant audio output level even though the station signal strength may vary from one station to another. When a stronger signal is tuned in, the detector furnishes an AVC voltage to the base of Q_1 that reduces forward bias and hence decreases gain to compensate for the increased signal (see also Sec. 3–11).

Capacitors C_2 and C_6 provide a ground return to the emitter circuit and minimize the tendency for common-signal coupling by the power supply. The base of Q_1 taps inductor L_2 for an improved impedance

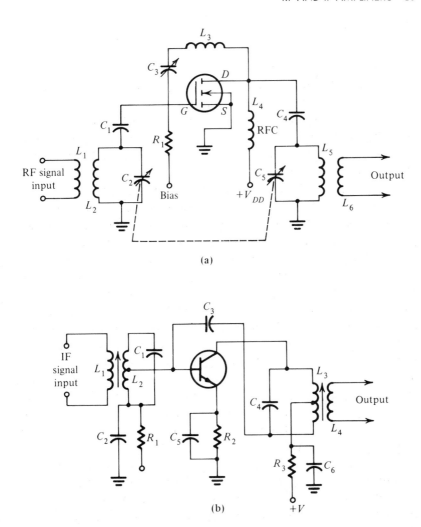

Figure 2-10   RF and IF Amplifiers

match. The tap on L_3, however, is for signal division so that an inverse signal can be coupled by C_3 to the base circuit for neutralization purposes. Resistor R_2 and capacitor C_5 are for minimizing thermal effects and hence stabilize the transistor function for a change of temperature. For an increase in the dc across R_2, the emitter becomes less negative and hence the forward bias is reduced. Consequently, there would be less conduction and hence compensation for the unwanted dc increase.

2–15. COUPLED IF STAGES

Intermediate-frequency amplifier stages employing capacitive coupling are shown in Figure 2–11. Transformer coupling could also be used as was shown for the RF amplifiers in Figure 2–10. The amplifier circuitry of Figure 2–11 has been used for video IF signals in television receivers. Transistors Q_1 and Q_2 are the dual-gate FET types and are particularly useful since they have a separate terminal for the automatic gain control (AGC) voltages obtained from the demodulator (see Sec. 3–12). Transistor Q_1 obtains its input signal from the tuner. Capacitor C_1 applies the signal to gate terminal G_1 as shown. Resistors R_1 and R_2 form a voltage-divider network for establishing the proper G_1 bias. The AGC input is applied to transistor gate G_2. Resistor R_3 and capacitor C_2 form a filter to bypass any signal variations. Hence, only the dc bias signal for gain control purposes appears at G_2. As with automatic volume control (AVC) for radio, the AGC regulates the gain of the IF stages to maintain a constant output level as preset by the viewer. When another station having a different carrier signal level is tuned in, the AGC provides a bias change to compensate for the difference and thus performs a correction.

The output signal from Q_1 is obtained from the FET drain element and appears across the parallel-resonant circuit composed of C_4 and L_1. The high impedance provides for a large voltage buildup for the signal

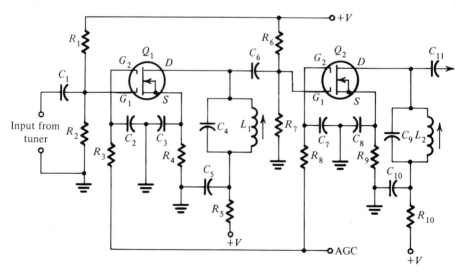

Figure 2–11   Video IF Stages

and the latter is coupled by C_6 to the G_1 terminal of Q_2. The basic function of the latter transistor is identical to Q_1. To obtain maximum signal transfer, inductors L_1 and L_2 have variable cores for peak tuning to the signal. Resistors R_4 and R_9 in conjunction with capacitors C_3 and C_8 are the conventional source-element stabilizing networks discussed in Sec. 2–2. Resistors R_5 and R_{10} in conjunction with C_5 and C_{10} are decoupling networks that provide a direct return to the source circuits for the signal energy and minimizes common coupling in the power supply.

2–16. CLASS B OR C (RF) AMPLIFIERS

A typical RF amplifier with resonant circuits is shown in Figure 2–12. This circuit is usually operated either Class B or C, as determined by the bias potentials applied. For Class B operation the circuitry is utilized in communication systems where amplification of a modulated RF carrier signal is necessary. The term Class B *linear* has been used to identify operation on the straight-line portion of the characteristic curve of the transistor. Once an RF signal is modulated, successive Class C amplifiers are unable to retain the complete modulated waveform because collector current flows for only portions of single-polarity alternations of the input signal (from zero to maximum in one direction). For Class B, however, the base–emitter bias is reduced to the cutoff point and only alternations of a particular polarity of the input signal are effective in collector current control. The resonant circuit utilizes the flywheel effect to reinstate the missing alternation of the signal polarities lost at the input.

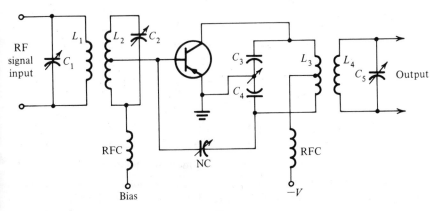

Figure 2–12 Class B or C (RF) Amplifier

For the circuit shown in Figure 2–12 the application of *reverse* bias at the input will drive the quiescent operating point sufficiently into the cutoff region for Class C operation. Consequently, collector current flows only for a portion of every other alternation of the input signal, contributing to the high efficiency of this system. As shown, the input RF signal is applied to the primary winding L_1 of the input transformer formed in conjunction with L_2. These inductors have shunting capacitors $(C_1$ and $C_2)$ that help form the resonant circuits required. Inductor L_2 is tapped for impedance-matching purposes between the inductor and the input of the transistor. At the output, the resonant collector circuit (sometimes referred to as the *tank* circuit) consists of L_3 shunted by variable capacitors C_3 and C_4. A single capacitor as was used for L_2 could be placed across L_3, but the dual-capacitor arrangement places the rotor section at ground and thus minimizes shock hazards during tuning. Since the rotors are connected to a common shaft and the stators are separated or split into two sections, such capacitors are also termed *split-stator* types. Bias and power supply potentials are applied in series with radio-frequency chokes (RFC) that offer a high reactance for signal energy and minimize common coupling among amplifier sections via the power supply.

Because interelement capacitances of transistors may provide regenerative coupling between input and output circuitry, amplifiers may oscillate and generate an unwanted signal. To eliminate such tendencies a neutralizing capacitor (N_c) is employed. Because the power supply feedline taps L_2 the resonant circuit is effectively split in half to produce at the bottom a signal 180° out of phase with that at the top. Hence, the neutralizing capacitor connects to the bottom of the collector resonant circuit and couples a portion of a signal to the base terminal of the transistor. The capacitor is tuned until neutralization is accomplished (see the discussion on *unilateralization* in Sec. 2–14).

2-17. PUSH-PULL RF AMPLIFIERS

As with the push-pull circuitry used with audio systems discussed in Sec. 2–12, push-pull can also be utilized for RF stages. A typical system is illustrated in Figure 2–13 utilizing two junction transistors (*npn* types). The incoming signal appears across inductor L_1 and is coupled to L_2. The secondary L_2 is tapped at center by the bias feed line as shown.

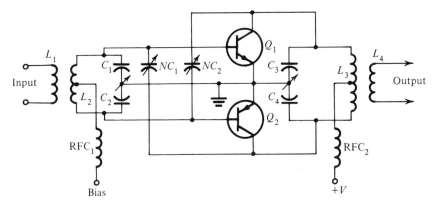

Figure 2-13 Push-Pull Class C Amplifier

Split-stator capacitors as discussed for the circuit shown in Figure 2-12 are convenient in push-pull because of the circuit symmetry that prevails. The center taps in the resonant circuits plus the centerline of the split-stator capacitors split the resonant circuits into dual sections to accommodate the push-pull transistors. As for the circuit shown in Figure 2-12, neutralization is utilized, although for the circuit of Figure 2-13 the dual process is usually termed *cross-neutralization*. Here, capacitor NC_1 connects from the bottom of the output resonant circuit to the base terminal of Q_1 while NC_2 connects from the top of the output resonant circuit to the base terminal of Q_2. Thus, the necessary degenerative signals are obtained for feedback purposes and their amplitude is established by the setting of the neutralizing capacitors.

In transmitting systems successive Class C amplifying circuits are used between the carrier oscillator and the final antenna system that transmits the signal. Thus, the low-amplitude signal initially generated is raised to the power level required for transmission. In practical systems appropriate ammeters (or milliammeters) are connected in series with the base and collector circuits to maintain a constant check of current levels. A current meter in a base circuit aids in the proper tuning of the resonant circuit and permits adjustment of the amplitude of the drive signal input. A current meter in the collector circuitry permits checking for the current dip that occurs when precise resonance is obtained during adjustment of the variable capacitors. For neutralization procedures the input RF signal is removed and the feedback capacitor is tuned for a minimum current reading in the base-current meters.

2–18. RF SIGNAL FREQUENCY MULTIPLIERS

The Class C amplifier circuits illustrated in Figures 2–12 and 2–13 can also be used for doubling or tripling the frequency of the signal applied at the input. Conventional circuitry is utilized as shown in Figure 2–14, except that the output resonant circuit is tuned to a *multiple* of the input-circuit frequency. If, for instance, the circuit were used as a frequency doubler, a 2.5-MHz signal would find resonance in both of the input parallel-resonant circuits. The output circuit in the collector, however, would be tuned to 5 MHz and consequently the flywheel effect of the resonant circuit would maintain this frequency and provide the secondary L_4 with the doubled output. For frequency doubling, the output circuit is pulsed at half the rate of the signal interchanged in its resonant circuits. Thus, the collector circuit furnishes power to its resonant circuit only half as often as would be the case if the input signal were also 5 MHz. If the output resonant circuit is tuned to triple or quadruple the frequency of the input signal, efficiency declines considerably because the circuit energy is not being replenished as often as in standard amplifiers. For frequency-multiplier circuitry, neutralization is not necessary because the dissimilarity in frequency between input and output signals inhibits regeneration.

2–19. AMPLIFIER FEEDBACK AND DEGENERATION

Many amplifiers utilize degenerative (inverse) feedback for diminished harmonic distortion, increased frequency response, improved stability, and noise reduction. The basic principle is illustrated in Figure 2–15, where a portion of the amplified output signal is fed back to an earlier circuit. For inverse feedback the signal that is fed back is out of phase with the signal where the feedback potential is applied as shown. Hence, the signal that is fed back has an inverse function in relation to the signal existing at the point of feedback. With such feedback, amplification is reduced in proportion to the amplitude of the fed-back signal.

For the circuit shown in Figure 2–15 the amplitude of the feedback signal is established by selection of the proper value of R_4 in the feedback line. Capacitor C_2 isolates the dc components at the output and input circuits. When the feedback signal appears across the emitter resistor R_3 of Q_1, there is a reduction of the signal voltage across R_3 proportionate to the amplitude of the signal fed back. For a positive alternation of

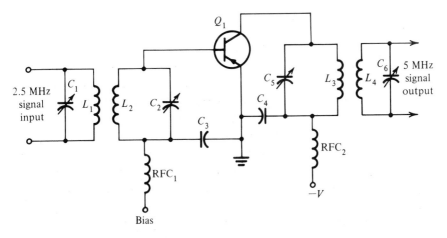

Figure 2–14 Frequency Multiplier (RF)

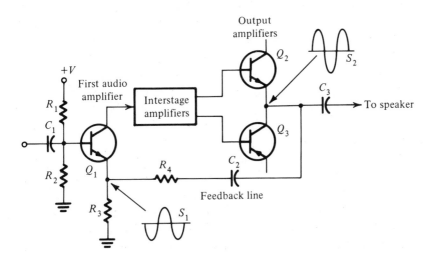

Figure 2–15 Inverse Feedback

an input signal the inverse feedback signal of negative polarity would alter the forward bias between emitter and base of Q_1, with a resultant decline in emitter–collector signal current. Distortion present at the output
would also be contained within the feedback signal and would inversely
affect the generation of such unwanted distortion (for additional feedback data, see Sec. 2–21).

2-20. DARLINGTON AMPLIFIER

The Darlington solid-state unit consists of two transistors, as represented by the symbol shown in Figure 2–16(A). The input transistor's circuitry is an emitter-follower type feeding the base input of the second transistor. Characteristics of this unit include exceptionally high gain. Total signal-current amplification (h_{fe}) is the product of the amplification obtained from each of the transistors within the Darlington structure (see also Sec. 1–18). Thus, $h_{fe_1} \times h_{fe_2} = h_{fe_d}$ (where the latter is the total Darlington gain). For Figure 2–16(A) resistors R_1 and R_2 form a voltage divider supplying bias to the base of the first transistor. The output is obtained from across emitter-resistor R_3 as shown.

The Darlington pair has many applications because of the high signal amplification and exceptional sensitivity. The output signal produces sufficiently high collector signal current levels to perform as an efficient driver even though fed by low-amplitude supply potentials. Hence, the device reduces the number of components that would otherwise be required for a given system. The Darlington pair is useful in audio circuitry as well as in switching devices. It is also useful for forming signal generators (oscillators). There is an impedance step-down between input and output as with the common-collector (emitter-follower) circuitry. The output impedance is usually equal to the resistance of R_3, while the approximate input impedance equals the amplification factor $\beta^2 \times R_3$.

2-21. OPERATIONAL AMPLIFIERS

The operational amplifier is a unit (usually direct coupled) utilizing an appropriate feedback loop. It is used where high gain (over 1 million possible) and a flat response are needed. The basic principles are illustrated in Figure 2–16(B). The lowercase Greek letter beta (β) usually used to indicate transistor gain is also employed to represent the decimal equivalent of the percentage of voltage fed back. Thus, the feedback loop consisting of R_2 is sometimes identified as β. Since the feedback is degenerative, only a small portion of the output signal is fed back; otherwise, the amplification of the circuitry would be reduced considerably. With a feedback signal applied to the input of a transistor stage, it is amplified and appears at the output of that stage to which it is applied as an amplified signal but out of phase with the distortion that develops within

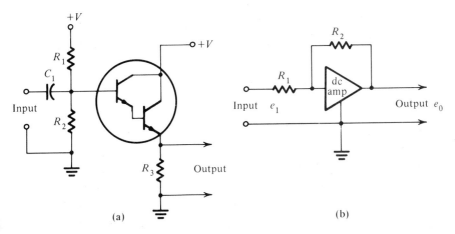

Figure 2-16 Darlington and Operational Amplifiers

that stage. Hence, distortion and noise signals are attenuated in proportion to the amplitude of the feedback signals.

In the absence of feedback, the input signal voltage e_i is increased by the amplification resulting in an output signal e_o. Thus, the open-loop amplification (without feedback) can be expressed as e_o/e_i. With inverse feedback (also termed *negative* feedback) the feedback symbol is often preceded by a minus sign: $-\beta$. Representing amplification as A, $A\beta$ represents the *feedback factor*. Thus, $1-A\beta$ is a measure of a feedback amplitude. When the feedback factor $A\beta$ is much greater than 1, the signal-voltage gain is independent of A and amplification with feedback becomes $1/\beta$ (see also Sec. 2–19).

2-22. DIFFERENTIAL AMPLIFIERS

The differential amplifier is useful for handling a wide-signal bandpass with excellent circuit stability. It is a versatile circuit and can be used as a mixer for heterodyning several signals, a limiter for signal clipping, a modulator, as well as a signal-frequency multiplier. The basic circuit is as shown in Figure 2–17(A) and contains no capacitor or inductor. Thus, because of the minimum number of components, it lends itself well in the design of integrated circuits and is frequently utilized as a companion circuit to the operational amplifier described in Sec. 2–21. As

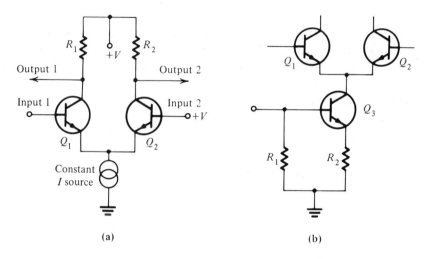

Figure 2–17   Differential Amplifier Circuits

shown in Figure 2–17(A), two transistors are used in an emitter-coupled arrangement wherein a constant-current source section is common to both. Two input and two output terminals are provided in a symmetrical system. Resistors R_1 and R_2 have matched values and both transistors have virtually identical characteristics.

There are several operational modes possible with this circuit. The signal can be applied to only one of the inputs, grounding the other. Hence, if a signal is applied to input 1, the amplified version would appear at the collection of Q_1. Similar characteristics prevail for transistor Q_2. In both instances there is a phase difference between input and output signals. Considering the constant-current source as resistive, or if it were replaced by a single resistor, signal-current variations would occur across it and provide common coupling. Consequently, the emitter–collector current of Q_2 would also contain signal voltages when the input to Q_1 is activated. Similarly, a positive alternation of the input signal at the base of Q_2 would raise forward bias for a current increase in the collector-emitter. Because of common coupling, similar current changes would prevail for the other transistor. For an input signal at the base of Q_1 and an output obtained from the collector of Q_1, the operational mode is designated as *single-ended input–output signal, inverting mode*. For an input at Q_1, but an output from Q_2, the mode is a *single-ended input–output, noninverting mode.*

The input signal can be applied across both base circuits to form a *differential-type mode.* An advantageous characteristic of the differential amplifier is the common-mode characteristic obtained for in-phase signals appearing at both input terminals simultaneously. Undesired signals picked up by the two inputs simultaneously would produce a voltage across an emitter resistor that tends to attenuate the common-mode signal without affecting a desired signal applied to a single input only. Because of this common-mode characteristic, the differential amplifier is highly stable. As shown in Figure 2–17(B), the constant-current-source symbol shown in (A) is represented by transistor Q_3 and associated components. For this circuitry the impedance between the collector and emitter of Q_3 is sufficiently high for constant-current purposes, yet resistor R_2 can have a much lower value than the conventional emitter resistor utilized in Figure 2–17(A). The reduction of the voltage drop across an emitter resistor also reduces power dissipation (see also Sec. 4–8 and Figure 4–7).

2-23. BANDPASS AMPLIFIERS

A bandpass amplifier is used in color television receivers to raise the gain of the color video signals while removing pulse- and sync-signal information so that the latter do not cause interference when applied to the picture tube. A typical circuit that performs these functions is shown in Figure 2–18. The bandpass amplifier is usually between the video amplifier output circuits and the color-signal demodulators. As shown, the video signal input is applied to the base of transistor Q_1 and amplified in the emitter–collector section in conventional fashion. A signal, obtained from the horizontal output transformer, is applied to the junction of the two capacitors C_4 and C_5. Such a signal is termed a *blanking signal* since it has a polarity that opposes the power supply voltage applied to R_3. When the blanking pulse appears it switches the transistor current off and thus prevents amplification of both the synchronizing signals and the 3.58-MHz burst signal accompanying all color transmission. Thus, the bandpass amplifier is momentarily inoperative during the presence of the blanking signal (which occurs only during the horizontal blanking interval). The blanking pulse is of sufficient duration to prevent amplification of the vertical sync pulses, equalizing pulses, horizontal sync signals, blanking signals, and the color burst carrier reference signal of 3.58 MHz.

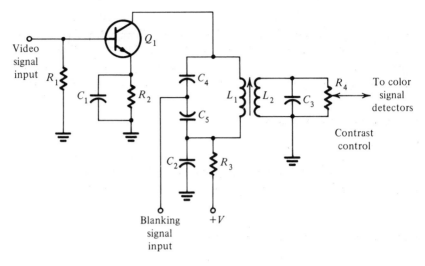

Figure 2–18 Bandpass Amplifier

The output signal is transferred from L_1 to L_2 and this transformer arrangement utilizes a variable core for tuning purposes. The output circuit is broadly resonant around the 3.58-MHz region to accommodate the chrominance sideband signal components. Resistor R_4 is a variable color control that permits adjustment of the amplitude of the output signal and compares to the contrast control in black-and-white television.

2–24. BURST-GATE AMPLIFIERS

The purpose for a burst-gate amplifier is to process the special synchronizing signal transmitted during color telecasting. This synchronizing signal of 3.58 MHz is transmitted as a nine-cycle segment situated on the latter part of the horizontal blanking interval. Because of its short duration it is termed a *burst* signal. This synchronizing signal is necessary to lock in the receiver's subcarrier oscillator so the latter produces a stable color-signal carrier as a needed substitute for the one that was suppressed at the transmitter. Once reformed in the receiver, the subcarrier is recombined with the color-signal sidebands to permit demodulation of the color video signals.

The burst signal must be removed from the composite video signal arriving at the receiver so that the burst signal can be routed to the required circuits. The undesired signals that accompany the synchronizing burst signal are removed by a gating circuit such as that shown in Figure 2–19. Here, transistor Q_1 receives the composite video signal via capacitor C_1 to the base terminal. At the same time a keying pulse, obtained from a tap on the horizontal output transformer, is also applied to the base terminal of Q_1 as shown. This keying pulse occurs only during the horizontal blanking interval and has a polarity that provides forward bias and causes the transistor Q_1 to conduct periodically. Thus, Q_1 conducts only during the time that the burst signal is present in the composite video signal and consequently only this burst signal appears at the collector output of Q_1. Although the output is amplified, an additional burst-signal amplifier (Q_2) is often used.

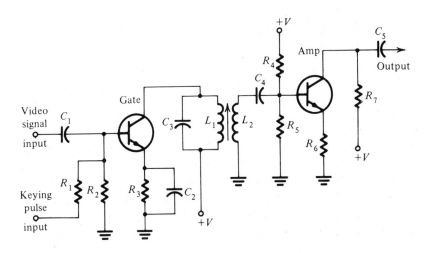

Figure 2–19 Burst Gate and Amplifier

The keying pulse is delayed approximately 3 to 5 μs to prevent entry of horizontal sync-pulse signals. Capacitor C_3 in conjunction with L_1 forms a high-impedance parallel resonant circuit for 3.58 MHz. Inductor L_1 is coupled to L_2 (transformer secondary) and a variable core permits precise tuning. Capacitor C_4 couples the burst signal to the base input of Q_2 and the amplified version appears across resistor R_7. Capacitor C_5 couples the signal to the phase detector and subcarrier oscillator system (described in Sec. 2–30) for automatic frequency control of the subcarrier generator.

2-25. SWEEP OUTPUT AMPLIFIERS

The purpose for sweep amplifiers is to raise the signal amplitude of the sweep signals utilized in television receivers and oscilloscopes. Sweep signals are needed in television to move the electron beam within the picture tube in both the vertical and horizontal planes at a rate established by the relaxation oscillators and synchronizing signals. It is necessary to sweep the beam both vertically and horizontally to form a rectangular lighted area referred to as a *raster*. It is upon the latter tracings that the picture information is impressed (see Sec. 8–5). For oscilloscopes the signal to be used is commonly applied to the input of the vertical amplifiers while an internal horizontal sweep system scans the signal across the face of the tube.

The basic circuitry necessary for television receivers is shown in Figure 2–20. Transistor Q_1 is the vertical sweep output amplifier that raises the signal level above that obtained from the vertical sweep-signal oscillator or driver stages. The amplifier system is conventional, with the amplified signals developing across R_3. Capacitor C_1 couples the amplified sweep signals to the vertical deflection coils consisting of L_1 and L_2. These coils are placed around the neck of the picture tube in combination with inductors L_3 and L_4. The latter are the horizontal deflection coils fed by the horizontal sweep amplifier system shown. Inductors L_1 through L_4 are combined in a common housing (termed a *yoke*) and are placed around the neck of the picture tube. The combined magnetic lines of the four sweep inductors move the beam within the picture tube to form the raster mentioned earlier.

The horizontal output system is more complex than the vertical output circuitry because of the multiple functions associated with Q_2. A high-voltage diode D_1 minimizes undesirable transient signals generated by the abruptly changing high-amplitude pulse signals. Another diode, D_2, supplies several thousand volts for the focus-control electrode of the picture tube. The amplitude of the sweep voltage developed is related to the size of the picture tube and the receiver design (black-and-white or color). For the circuitry shown in Figure 2–20, a black-and-white receiver is assumed, although similar circuitry is utilized for color receivers.

The output from Q_2 is applied to a horizontal transformer consisting of a primary (L_6) and several secondary windings. Although the sweep signals are coupled by capacitor C_3 to the horizontal deflection coils, they are also used to produce the focus electrode potentials as well as the potentials needed by the second anode of the picture tube. Thus,

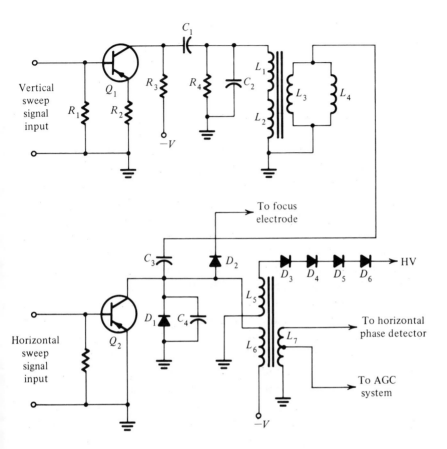

Figure 2-20 Sweep Output Amplifiers

the secondary winding L_5 steps up the voltage to a value ranging between 15 and 30 kV, depending on picture tube size. Color receivers require a higher-amplitude second anode potential than black and white. A series of diodes (D_3 through D_6) serve as rectifiers for the high voltage potentials. Additional windings are present for pulse signals needed by the horizontal phase detector, gating circuits, and AGC systems.

2-26. ARMSTRONG OSCILLATOR

A variety of signals must be generated in electronic systems for gating, counting, and control purposes. Such signals consist of both RF and audio types and include sine-wave, pulse, and square-wave formations. The generators used to produce signals are also termed *oscillators* and there are two primary categories: *resonant-circuit* types and *relaxation* types. For the resonant-circuit types the frequency of the generated signal is determined by the value of resonant circuitry components plus circuit inductances and capacitances in aggregate. The relaxation oscillators produce signals that have a frequency related to circuit component values usually without resonant systems. Two basic RF signal generators are illustrated in Figure 2–21.

The oscillator shown in Figure 2–21(A) was one of the first resonant-circuit types and is identified as the Armstrong feedback type. Note that the output signal develops across the resonant circuit consisting of C_3 and L_3. A pickup inductor L_2 samples a portion of the signal and couples it back to the base terminal of the transistor using capacitor C_1. Thus, a continuous input–output loop is formed to sustain oscillations. When the circuit is switched on, the initial rise of potentials is sufficient to initiate the oscillatory processes. The phase relationships between signals appearing across L_2 and L_3 determine the polarity of the feedback. If L_2 is reversed, the feedback will be degenerative and hence will prevent oscillations. Capacitor C_2 provides for a direct signal return from the collector circuitry to the emitter. Inductor L_1 is a radio-frequency choke having a high reactance for the signals and thus minimizing their leakage to the power supply. The frequency of oscillations is determined by Eq. 1–40.

2–27. HARTLEY OSCILLATOR

The circuit shown in Figure 2–21(B) is termed a Hartley oscillator, after its originator. This signal generator utilizes a tapped inductor (L_1) that forms a resonant circuit with capacitor C_1. The tap splits the inductor into two sections and sets up a division of components between the input and output circuitry. Capacitor C_1 plus the upper portion of L_1 form the base–emitter portion, while capacitor C_1 and the lower section of L_1 form the collector–emitter portion. Thus, the output signals are coupled to the input section by virtue of the mutual inductance existing across the tapped L_1 winding. Consequently, feedback is established in similar fashion to the circuit shown in (A).

Capacitors C_3 and C_4 isolate the dc circuits and prevent such potentials from being grounded through inductor L_1. Inductor L_3 is an RF

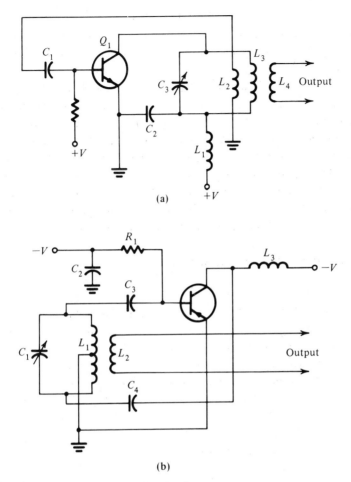

(a)

(b)

Figure 2-21 Armstrong and Hartley Oscillators

choke isolating signals from the power source. Resistor R_1 is in series with the feed line for the bias to the base of the transistor.

2-28. COLPITTS OSCILLATOR

The Colpitts oscillator is another version of the RF types designed to generate high-frequency signals. A typical circuit is shown in Figure 2–22(A), using an FET. [A junction transistor could also be utilized for this circuit in similar fashion to that shown in Figure 2–21(B).] For the

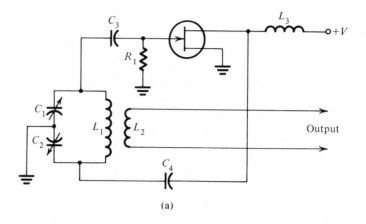

(a)

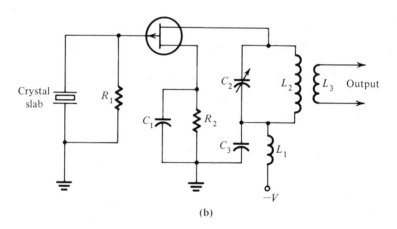

(b)

Figure 2–22 Colpitts and Crystal Oscillators

Colpitts oscillator, L_1 is not tapped as was the case for the Hartley oscillator, but instead dual capacitors C_1 and C_2 are utilized. The rotor sections of these capacitors are connected to a common shaft and placed at ground potential as shown. Thus, the capacitors and L_1 form the resonant circuit. Because of the grounding of the rotor sections the resonant circuit is electrically split in half just as was the case of splitting the resonant circuit of the Hartley oscillator by a tapped inductor. The split resonant circuit provides coupling of the output signal obtained from the source element of the FET to the gate input terminal to sustain oscillations. Capacitors C_3 and C_4 provide signal coupling with dc isolation. Inductor L_3 is an RF choke for isolation of the circuitry signals from the power section.

2-29. CRYSTAL OSCILLATORS

For increased frequency stability, piezoelectric quartz crystals are ground to a specific thickness and utilized to stabilize the signal frequency of an oscillator. The quartz crystal is a *transducer* that produces a signal voltage when subjected to mechanical vibrations, or it undergoes a vibration when voltages are applied across it. It is usually mounted between two metal plates forming the contacting elements for the unit. The mounting plates plus the crystal structure produce a resonant circuit characteristic wherein the mass of the crystal can be considered the inductance, and the holding plates as the capacitance. A typical circuit is shown in Figure 2–22(B).

Resistor R_1 is the dc ground return for the gate element, and capacitor C_1 and resistor R_2 form the conventional stabilizing circuitry to minimize the effects of thermal changes (see Sec. 2–2). The output resonant circuit consists of C_2 in parallel with L_2, with the output obtained from the secondary winding L_3. Capacitor C_3 is a ground return to the drain element to provide for a short signal path. Inductor L_1 is an RF choke often utilized in RF circuits to provide a high reactance for signal energy and prevent coupling to the power supply. For increased stability in transmitting systems the crystal slab is often encased in a heated container. Since thermal variations alter the crystal frequency, a stabilized crystal temperature helps maintain the signal frequency near or at its precise point. In other instances synchronizing signals are utilized to lock in the oscillator, as discussed in Sec. 2–30.

2-30. SUBCARRIER OSCILLATORS

The purpose for a subcarrier oscillator in color television systems is to generate another carrier signal independent of the primary video carrier signal. In color transmitting systems the subcarrier signal is modulated by the color signals to produce sidebands. After modulation, the subcarrier is suppressed and only the color sideband signals are transmitted. Consequently, the missing subcarrier must be generated in the receiver and combined with the incoming sidebands so that demodulation of the color video signals can be accomplished. In the receiver the subcarrier oscillator frequency must be locked in precisely with the frequency of the subcarrier signal at the transmitter. This is accomplished by utilizing the 3.58-MHz burst signal transmitted and processed by the burst-gate circuitry discussed in Sec. 2–24.

A typical system for generating a subcarrier and controlling its frequency is illustrated in Figure 2–23. Associated with the system is the phase detector (also called a discriminator), explained more fully in Sec. 2–31, and the reactance-control circuit utilizing transistor Q_1, described more fully in Sec. 2–32. The oscillator transistor (Q_2) has a feedback loop from the collector terminal to the base terminal consisting of C_9 and R_{10}. A fixed-frequency quartz crystal is in series from the output section of Q_1 to the base of Q_2 using coupling capacitor C_7. The crystal is ground for a 3.58-MHz frequency and thus stabilizes the circuit for oscillation at that frequency. Rigid control with respect to frequency and phase is not possible, however, because thermal effects cause a crystal frequency change, as do variables in circuit component values for temperature changes in the area of the oscillator circuit.

The exact subcarrier frequency is 3.579,545 MHz and for proper color rendition the subcarrier oscillator in the receiver must be locked in synchronization with the transmitted subcarrier burst signal. The lock-in must be precise and correction must be performed automatically for any slight drift wherein phase differences occur between burst and subcarrier signals. Such rigid frequency control is accomplished by comparing the output signal frequency of the subcarrier oscillator with the incoming burst signal frequency in a phase-detector circuit. When a difference occurs, a correction voltage is produced by the phase discriminator and applied to the input circuit of Q_1, the reactance-control circuit. The latter then alters the subcarrier oscillator frequency to make the necessary correction. Note that the output from the Q_2 oscillator has a circuit loop back to the phase detector, and the latter connects to Q_1. Thus, a continuous circuit loop is present and is often referred to as a *phase-locked loop* (PLL). The output from Q_2 is also applied to the color signal detectors where the demodulation process produces the color video signals.

2–31. PHASE DISCRIMINATORS

A typical phase discriminator using dual diodes is also shown in Figure 2–23, where it is used to compare a synchronizing burst signal frequency

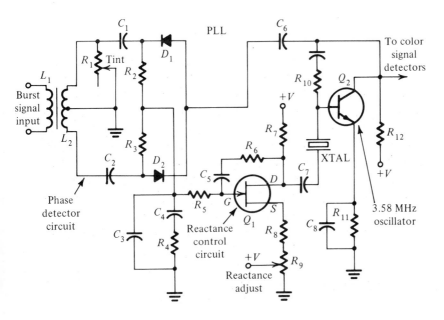

Figure 2–23   Subcarrier Oscillator and Control

with a subcarrier oscillator frequency. In such a system the phase detector generates a correction voltage when phase differences occur between the two signals. As shown, the synchronizing input signal is applied across a transformer primary L_1 and hence appears across the secondary L_2. The output applied to the reactance transistor Q_1 is obtained from the junction of R_2 and R_3 as against the center tap of L_2 (ground return). The sampled signal from the oscillator is applied to the junctions of diodes D_1 and D_2, thus forming balanced input and output systems. The circuit is symmetrical, with equal values for resistors R_2 and R_3 as well as equal values for capacitors C_1 and C_2. Although the circuit is sensitive to phase changes, it resembles the conventional bridge circuit wherein a balanced bridge produces a null voltage across specific terminals. For the phase discriminator, a zero voltage exists when the synchronizing signal coincides with the oscillator signal. An output correction voltage is produced when phase differences occur because of oscillator drift. Whether the correction potential is positive or negative depends on whether the oscillator frequency rises above or falls below that of the synchronizing burst signal. The correction voltage is applied to the reactance transistor Q_1, and the value of the reactance increases or decreases as needed, causing a slight change in the subcarrier oscillator frequency for correction. The mass of the crystal can be considered the inductive reactance and the holding plates the capacitive reactance to form the oscillator's resonant circuit. Thus, the output from the reactance control circuit can alter the reactances of the oscillator circuit and thus control frequency (see also Sec. 2–32).

2–32. REACTANCE-CONTROL CIRCUITS

The purpose for a reactance-control circuit is to simulate either capacitive or inductive reactance with a value related to a specific amplitude of input potential. Thus, such a circuit can alter reactive and resonant characteristics of other circuits by electrical rather than manual control. A typical example is the reactance-control circuit shown in Figure 2–23. Resistor R_6 helps establish the reactance characteristics, with capacitor C_5 blocking dc potentials. Essentially, the oscillator signal is applied across the output of Q_1 and consequently also appears across the R-C network coupled to the input gate terminal. If R_6 is 10 times that of the gate input impedance of Q_1, the R-C network of resistors and capacitors from the gate circuit to ground will have a signal *voltage* lag since *current* leads in a network that is predominately capacitive. Thus, the signal at the gate terminal of Q_1 has its phase altered to lag the oscillator signal. Hence, the circulating signal developed in the source–drain output section has a current-lag characteristic as compared to the oscillator signal. Consequently, the reactance circuit appears to have inductive characteristics. This factor can be more readily understood by reference to the reactance circuitry illustrated in Figure 2–24.

A reactance circuit using a junction transistor is shown in Figure 2–24(A). This circuit simulates a capacitive reactance and when shunted across an oscillator it can regulate the frequency within certain limits. The reactance-forming components consist of C_1 and R_1. These two components essentially are coupled across the oscillator circuit. Hence, the RF signal generated by the oscillator appears across this network of C_1 and R_1. The values of the latter two components are selected to have a certain component-value ratio. Capacitor C_1 has a reactance that is substantially greater than the resistance of R_1 for the frequency of signals involved. If the oscillator voltage is represented as E_o along the x axis of a graph, it is shown as in Figure 2–24(B). The current for C_1 and R_1 is

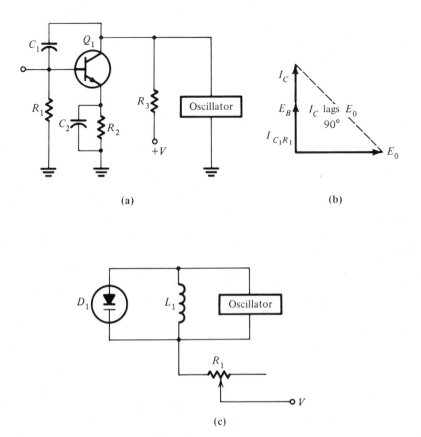

(a)

(b)

(c)

Figure 2–24   Reactance-Control Circuits

shown at right angles along the y axis. The graph thus depicts the current for the R_1-C_1 network leading the oscillator voltage by 90°. Across resistor R_1, however, both voltage and current are in phase, since pure resistance does not alter such phase relationships. Hence, the signal voltage at the base terminal input of transistor Q_1 leads the oscillator voltage by 90° as shown in (B). Since collector *current* is in phase with base-terminal *voltage*, the collector current (I_C) is also shown along the y axis of the graph. Thus, it is obvious that collector current leads oscillator voltage and thus introduces a capacitive reactance across the resonant circuit of the oscillator. In practical applications, the resistance of R_1 is selected to have an ohmic value of approximately one-tenth of the capacitive reactance of C_1, thus making the network C_1-R_1 primarily capacitive.

An input potential applied to the base of Q_1 alters emitter–collector current within a range established by the amplitude of the input signal. Thus, collector current can be raised or lowered by applying either a positive or negative voltage across R_1. Thus, the simulated capacitance value is changed accordingly. If a sine-wave type signal is applied to the input of Q_1, the frequency of the oscillator signal will change at a rate dependent on the frequency of the input signal. For an audio-signal input, a *frequency modulation* of the oscillator's RF signal is produced.

Another method for varying reactance by voltage changes is illustrated in Figure 2–24(C). Here a varactor diode is utilized as a shunt across an inductance L_1. The varactor diode exhibits a capacitance directly proportional to an applied reverse-bias voltage. Thus, diode D_1 and inductor L_1 comprise the resonant frequency-determining circuit of the oscillator. A voltage change will alter the capacitance of the diode and hence can regulate the frequency of the oscillator signal generated. A variable resistor (R_1) can be utilized for tuning purposes or a number of fixed-value resistors can be switched in the circuit so that pushbutton tuning selection can be utilized.

2–33. MULTIVIBRATORS

The multivibrator is a signal generator of the nonresonant type wherein the frequency of the generated signals is established by the values of circuit resistances and capacitances. The multivibrator, as well as the blocking oscillator described in Sec. 2–34, are known as *relaxation oscillators*, and they are useful in a wide variety of circuitry for signal production.

As shown in Figure 2–25, the basic multivibrator circuit usually contains two transistors in typical amplifier circuitry. As shown, however, instead of provisions for an input signal at Q_1, the output from Q_2 is coupled back to the base input of Q_1 using capacitor C_1. Thus, the signals fed back to Q_1 are continuously amplified and recirculated to produce and maintain signal generation.

Relaxation oscillators can be locked into synchronization with an external signal for precise frequency-control purposes. This is done in television receivers where synchronizing pulses are transmitted to lock in the vertical and horizontal sweep generators of the relaxation type. For synchronization of the circuit in Figure 2–25 an unbypassed emitter resistor R_4 is utilized. The synchronizing signal is applied across this resis-

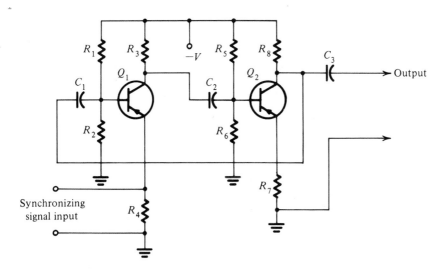

Figure 2–25   Multivibrator Oscillator

tor and if the sync-signal frequency is at or near the free-running frequency of the multivibrator, frequency lock-in will result. The circuit can also be synchronized by a signal having a frequency twice that of the free-running signal frequency. As shown, the output signal is obtained from the collector of Q_2 and coupled by capacitor C_3 in conventional fashion. The circuit is symmetrical in design; hence an output could be obtained from the collector of Q_1 and the synchronizing signal applied across R_7.

2–34. BLOCKING OSCILLATORS

As with the multivibrator discussed in Sec. 2–33, the blocking oscillator is a relaxation type. It is useful in applications where it is necessary to synchronize the frequency of the generated signal with that of an external signal. A typical blocking oscillator using a single *npn* transistor is shown in Figure 2–26. The operating principle consists of periodically blocking the transistor conduction by having the circuit continuously change the emitter–base forward bias. As shown, a transformer is utilized in the collector circuit with L_2 providing for a signal output as well as a feedback coupling loop. An additional winding, L_3, provides for signal synchronization.

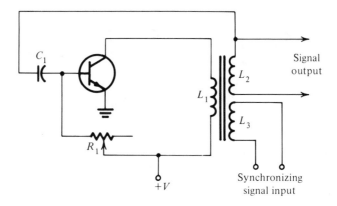

Figure 2-26 Blocking Oscillator

During operation, the feedback loop charges capacitor C_1 with a polarity that is negative at the transistor base. Since such a voltage rise across C_1 applies reverse bias to the base–emitter circuit, conduction for the transistor ceases. The capacitor discharges at a rate depending on the amount of energy stored and the time constant of the circuit components. When the capacitor has discharged across R_1 normal forward bias prevails and the transistor conducts again. The feedback loop again builds up a reverse bias to stop conduction and the operating cycle is thus repeated continuously as long as the power is applied to the circuit. Proper operation depends on the polarity of the signal fed back from L_2. For proper synchronization, the sync-signal frequency must be at or near the free-running frequency of the blocking oscillator. The sync signal appearing across L_1 from L_3 can trigger the transistor into conduction slightly prior to when it would normally do so. Thus, control of the frequency of the generated signal is maintained.

2-35. HALF-WAVE POWER SUPPLY

The half-wave power supply, as well as the full-wave type described in Sec. 2–36, is widely utilized to convert the ac from the power mains to dc for utilization as needed in electronic circuits and systems. As shown in Figure 2–27, transformers are utilized for increasing or decreasing the voltage levels obtained from the power mains. Additional secondary windings may be utilized where intermediate voltage levels are required.

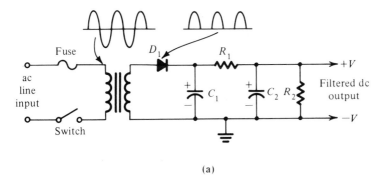

(a)

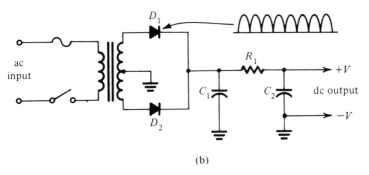

(b)

Figure 2–27 Basic Power Supplies

In television receivers, for instance, an additional winding is necessary to furnish the low-voltage ac needed for the picture-tube filaments. For such devices as radio receivers, tape recorders, and high-fidelity stereo amplifiers, power supply voltages may range from several volts to 100 V or more. For industrial application, however, heavy-duty components are utilized because kilowatts of power may be needed.

The circuit shown in Figure 2–27(A) is a half-wave type using a single diode rectifier (D_1). This circuit is a basic economical type satisfactory for low-priced equipment. Generally, a fuse is utilized in the input line to protect against overloads that may occur when power-supply components become defective. A switch is also present in the primary winding to turn the power supply on and off. The alternating current from the line is in the form of a continuous sine-wave signal, as shown. When this appears across the secondary of the power-supply transformer, diode D_1 permits passage of only the positive alternations. These half-alternations are termed *pulsating dc.* A continuous path is provided by R_1 and R_2 (plus the load system across R_2). Capacitors C_1 and C_2 are termed *filter capacitors* and have a low reactance for the ripple frequency of the pulsating dc. Hence these units tend to smooth out current fluctuations. Also, these capacitors charge to the peak amplitude of the pulsating dc and tend to assure a continuous-value output current flow, depending on the load characteristics. If the load draws current at a rate above that by which the capacitors can be charged, the filtered dc output would contain a significant ripple.

Resistor R_1 may be replaced in some commercial applications by a filter inductor having a high series reactance for the ripple frequency. The rectification action of diode D_1 charges the filter capacitors each time a positive pulse is produced. Because the pulsating dc has intervals between pulses, the power-supply regulation is somewhat inferior to that of the full-wave type discussed in Sec. 2–36. In power supplies *regulation* is the term applied to indicate to what degree (as a percentage) the filtered dc output voltage varies as the current drain on the power-supply changes. Voltage regulation is the ratio of output voltages that prevail for the minimum and maximum current drains (see Sec. 2–40).

The filter capacitors are of the electrolytic types and to prevent damage, their polarity markings must coincide with the potentials appearing across them. Since the filter capacitors are charged to the peak values of the pulsating dc, the output voltage will be somewhat higher than the rms value of the ac power input for no-load conditions. As the load is increased the additional current drain depletes the charges of the capacitors and output voltage will then decline to a level dependent on regulation.

2–36. FULL-WAVE POWER SUPPLY

A full-wave power supply is illustrated in Figure 2–27(B). This term is applied because dual diodes are employed so that each alternation of the ac signal is utilized. The result of the dual diode function is the formation of an unbroken sequence of unidirectional pulses, as shown. Since the pulsating dc amplitudes are continuous, the filter capacitors are charged at twice the rate of the half-wave power supply. Consequently, regulation is improved and a smoother filtered dc output can be obtained. Thus, the filter capacitors can have lower values than that needed for the half-wave supplies while maintaining the same degree of ripple-filtering process.

For the circuit shown in Figure 2–27(B), the secondary of the transformer is center tapped to ground for an equal division of the voltage at D_1 and D_2. Thus, to obtain approximately the same output voltage from the full-wave circuit as for the half-wave, the secondary winding would have twice the number of turns. Where the secondary for the circuit in (A) may have a 30-V potential, the secondary winding in (B) would have a 30-V potential on each side of the center tap. The dual diodes have a common junction for the voltage output line feeding the typical series resistor and filter capacitors as shown for the circuit in (A). When a positive alternation of the ac line voltage appears across the secondary, the center tap has a negative potential with respect to the top of the secondary. In this instance electron flow would be from center tap through the load circuit, through R_1, and to the rectifier. Since the bottom of the secondary winding is negative, diode D_2 does not conduct. When the next alternation of the ac line potential appears across the secondary, its negative polarity at the top of the transformer indicates a positive polarity at the anode of D_2 with respect to ground. Consequently, electron flow through the ground network, through the load, and through resistor R_1 completes its return flow to the bottom of the transformer utilizing the conducting D_2.

Thus, for each alternation of the ac line signal, a positive alternation of rectified signal energy is produced by the full-wave system. The diodes conduct alternately and convert the positive and negative ac line signals to unidirectional pulsating dc. The disadvantages of the full-wave system are the need for an additional rectifier and a center-tap transformer, but the advantages over the half-wave type are improved filtering and regulation.

2–37. VOLTAGE-DOUBLER CIRCUIT

The purpose for a voltage-doubling power supply is to obtain approximately twice the filtered dc output potential than can be realized from the half-wave or full-wave power supplies. The voltage-doubler circuit utilizes two diodes, as shown in Figure 2–28(A). Capacitors C_1 and C_2 are an integral part of the doubling procedure since they receive alternate charges and apply their additive charges to the output lines. Capacitor C_3 charges to the full output voltage and provides filtering of the ripple components.

When a positive alternation appears across the secondary of the transformer, the top line applied to D_1 is positive and the bottom line feeding the junction of C_1 and C_2 is negative. Under this condition diode D_1 conducts and in so doing charges capacitor C_1 to the peak of the potential across the secondary winding. For the second alternation of the incoming ac, the top of the secondary is negative and the bottom positive. Now, electron flow is through diode D_2 and its return path is to the bottom of the secondary winding. Consequently, capacitor C_2 is also charged to the peak of the voltage appearing across the secondary winding. Thus, successive alternations of the sine-wave ac across the secondary alternately charge capacitors C_1 and C_2 with a polarity as shown.

Since the two capacitors can be considered as two voltage sources in series, the sum of the charges provides for approximately double the voltage appearing across the transformer secondary winding. Under load conditions the voltage would decline slightly, depending on the efficiency of the filtering system and the nature of the load applied. If the load circuit drains a substantial amount of current in a given time, the two rectifiers would be unable to replenish the successive charges across C_1 and C_2 rapidly enough to maintain a peak output potential. Thus, the value of the output potential depends on the degree of regulation available from the system.

2–38. VOLTAGE-TRIPLER CIRCUIT

In addition to the voltage multiplication system described in Sec. 2–37, a voltage-tripling circuitry has also been utilized. A typical example is shown in Figure 2–28(B) and it is useful for obtaining approximately three times the voltage delivered by the secondary winding of the power transformer. Note that three diodes are required here, in conjunction with capacitors C_1 and C_2. Capacitor C_3 is part of the filter system and an extension of the filter system can be employed by adding resistor R_1 and capacitor C_4 shown by the dashed-line formation.

For a positive alternation of the ac line signal appearing across the secondary of the transformer, the anode of D_1 would have a positive potential applied with respect to the bottom of the transformer (negative). Thus, electron flow is from the lower line of the secondary winding charging capacitor C_1 with a polarity as shown, with the return electron

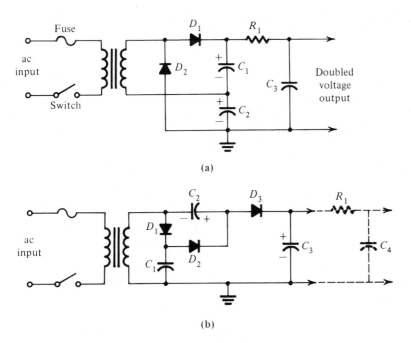

(a)

(b)

Figure 2–28   Voltage-Multiplier Power Supplies

flow through the conducting D_1 to the upper positive secondary line. For the next alternation of ac, the upper terminal of the secondary is negative and the bottom positive. Now diode D_1 is unable to conduct but diode D_2 has the proper forward bias for conduction. Consequently, capacitor C_2 is charged with a potential polarity as shown. The charge across C_2, however, is *twice* that which formed across C_1 because C_2 was charged not only by the potential across the secondary winding, *but also* by that which prevailed across C_1.

When the third alternation appears across the secondary winding the top is again positive and the bottom negative. Now, C_1 is charged again to the peak voltage and diode D_3 also conducts. Consequently, capacitor C_3 is charged to a potential that is the *sum* of the voltage across C_2 *plus that appearing across* the secondary winding. Thus, the voltage appearing across C_3 is approximately three times that of the line voltage under no-load operating conditions. As with the other power supplies discussed in previous sections, the output voltage level is determined by the load current drawn from the power supply and the degree of filtering that aids regulation.

2–39. BRIDGE-RECTIFIER CIRCUIT

The purpose for a bridge-rectifier circuit is to obtain full-wave power supply operation without needing a center-tap transformer. The disadvantage is that four diode rectifiers are needed as shown in Figure 2–29(A). Note that the diodes form a balanced bridge network with the output applied to a conventional ripple filter section composed of two capacitors and a series resistor. Two diodes are used for rectifying the positive half-cycles of the alternating current and another two for the negative alternations. When a positive alternation appears across the secondary winding (L_2) electrons leave the negative bottom terminal of L_2 and flow through D_2, through the ground circuit, up through the load, through R_1, and through diode D_3 for a return to the top of L_2. When a negative alternation appears across L_2, electron flow is through diode D_1, through the ground-return circuit and load, and through diode D_4 for the return to the transformer. Thus, the bridge power supply rectifies both the positive and negative alternations of the incoming alternating current for full-wave rectification.

2–40. ZENER REGULATOR

The purpose for a zener diode is to regulate the output voltage from a power supply and thus maintain a fairly constant level within certain limits of current drain variations. The zener is a silicon diode that conducts current when forward bias is applied, as with the conventional rectifying diode. The zener function, however, occurs when a reverse-bias voltage of proper amplitude is applied. For a low reverse bias the resistance of the zener diode is high and only a minimal amount of current flows. As the reverse-bias potential is raised, there is only a slight and insignificant increase in conduction. As the bias voltage is gradually increased, a critical point is reached where the internal resistance of the diode undergoes a sharp drop to an ohmic value almost zero. Consequently, current immediately flows through the diode in an amount that would constitute a damaging breakdown in a conventional diode of comparable dimensions. For the zener diode, however, the sudden conduction, even though in the reverse direction, is not harmful to the internal structure if the applied voltage lies within specified limits. If the reverse-bias voltage is removed, reverse conduction ceases. The breakdown point achieved for a certain bias potential is referred to as the *zener region*.

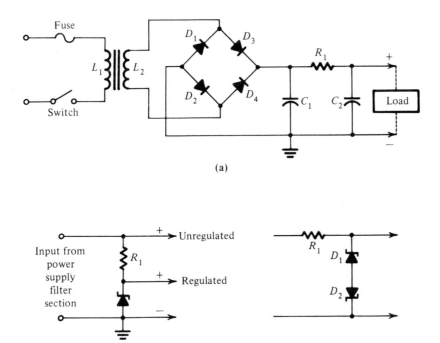

(a)

(b)   (c)

Figure 2-29   Bridge-Type Supply and Regulation

The amount of bias required to reach this region (and the amount of current that would flow) depends on the degree of resistivity designed into the silicon diode and to the bulk of the solid-state structure.

Once the zener region has been achieved, the voltage drop across the diode will remain constant and hence the unit is used for regulation of voltage output. A typical circuit is shown in Figure 2–29(B). Resistor R_1 is a voltage-limiting type having an ohmic value selected to provide a voltage for operation within the zener region. The zener diode is connected into the circuit so that the voltage across the diode forms a reverse bias. The regulated output voltage is obtained from across the diode as shown. The voltage at the top of resistor R_1 is unregulated. When the load circuit draws additional current from the regulated output terminal, the voltage drop across R_1 increases and under normal circumstances less voltage would appear at the output. The zener, however, alters its conduction to the degree necessary to maintain the output voltage at the value established before the load current drain changed. Such zener diodes operate within specified limits and units are designated by voltage and power ratings, so particular ones can be selected as needed.

The zener diode can be paired so that voltage regulation of alternating current can be obtained. The basic circuit is shown in Figure 2–29(C). Note that the two diodes are wired in opposing fashion so that they conduct alternately for respective positive and negative alternations of the alternating current from the line. Units are available containing two matched diodes which are already connected back to back for commercial purposes.

2–41. POWER-SWITCHING DIODES

When it is necessary to apply power to a load at predetermined intervals rather than continuously, special power-switching diodes are utilized. Such diodes come in a variety of sizes and permit use of low-power gating potentials to turn on or off a comparatively much higher power. A basic switching circuit for the silicon-controlled rectifier (SCR) is shown in Figure 2–30(A). As with other diodes, the symbol is representative and does not indicate the power-handling capability of the unit. The SCR devices are available in small units for low current capabilities as well as large units having higher voltage and current ratings.

As shown in Figure 2–30(A), the SCR represents a basic diode with an additional element referred to as the gate. The power source applied across the SCR circuit has the polarity shown. Current will not flow, however, and hence the circuit is in a nonconducting state. When a steady-state or pulse gate signal is applied between the gate terminal and ground, the positive gate potential causes the SCR to switch into its conducting mode. Thus, voltage is applied across the load and current flows in an amount determined by internal resistance of the latter. If the gating voltage is removed, the SCR continues to conduct and remains in this gated-on position until measures are taken to stop conduction, as explained later. Thus, whether a short-duration pulse or a dc gating signal is applied, conduction continues and the gate signal loses control.

Conduction will cease when the circuit is momentarily opened to remove the voltages across the anode and cathode of the SCR. When potentials are reapplied, the SCR remains again in a nonconducting state until a new gating potential is applied. With dc input to the SCR circuit, the diode latches on when gated and continues conduction; if ac is applied, however, the voltage across anode and cathode changes polarity

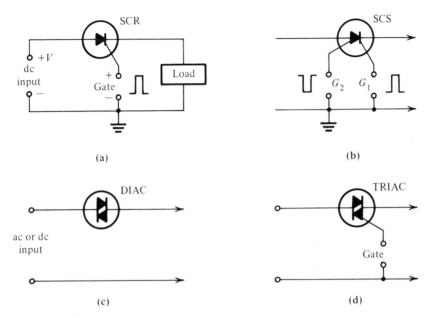

Figure 2–30   Electric Power Switching Circuits

continually and the alternations with reverse bias will periodically cause SCR nonconduction (assuming the presence of the gating signal). The amount of output power from the circuit can be controlled by utilizing an ac gating signal and shifting its phase with respect to that of the input ac power.

Another switching diode is the silicon-controlled switch (SCS) as shown in Figure 2–30(B). Here, either a positive or negative pulse can intitiate the switching mode, depending on whether G_1 or G_2 is used. As opposed to the SCR, the SCS can be switched *off* by a specific gating signal. A dual-diode switching unit is shown in Figure 2–30(C). This device is termed a Diac and the input can be either ac or dc as shown. This special diode can be used to switch power automatically since it conducts only when a predetermined voltage level is reached. Once this voltage is applied, the diode conducts in either direction. When a gate electrode is added to the Diac as shown in Figure 2–30(D), the unit is termed a Triac. This diode unit is similar to the SCR and does not conduct until a gate signal is applied. For the Triac, however, either ac or dc can be switched, and the latter can be applied in either polarity (plus to the Triac and negative to the bottom line, or negative to the Triac and plus to the bottom line).

2–42. AM DETECTORS

The purpose of an AM detector is to extract from an amplitude-modulated RF carrier the audio or video signal information. A typical circuit is illustrated in Figure 2–31 and it performs a rectification of the RF signal in similar fashion to that for the half-wave power supply discussed in Sec. 2–35. The amplitude-modulated carrier is applied across the primary (L_1) of the input transformer as shown. The radio-frequency signal in this case is indicated as the *intermediate-frequency* (IF) signal, since this is the result of signal mixing in the tuner—a characteristic of the *superheterodyne* receiver (see Chap. 11). The signal appears across the secondary winding (L_2), which is shunted by capacitor C_1 to form a resonant section tuned to the IF signal.

A solid-state diode performs the half-wave rectification and the demodulated audio or video signal develops across resistor R_1, which also serves as the volume or gain control. As shown in Figure 2–31, the incoming IF signal is an amplitude-modulated carrier and for purposes of illustration, the first segment shows the unmodulated state. The diode rectifier converts the signal to a series of unidirectional pulses, as shown for the rectified RF. The pulsating dc is filtered by capacitor C_2 and hence the pulses are converted to a low-frequency signal that follows the amplitude changes of the rectified RF signal. The result is an output signal having amplitude changes but of a unidirectional nature such as pulsating dc. Coupling capacitor C_3 not only transfers the demodulated signal to an amplifying stage, but converts it to one having ac characteristics.

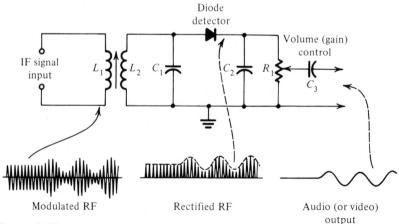

Figure 2–31 AM Detector Circuit

2–43. FM DETECTORS

The purpose for the FM detector is to extract from a frequency-modulated RF carrier the audio information (or whatever other modulating signal had been used). The most widely used circuit for this purpose is the ratio detector shown in Figure 2–32. Two diodes are utilized as shown plus an output filter network for extracting the audio information. The incoming frequency-modulated signal is applied across the primary of the input transformer. The secondary winding is split into two sections by a center tap and the latter is connected to a series inductor (L_4) coupled to the primary L_1 as shown. The secondary sections of L_2 and L_3 form a dual symmetrical circuit and in the presence of an unmodulated RF carrier signal, both diodes conduct equally for successive negative-signal alternations. Consequently, a steady-state output voltage prevails across resistors R_1 and R_2. Capacitors C_2 and C_3 charge to the peak amplitude of the rectified signals. For positive alternations (during which the diodes are nonconducting) capacitors C_1 and C_2 discharge across the resistors and maintain a steady-state output voltage.

For a frequency-modulated input signal, there is a constant change of signal frequency above and below the resonant frequency established by the tuned circuit composed of L_2, L_3, and C_1. Now, the coupling of L_4 to L_1 produces a circuit imbalance resulting in greater conduction for one diode with respect to the other. The result is an uneven voltage distribution across R_1 and R_2. As an example, assume that an unmodulated signal produces 0.25 V across R_1 and the same voltage across R_2. Total voltage would then be 0.5 across the resistive network. For a specific frequency deviation of the incoming signal the voltage drop across R_1 may drop to 0.2 V while that across R_2 may rise to 0.3 V. For a greater frequency deviation of the incoming carrier the voltage across R_1 may drop

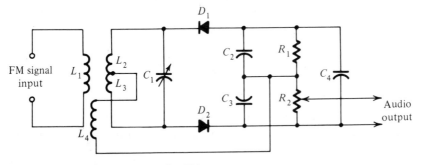

Figure 2–32 Ratio Detector for FM

to 0.1 V and that across R_2 rise to 0.4 V. For a carrier shift in the opposite direction, the voltage across R_1 would rise whereas that across R_2 would decline. Note that the *total voltage* across the two resistors remains the same although the *ratio* of voltages changes. By utilizing one of the output resistors as the output audio source the voltage variations can be tapped.

Capacitor C_4 shunts the resistive network and it has a much higher capacitance than C_2 and C_3. The purpose of C_4 is to charge to the peak voltage (such as the 0.5 V in the preceding example). Since a capacitor opposes an abrupt change of potential, it absorbs undesired transients such as static or interference from amplitude-modulated signals that may be accompanying the frequency-modulated carrier. Thus, capacitor C_4 is an effective noise-suppression device and hence eliminates the necessity for the noise clipper stage that was required for the older-type discriminator FM detector. The latter circuit resembles the ratio detector except that both diodes are wired in the same direction and no shunting capacitor such as C_4 is used. Instead, the discriminator required a limiter circuit that preceded the detector and clipped off amplitude-modulated peaks and noise signals. The limiter stage was also referred to as a clipper. Although performance equaled that of the ratio detector, the simplification of the latter has resulted in widespread usage.

2–44. REGENERATIVE DETECTORS

The purpose for a regenerative detector is twofold; it can demodulate the incoming RF signal and can also be switched into an oscillatory state for the production of an independent signal. The generated signal can then be utilized to heterodyne with signals such as the Morse code continuous-wave (CW) type. Such signals consist of unmodulated RF coded into segments and would be inaudible when processed by the average detector. The regenerative detector, however, mixes its signal with the incoming signal and by adjusting the detector to produce a difference in the frequency of the two signals, an audible signal is produced. If the regenerative detector signal and the incoming signal have the same frequency, the condition known as *zero beat* occurs and no audio signal would be produced. The mixing of signals having dissimilar frequencies, however, produces an audio output when the difference is within the audible signal range.

A typical circuit is shown in Figure 2–33 and a feedback inductor (L_2) is used to couple a portion of the amplified signal from L_4 back to the input circuit composed of L_3. The phase of the signal fed back must be such that oscillations occur. The incoming signal is transferred to the resonant circuit composed of L_2 and C_1 and rectification (detection) occurs between the base and emitter sections of the input circuit. The varying signals between base and emitter of the transistor influences current flow in the collector–emitter section and produces an amplified output. The audio signal thus develops across L_4 and hence is available from the secondary L_5 as shown.

The degree of coupling between L_2 and L_3 can be varied to establish the amount of regeneration; or the inductors can be at a fixed separation and the degree of regeneration adjusted by variable resistor R_1. When this resistor increases positive feedback, the circuit attains maximum efficiency at a point *immediately below* the oscillatory point. When oscillations do occur, the circuit generates its own signal for use in the detection of unmodulated carriers that contain code information as mentioned earlier.

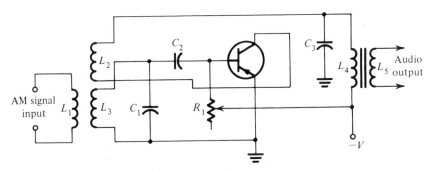

Figure 2–33   Regenerative Detector

2–45. COLOR-SIGNAL DETECTORS

In color television systems three color signals are utilized: red, blue, and green. These three signals are converted into two signals, termed I and Q (in-phase and quadrature). Thus, spectrum space is conserved by transmitting two instead of three sideband signals and in addition also suppressing the subcarrier that was modulated to produce the color-signal sidebands. Consequently, it becomes necessary to generate a substitute color subcarrier in the receiver as well as reestablishing the original three color signals that were used to produce the I and Q signals (see also Secs. 11–7 through 11–9). At the receiver, color-signal detectors are utilized as shown in Figure 2–34 to demodulate the composite RF signals and produce R–Y and B–Y components. As shown, the 3.58-MHz color subcarrier is injected into the circuitry of the demodulators and recombines with the incoming I and Q signals. The detection produces the red signal minus the luminance (Y) and the blue minus the luminance (Y) components. A matrix circuit such as that described in Sec. 2–46 is then used to mix the correct proportions of the red and blue to obtain the required green (G–Y).

For the circuit shown in Figure 2–34 transistors Q_1 and Q_2 represent the R–Y and B–Y demodulators. Some manufacturers designate these as X and Y when certain color-signal phase relationships are established for a particular receiver (See Secs. 8–6 and 11–7). As shown, the chroma signals are applied to the inputs of Q_1 and Q_2 simultaneously and signal variations appear across the emitter resistors R_4 and R_5. In turn, the signals across the resistors are modified by the subcarrier signal.

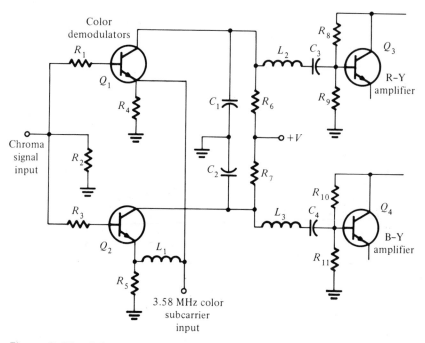

Figure 2–34 Color-Signal Detectors

Thus, the sideband color components are mixed with the subcarrier and the respective R minus Y and B minus Y signals are detected and developed across the collector resistors R_6 and R_7. Inductor L_1 introduces the required phase shift for the Q_2 circuitry. The respective red and blue signal components are amplified additionally by Q_3 and Q_4 and processed as described in Sec. 2–46.

2–46. MATRIX CIRCUIT

The purpose for a color-signal matrix circuit is to combine proportions of the R minus Y and B minus Y signals to produce a G minus Y signal representative of the green color-signal component. A typical circuitry is shown in Figure 2–35. Transistors Q_3 and Q_4 are a continuation of the circuitry shown in Figure 2–34. These are conventional amplifiers and develop the output signal across R_{14} and R_{15}, and from there transfer

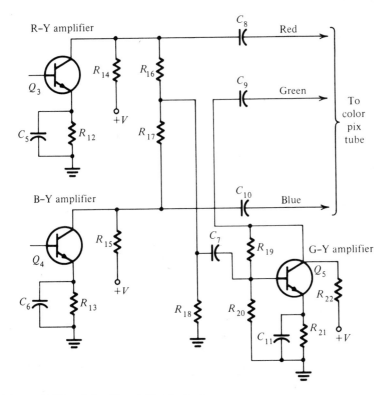

Figure 2–35   Color-Signal Matrix System

them to the input of the color picture tube. Resistor R_{16} has a lower value than R_{17} for proper signal amplitude apportionment. Thus, a tap at the junction of these resistors couples a portion of each signal amplitude to the base input of transistor Q_5. Resistors R_{16} and R_{17}, as well as resistor R_{18}, form the matrix for mixing required amplitudes of the red and blue signals for forming the G minus Y composite for the green color. The output from Q_5 is the amplified G–Y signal, which is now coupled to the input of the color picture tube in conjunction with the other two signals. (The proper proportions of chroma and luminance signals are listed in Table 7–30.)

3 Signal Modification, Routing, and Control

3–1. INTEGRATING CIRCUITRY

A simple R-C circuit utilized for pulse-signal modification is shown in Figure 3–1(A). This circuit is an *integrator* and is widely used in various branches of electronics. The degree to which the circuit modifies signals depends on the RC time constant of the circuit. The pulse modification consists of attenuating the high-frequency signal components to produce the results shown in (B), (C), and (D). Essentially, the integrator performs as a low-pass filter that attenuates high-frequency signals or signal components. When sinusoidal signals are applied, those of higher frequency are diminished to a greater degree than lower-frequency types. Signal modification is primarily attenuation for sine-wave signals, although some phase shifting occurs. Square-wave and pulse signals, however, have their waveshape altered due to high-frequency component filtering.

From the calculus we can establish a formula relating to the signal voltage applied to the integrator capacitor (e_c) and the capacitor signal current (i_c):

$$e_c = \frac{1}{C} \int i_c \, dt \tag{3–1}$$

where e_c is the signal voltage across the capacitor
C is the capacitance in farads
i_c is the capacitor signal current

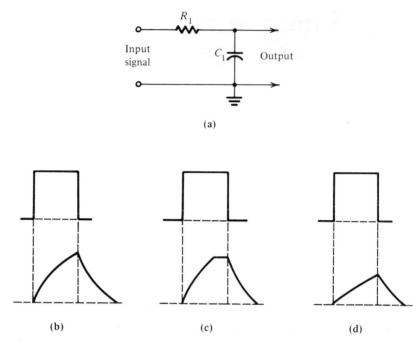

Figure 3–1 Integrating Circuit and Waveforms

Thus, Eq. 3–1 indicates that the capacitor voltage e_c is proportional to the time interval of capacitor current i_c. The time constant is long compared to the width of the pulse signals applied. Pulse waveforms contain numerous signal components which are harmonically related to the fundamental frequency. For the upper harmonic components, where the value of the resistor in ohms is considerably higher than the reactance of the capacitor, the following relationships exist:

$$e_c = \frac{1}{RC} \int e \, dt \qquad (3\text{–}2)$$

From Eq. 3–2 it is shown that the output signal voltage of an integrator is proportional to the integral of the input signal current. Note Figure 3–1(B), where a positive pulse represents the input signal. The steep leading edge of the pulse as it attains full amplitude applies this potential across the input. The rise time is of short duration, but the flat top holds the voltage at a fixed level for the duration of the pulse width. In a capacitor, voltage lags current, and the voltage rise is exponential.

The capacitor reaches 63% of the full charge in one time constant. After approximately five time constants the capacitor is charged fully. Because of the long time constant of this circuit the voltage of the output signal does not attain a leveling off unless a shorter time constant is present compared to pulse width, as shown in (C). For a longer time constant an almost pure sawtooth waveform is attained as in (B).

An inductor and resistor can also be used to form an integrator circuit. For the one shown in Figure 3–1(A), resistor R_1 would be replaced by an inductor and C_1 with a resistor. A long time constant would still prevail and the same type of output waveform is obtained. Since inductors also have resistance as well as reactance, design factors are more critical and in practical circuits the series resistor and shunt capacitor are used primarily.

3–2. DIFFERENTIATING CIRCUITRY

The basic differentiating circuit consists of a series capacitor and shunt resistor, as shown in Figure 3–2(A). Compared to the integrator discussed in Sec. 3–1, the time constant of the differentiating circuit is short

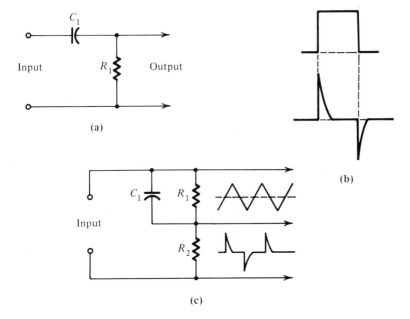

Figure 3–2   Differentiating and Dual Output

in relation to the width of the pulse signal applied. The integrating circuit can be compared to a high-pass filter because it diminishes the lower-frequency signal components of a pulse and hence modifies it. The differentiator circuit is widely used to convert wider-than-desired pulses to sharply rising, narrow pulses suitable for rapid switching and triggering in digital electronics. The differentiator retains the sharply rising leading edge of the input pulse signal as shown in (B). For this circuit, a voltage applied to the capacitor causes a current flow proportional to the time derivative of the voltage across the capacitor:

$$i = C\frac{de_c}{dt} \qquad (3\text{--}3)$$

Because of the short time constant, some signal components of the input pulse create a situation where the circuit resistance has a value much lower than the capacitive reactance in ohms. Thus, these quantities can be set down as follows to indicate the voltage across the resistor (e_R):

$$e_R = IR = RC\frac{de}{dt} \qquad (3\text{--}4)$$

For an applied pulse, the leading edge represents a sharp rise and since current leads voltage in a capacitor, the high initial current produces a voltage drop across R_1, representing a spike-type waveform. For the flat top of the input pulse the capacitor current declines as the capacitor charges at a rate dependent on the time constant. Because the time constant is short, the capacitor charges very rapidly and current flow drops to zero. Consequently, the voltage across R_1 also drops to zero. For the trailing edge of the pulse the input voltage suddenly drops to zero and the capacitor discharges across R_1. The discharge direction is opposite to the charge direction; hence, the voltage across R_1 is in the form of a negative spike, as shown. As with the integrator circuit discussed in Sec. 3–1, pulse signals are usually applied to the differentiator. If sine-wave signals are applied, the amplitude is attenuated progressively as the signal frequency rises. Some phase shifting would also occur.

An inductor and resistor can also be used to form a differentiating circuit, in which case C_1 is replaced with a resistor and R_1 with an inductor. Because of the inherent internal resistance of an inductor, the design is less desirable and usually avoided in practical circuitry.

3–3. DUAL *I* AND *C*

In Figure 3–2(C) a dual circuit is shown performing both differentiation and integration. For a pulse-signal input, the upper two terminals produce an integrated signal output, while the lower two terminals provide a differentiated signal output. The time constant (τ) for this circuit utilizes the following equation:

$$\tau = \frac{R_1 R_2 C_1}{R_1 + R_2} \tag{3-5}$$

3–4. DIODE SIGNAL MODIFIERS

Diodes can also be used in special circuits for modification of signals or for removing transients, noise-signal components, or excessive amplitude peaks of signals. Diodes can also perform signal clipping for sine waves so that they attain square-wave characteristics. The circuit shown in Figure 3–3(A) clips the peak amplitudes of input waveforms so that the out-

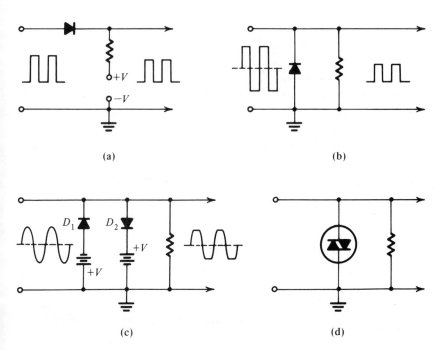

(a)   (b)

(c)   (d)

Figure 3–3   Diode Signal Modifiers

put signal amplitude is proportional to those values of the input waveform exceeding a specific value. For the one shown in (A), a series type is indicated since the resistor is in series with the diode. When a bias voltage of proper polarity is applied to the terminals below the resistor, a reverse bias prevails for the diode and no conduction occurs unless this bias amplitude is nullified. When a positive polarity signal appears at the input, current will flow only for amplitudes that exceed the reverse bias voltage. If, for instance, the reverse bias is 5 V and the input signal is 12 V, a 7-V output is obtained, since 5 V of the input waveform must overcome the reverse-bias potential.

A shunt clipper is shown in Figure 3–3(B). Here, the negative-signal portions of a square wave are clipped. This comes about because the positive-polarity portions form a nonconducting reverse bias for the diode and hence the signal passes through to the output. For negative portions of the input signal, however, the diode conducts because of the forward bias applied. Consequently, the diode shunts the negative portions of the signal and hence the output consists of a series of positive-polarity pulses as shown. If negative-polarity output pulses are required, the diode is reversed in the circuit.

By using dual-shunt clippers, with one diode reversed as shown in Figure 3–3(C) both negative and positive clipping is possible. Thus, square waves can be reduced in amplitude, or sine waves can be clipped to resemble square waves as shown. Such a parallel clipper is sometimes termed a *slicer*. The degree of clipping is adjusted by regulating the amplitude of the bias potentials employed in series with each diode. For a negative alternation exceeding the applied bias, D_1 conducts. The other diode, D_2, conducts for a positive alternation exceeding the bias potential. The combined clipping of the dual diodes modifies the input signal as shown. Dual diodes in a single housing (a *Diac*) conduct only when a certain specific potential is reached; hence the function for the circuit shown in (D) is similar to that shown in (C).

3–5. TRANSISTORIZED SIGNAL CLIPPER

A transistorized circuit signal clipper is shown in Figure 3–4. The circuitry is a conventional Class A type amplifier with the bias set on the linear portion of the characteristic curve. For clipping purposes, the input signal must have an amplitude sufficiently high in both its negative and positive directions to drive the transistor into both the cutoff region

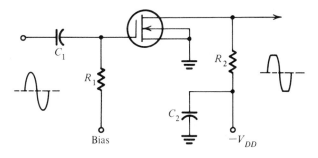

Figure 3–4   Transistorized Signal Clipper

and the saturation region. Thus, the circuit is essentially an overdriven amplifier that produces limiting or clipping functions for an input signal. Depending on the amplitude of the input-signal drive, a portion of each alternation peak of the output signal is clipped. If the input signal drive is sufficiently high, the output becomes more nearly a square wave with sharply rising leading and trailing edges. A junction transistor could, of course, be used instead of the FET shown.

3–6. SAWTOOTH SIGNAL FORMATION

A method for forming sawtooth signals is shown in Figure 3–5(A). The principle involved is the slow charge and rapid discharge of a capacitor (C_1) and hence the circuit is sometimes called a *discharge circuit*. No dc bias is present between the base and emitter and hence the transistor is at or near current cutoff. During nonconduction of Q_1 a closed-circuit loop exists in the circuit composed of the battery, capacitor C_1, and resistor R_2. Consequently, the battery charges the capacitor and the electron flow is in such a direction that the collector side of C_1 has a gradually rising positive potential. Thus, the initial portion of the sawtooth waveform is generated. The rate of charge depends on the time constant of the circuit and during the initial charge (to about 1% of full charge) the potential rise is virtually linear after which the voltage build-up would follow an exponential curve. Thus, the sharp drop in amplitude which forms the complete sawtooth is initiated during the linear portion of the voltage rise.

The input to the discharge circuit is obtained from a relaxation circuit such as a blocking oscillator. The signal consists of a sharp rise in

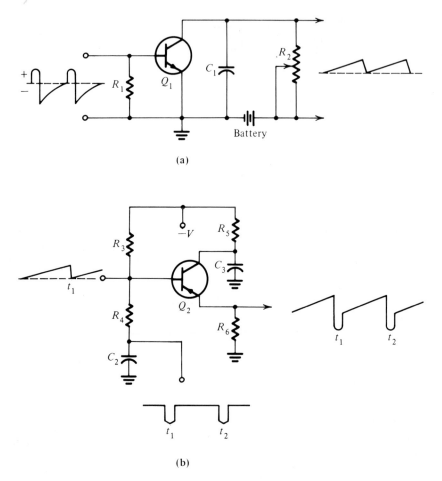

Figure 3-5 Sawtooth Formation and Modification

the positive direction followed by an abrupt change in the negative direction as shown. For the positive portion of the input signal the base terminal of the transistor is positive with respect to the emitter and hence a
temporary forward bias is present that permits transistor conduction.
During the latter the transistor's impedance drops to a low value and
behaves as a shunt across C_1. Consequently, the capacitor discharges
through the transistor and the output voltage of the sawtooth waveform
drops abruptly to zero. During the negative excursions of the input signal the transistor is again in a nonconducting mode and capacitor C_1

charges again to form the rising amplitude of a new sawtooth signal. In design practices the sawtooth-forming characteristics can be evaluated by solving for the instantaneous potential across the capacitor for a given time constant:

$$e_c = E(1 - \epsilon^{-t/RC}) \qquad\qquad (3\text{–}6)$$

where e_c is the instantaneous voltage across the charging capacitor
   E is the maximum voltage (source voltage)
   ϵ is the Naperian log base and equals 2.718
   R is the total series resistance in ohms
   C is the capacitor value in farads
   t is the time in seconds

If transistor Q_1 is held at cutoff (by the absence of a bias or by the application of a low value of reverse bias) the input signal can consist of a series of positive pulses. The time interval between pulses thus determines the amplitude and duration of the leading incline of the sawtooth.

3–7. SAWTOOTH SIGNAL MODIFICATION

In electrostatic-deflection oscilloscope tubes the sweep potential applied to the deflection plates consists of a sawtooth waveform as depicted at the output of the circuit in Figure 3–5(A). For magnetic deflection such as used in television picture tubes, however, a sawtooth voltage applied to the inductors may result in a distortion of the sawtooth *current* needed for magnetic deflection. Consequently, it is often necessary to modify the sawtooth voltage in a manner that will assure the creation of a current sawtooth. A typical circuit for doing this is shown in Figure 3–5(B). Here an emitter-follower circuit has a sawtooth applied to the base input terminal as shown, and the output develops across resistor R_6 in the emitter line. At the same time a negative-polarity pulse train is obtained from the transformer of the horizontal output amplifier (see Figure 2–20) and applied to the junction of R_4 and C_2 as shown. The applied inverted pulse also appears at the base of Q_2, where it combines with the incoming sawtooth. The timing of the pulse is such that the time interval t_1 of the inverted pulses appear at time interval t_1 of the sawtooth waveform. Consequently, it modifies the sawtooth as shown at the output from Q_2.

3–8. GAIN AND TONE CONTROLS

A variable resistor such as R_1 shown in Figure 3–6(A) is an *attenuator* for regulating the level of signal amplitude applied to the transistor. In radios and high-fidelity equipment it is known as a *volume* control and in television it is a *gain* control. Thus, such devices modify the signal amplitude from its maximum potential value to some lower amplitude to suit the individual taste (see also Sec. 3–10). A similar variable resistor can be used for tone control purposes as shown at (B). This resistor in conjunction with capacitor C_2 attenuates higher-frequency signals because the capacitor has a decreasing value of reactance for higher-frequency signals. In conjunction with C_2, the impedance can be varied for a greater or lesser high-frequency signal attenuation. When high-frequency signals are diminished, the base tones are accented in comparison and hence this circuit is sometimes called a *base tone control*. A treble tone control can also be formed, as shown in Figure 3–6(C). Here, capacitor

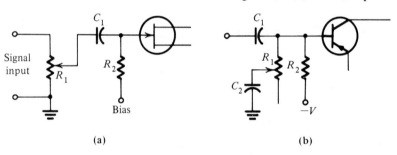

(a)   (b)

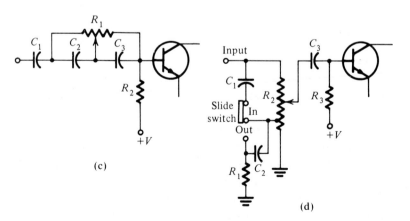

(c)

(d)

Figure 3–6   Gain and Tone Controls

C_1 is the conventional coupling capacitor and the treble control is made up of R_1, C_2, and C_3. Capacitor C_3 is usually a higher value than C_2 (for example, 2.2 μF for C_3 and 0.1 μF for C_2). When the variable arm of R_1 is at the left capacitor C_2 is shorted out and the larger value of C_3 has a sufficiently low reactance so that it has little effect on all signals. However, when R_1 is at the right, it shorts out C_3 and leaves C_2 in series with the signal. The lower capacitance value creates an increasing attenuation for lower-frequency signals and by comparison the higher (treble) signal frequencies appear more predominant. Obviously, intermediate settings of R_1 permit selection of different degrees of attenuation.

Most higher-quality high-fidelity radio receivers and audio amplifiers have a switch identified as the *loudness* control. When the switch is thrown to the *in* position the circuit increases the base response, particularly at low volume levels, to compensate for the decreased sensitivity of the human ear to low-frequency tones. The circuit shown in Figure 3–6(D) exemplifies the basic components utilized. The circuit is associated with the volume control R_2 and a slide-type (or pushbutton) switch selects the *in* or *out* for the loudness control function. With the switch in the *in* position, capacitor C_1 is placed in series with C_2 and R_1. Now the higher-frequency signals encounter a lower reactance for the shunt capacitors and are attenuated, thus producing an equivalent base signal boost. As the volume control arm is turned down it reaches the tap connected to C_2 and resistor R_1; thus, it provides for an increased shunting effect for high-frequency signals. In the *out* position the slide switch shorts out capacitor C_2 and also disconnects capacitor C_1, thus providing for normal response.

3-9. PRE- AND DEEMPHASIS CIRCUITRY

Special signal-modifying circuits are often used in audio and radio transmission practices for noise-reduction purposes. In public-entertainment FM radio, for instance, a special noise-reduction system utilizes a *preemphasis* circuit at the transmitter for special signal modification and hence at the receiver it is necessary to employ a circuit that restores the signal to its original status. For the latter purpose a circuit, termed a *deemphasis* network, is utilized. The two circuits are illustrated in Figure 3–7. Such circuits help reduce the noises present in the interelements of transistors as well as circuit noises generated by certain electronic components. Since these noises are usually generated at a fixed level, the sig-

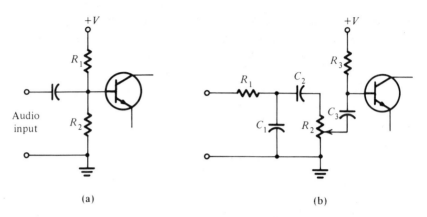

Figure 3–7 Pre- and Deemphasis Circuit

nal-to-noise ratio can be improved by a process whereby the level of the signals (whose frequencies are in the noise regions) is raised above the constant-level noise. Since the generated noise signals have a rising amplitude at higher-frequency audio signals, the latter are raised in level at a rate that increases for higher-frequency signals. This is termed *preemphasis* and can be accomplished by the simple circuit shown in Figure 3–7(A). Here a capacitor (C_1) has a lower capacitance than normal for a coupling capacitor. Hence, there is a rising reactance for signals of lower frequencies. Thus, higher-frequency signal amplitudes rise.

In the United States the Federal Communications Commission (FCC) has established certain specifications for the pre- and deemphasis systems. The incline in the signal amplitude beyond its normal value for the audio signal starts at approximately 400 Hz and rises gradually. Thus, at 1 kHz the increase is 1 dB; at 1.5 kHz the rise is almost 2 dB, and at 2 kHz the rise is about 3 dB. For 2.5 kHz there is almost a 4-dB increase and from then on the rise is virtually linear, reaching 8 dB for a 5-kHz signal and 17 dB for a 15-kHz signal. The time constant for the preemphasis network of C and R is 75 μs; that is, $\tau = 75 \times 10^{-6}$ s. In FM, the increase of signal amplitude at the higher frequencies for preemphasis purposes produces an increase in the frequency deviation of the carrier and the values selected by the FCC produce optimum benefits without undue frequency shifting of the carrier.

At the receiver a deemphasis circuit is required so that the excessive rise in the levels of the high-frequency signals are restored to normal. Otherwise, the audio reception would be harsh and shrill for the high-frequency end of the treble response. A deemphasis circuit is shown in Figure 3–7(B) and consists of a series resistor R_1 and a shunting capacitor C_1 having the same time constant of 75 μs as used in the preemphasis. Thus, the excessive levels of the higher-frequency signals are effectively brought down to normal amplitude. Capacitor C_2 is the conventional coupling capacitor and R_2 is the volume control. Capacitor C_3 prevents shorting of the base bias potential furnished via R_3 when the variable arm of R_2 is at ground.

In FM public-entertainment broadcasting another preemphasis system that is widely utilized incorporates the *Dolby* noise-reduction principle. This is an extension of the widely used Dolby-B noise-reduction system employed in stereo cassette tape recorders and other tape decks. For the latter the Dolby circuitry is conveniently encapsulated within an integrated circuit and becomes a unified section of the circuitry associated with the tape system. During recording, the level of a group of high-frequency signals is modified by successfully boosting the level to a degree related to the original amplitude. Basically, the system raises noise-prone higher-frequency signals above the constant-level noise. During playback a decoder within the IC reverses the signal amplitude rise and brings it to normal levels. The reduction also drops the noise signals, and hence the usual tape background noises, including high-frequency hiss, are reduced by as much as 10 dB.

In FM broadcasting the preemphasis utilized has the drawback that bandwidth is increased due to greater carrier deviation caused by the higher-frequency signals, which have an increased amplitude. In Europe the 75-μs time constant for preemphasis is replaced with a less objectionable 50-μs time constant. In high-fidelity practices, however, problems prevail because of the wide band of audio-frequency response desired (20 to 20 kHz or more). Thus, broadcast stations often use circuits that compress higher signal amplitudes (or employ automatic peak-limiting circuits) to prevent overextended band widths. In utilizing the Dolby system for transmission, the selected time constant for the preemphasis and the deemphasis is 25 μs. The latter was found to be adequate to form a noise-reduction system in transmission. The Dolby system used for transmitting, however, requires a special decoder at the receiver to realize optimum noise-reduction benefits. Without the decoder, the treble tones of music would be modified perceptibly. Receivers using the decoding network have a switch for selection of either the 75- or the 25-μs deemphasis system, with the latter decoded by the built-in Dolby circuitry.

3–10. ATTENUATORS (PADS)

As mentioned in Sec. 3–8, gain and tone controls are essentially *attenuators*, utilizing variable resistors. Attenuators (also called pads) are also formed by fixed-resistor values designed to perform dual functions: to diminish the level of the signal amplitude, and to match the impedance of the input circuit with that of the output. A typical three-resistor pad is shown in Figure 3–8(A). This is an unbalanced network, since one line is above ground. This pad is also known as a *T pad*. A balanced pad is shown in (B) and if the shunting resistor is center tapped, as shown by the dashed lines, the upper and lower lines are equally above ground.

Variable resistors can be used for the T pads, with a typical schematic representation as shown in Figure 3–8(C). In practical applications, however, the three variable resistors are wired as shown in (D). The advantage of such an attenuator system is the maintenance of a fixed-value resistance at the base of the transistor. For maximum volume level the positions of the variable arms would be as shown, hence the input signal is transferred to the base input. If each resistor is 25 kΩ, the setting shown in (D) would have R_3 from base to ground for this resistance. At minimum volume the variable arms of R_1 and R_2 would be at the open

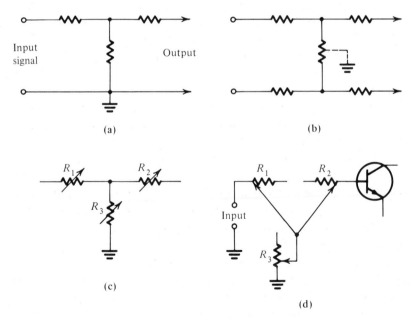

(a)

(b)

(c)

(d)

Figure 3–8 Fixed and Variable Pads

ends of the resistors while the variable arm of R_3 would be at ground. Thus, between the base and ground R_2 would now provide 25 kΩ. For intermediate volume levels the same resistance would be maintained between base and ground.

3–11. AUTOMATIC VOLUME CONTROL

Automatic volume control (AVC) circuits are used in communications receivers to maintain the volume level at an amplitude level selected by the volume control setting. Thus, the system holds to the preset output volume despite variations in the strength of the incoming signal to the detector. Thus, AVC compensates for the fading of transmitted signals, or the difference in the amplitude of RF signals coming from different stations and locations. Essentially, automatic volume control can be considered as an automatic gain (AGC), although the term "AVC" is utilized primarily in radios while AGC generally designates the system utilizing television receivers, as discussed in Sec. 3–12.

The principle utilized in AVC consists of sampling the signal amplitude at the detector and utilizing this sample for regulating the bias of the transistors for the RF and IF amplifier stages. When the incoming signal strength rises, a higher signal is also developed in the detector system and thus a voltage of proper polarity can be obtained from the detector for altering the bias of the early stages to cause a signal amplitude reduction. Thus, the AVC automatically brings the output signal level down to that set by the volume control.

The AVC bias takeoff section is illustrated in Figure 3–9(A). As discussed in Sec. 2–42, diode D_1 rectifies the incoming RF signal and the result appears across resistor R_1. The average value of the rectified signal is maintained by capacitor C_3. The output from the volume control R_1 is coupled to a subsequent stage by C_5. The takeoff network consists of capacitor C_4 and resistor R_2. These two components form a filter section that virtually eliminates audio-signal variations. Capacitor C_4 has a low reactance to bypass audio-signal components; consequently, a negative-polarity dc signal is formed. If the volume stabilization bias must have a positive polarity, diode D_1 can be reversed to alter the electron flow direction and hence the polarity of the AVC signal. In some industrial electronic systems, the terms *automatic signal amplitude control* or *automatic level control* are used.

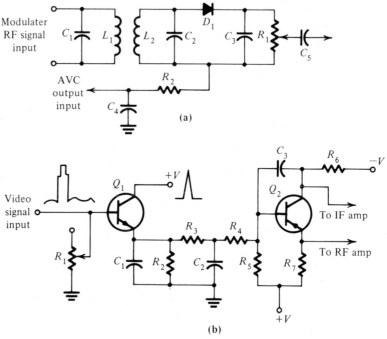

Figure 3–9 Automatic Gain Controls

3–12. AUTOMATIC GAIN CONTROL

The purpose of an automatic gain control (AGC) system is to maintain the signal level (contrast) of a television picture to that preset by adjustment of the contrast control. As with the AVC circuit discussed in Sec. 3–11, the AGC circuitry develops bias for the RF and IF stages to correct for any increase or decrease in gain above the preestablished value. The basic circuit could be in the form of the AVC section shown in Figure 3–9(A), although the system known as *keyed* AGC illustrated in (B) is the preferred method. Here, transistor Q_1 functions as the AGC *gate* and transistor Q_2 performs the amplification of the AGC bias signals.

As shown in (B), the video signal input is applied to the base terminal of Q_1 and consists of horizontal blanking and sync signals, vertical blanking and sync signals, and the video signal, which contains picture information. A positive-polarity pulse obtained from the horizontal output circuit is applied to the Q_1 collector terminal as shown. Thus, the signals at the base and collector have positive polarities. If negative-polarity signals were to be used, a *pnp* transistor would be employed for Q_1. Resistor R_1 is set to the point where Q_1 does not conduct during the absence of base and collector signals. Thus, for Q_1 to conduct, both base and collector signals must be present.

The precise adjustment of R_1 sets the input terminals of Q_1 to the point where only the sync tips of the composite video signal arriving at the base terminal have sufficient amplitude to permit conduction. However, without the presence of the reverse bias (furnished by the positive pulse at the collector), conduction cannot occur. Since the pulse is obtained from the horizontal output circuitry, and since the horizontal blanking occurs periodically, conduction occurs at the horizontal sweep rate. (The latter is 15,750 pulses per second for black-and-white transmission and 15,734 for color.) When conduction does occur, electron flow occurs through resistor R_2 as well as R_3, R_4, and R_5 (the latter connecting to the positive supply terminal shown). Thus, the base side of R_5 develops a negative potential and establishes forward bias for Q_2. The periodic output signal obtained from the emitter of Q_1 is filtered by the capacitor–resistor network that couples the signal to the base of Q_2. Thus, a steady-state signal is maintained at the base of Q_2 and is amplified for applications to the IF amplifiers (from the collector) and the RF amplifiers (from the emitter) as shown. Since transistor Q_1 does not conduct between horizontal sync pulses, any noise signals present in the incoming signals to the base of Q_1 are eliminated because the transistor is nonconducting at that time. When the incoming signal rises in amplitude, the base of Q_1 obtains a higher-amplitude signal. The latter causes an increase in forward bias and thus increases the conduction amplitude. As a result, a higher-amplitude AGC bias is developed with a polarity established so that it will decrease the signal gain to the preset level.

3–13. SIGNAL-DELAY SYSTEMS

Often in electronic digital systems it is necessary to delay a signal (such as a pulse or spike waveform) for a specific time interval. Several methods for doing this are shown in Figure 3–10. A transmission-line delay is shown in (A) and consists of a number of series inductors and shunt capacitors. Such a line need not consist of discrete components but could utilize equivalent forms of inductance and capacitance formed by any length of transmission line needed. For higher-frequency signals the series inductance inherent in any length of wire becomes appreciable, as

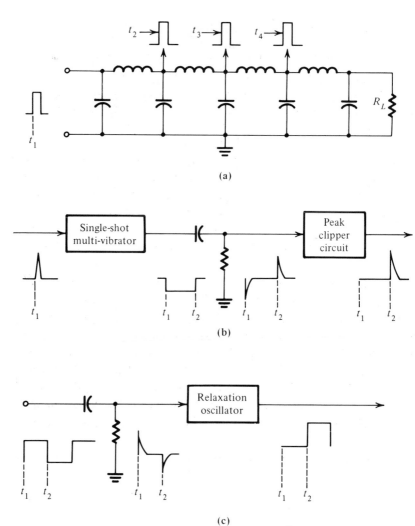

Figure 3–10 Signal-Delay Circuits

does the shunt capacitance formed whenever two conductors are placed into close proximity.

For a length of line such as that shown in Figure 3–10(A), any signal applied to the input will travel the length of the line in a time interval determined by the line length and the reactances formed by series conductors and shunt capacitors. When the line is tapped at specific intervals, as shown, output terminals are obtained that furnish a signal delay that is longer for the terminals farther away from the input. For the system shown, a pulse entering at time t_1 can be obtained at the first output terminal with a delay of t_2 as shown. Subsequent taps produce the same signal at later time periods than that of the input pulse. The line is terminated by the shunt resistor, R_L, which has an ohmic value equal to the line impedance $(Z = \sqrt{L/C})$.

The load resistance at the end of the line absorbs the signal energy reaching it. When R_L has an ohmic value equal to the line impedance (Z_0) the resistor prevents any signal reflection back along the line. Line reflections cause *standing waves* of signal amplitude along the line and disturb proper signal-delay function.

Another method for signal delay is shown in Figure 3–10(B). Here a spike pulse having a leading edge identified as time t_1 is applied to a single-shot multivibrator (see Secs. 3–2 and 6–19). The output from the latter is a negative-polarity pulse with its leading edge coinciding in time with the input spike signal. This pulse is differentiated by the series capacitor and shunt resistor as shown, producing a negative spike at time t_1 and a positive spike at time t_2. This signal is applied to a peak clipper circuit, which eliminates negative excursions of the incoming signal. Consequently, the output consists of a single spike pulse having a leading edge delayed to time t_2 in relation to the input pulse time t_1.

Another method is shown in Figure 3–10(C). Here the input pulse having a duration referenced as t_1 and t_2 is differentiated to produce a sharp positive spike at t_1 and a negative spike at t_2. This signal is applied to a relaxation oscillator that requires a negative-polarity pulse for pulse repetition synchronization. Consequently, the output pulse is initiated by the negative spike input t_2, and hence the leading edge of the output pulse has been delayed as shown.

3–14. COMBINING CIRCUIT

There are many occasions in electronic systems where certain pulse or spike waveforms must be inserted into another group of signals at precise time intervals. A typical example occurs in television transmission, where it is necessary to insert blanking pulses at specific time intervals in the video signal. In addition, sync pulses are then mounted on top of the blanking pulses. These and other combining tasks are performed by *gating circuits* which consist of several transistors with individual inputs combined in a single output, as shown in Figure 3–11. Here transistor Q_1 has forward bias applied to it via resistor R_1 and conducts continuously.

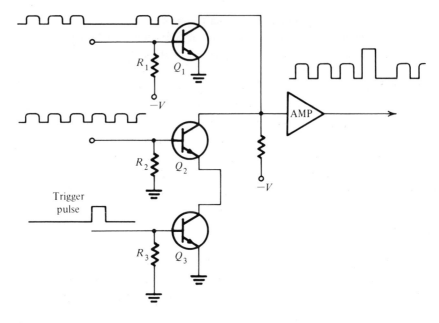

Figure 3–11   Combining Circuit

Assume that the input signal consists of the five pulses shown, with a two-pulse time interval between the third and the fourth pulse. This pulse train is amplified by Q_1 and would appear in the collector circuit as an amplified inversion of the input signal. The positive polarity is restored by the subsequent amplifier stage as shown. Transistor Q_2 has an uninterrupted train of positive pulses applied to the base circuit as shown. No dc forward bias is applied, but the pulse train has sufficient amplitude and is of correct polarity to provide forward bias for Q_2. Since the latter, however, is in series with Q_3, it is unable to conduct unless Q_3 also conducts. For Q_3, however, conduction does not occur until the solitary positive pulse appears, having a time coincident with the fourth pulse of input signal to Q_2. Thus, the *trigger pulse* at Q_3 input and the *fourth pulse* in the signal train at Q_2 form a *coinciding forward bias* that permits Q_2 and Q_3 to conduct simultaneously. Consequently, these two transistors develop an output signal that combines the added pulse amplitude triggered at the time interval illustrated. Consequently, the output waveform now has this additional pulse inserted as illustrated at the output amplifier terminal.

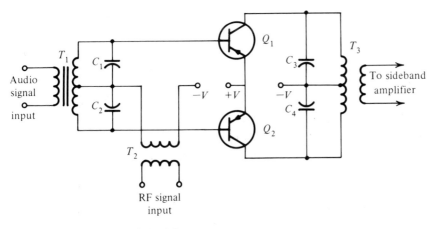

Figure 3–12   Balanced Modulator

3-15. BALANCED MODULATOR

A balanced modulator using *pnp* transistors is shown in Figure 3–12. The purpose for this circuit is to modulate an RF carrier, generate sidebands, and suppress the original carrier and the modulating signal. As shown, for this particular circuit the audio signal input is applied to transformer T_1 and transferred to the base inputs of the two transistors. The RF carrier signal is injected utilizing transformer T_2 and appears in series with the power supply potential and the center tap of transformer T_1. Since the RF signal is applied at the center tap of the T_1 secondary, the signal is applied *in phase* to *both* base terminals of the transistor. The amplified RF signal energy appears at the collectors of both Q_1 and Q_2. Since the latter are connected in push-pull configuration, *electron flow* through each transistor is from the $-V$ terminal to the center tap of T_3. Hence, current changes caused by the applied RF signals at the base terminals are equal and opposite for each side of the center tap at T_3. Thus, cancellation occurs for the RF signal at the output.

For the audio signals appearing across the secondary of T_1 a phase division occurs because of the center tap; hence, each base terminal receives a signal 180° out of phase with the other. Because the audio signals alter collector-current amplitudes for both Q_1 and Q_2, the carrier-frequency currents within each transistor are altered by modulation. The resultant sidebands encounter resonant circuits made up of C_3 and the upper winding for the primary of T_3 for Q_1, and C_4 and the lower winding of the primary of T_3 for Q_2. These parallel-resonant circuits have a low impedance for the off-resonant audio signals and thus attenuate them. Because the output circuit also suppresses the carrier, only the sideband signals appear in the secondary of T_3.

At the input, capacitors C_1 and C_2 have a low reactance for the RF signals and thus provide for a low-impedance coupling to the base elements of the transistor. For the audio signals appearing across the T_1 secondary, however, the capacitors have a high reactance and hence do not effect audio-signal amplitudes (see Sec. 11–2).

4 Integrated Circuits

4-1. INTEGRATED-CIRCUIT FACTORS

Integrated circuit (IC) is a term describing a micro-miniaturized electronic-circuit system. The finished unit may contain thousands of transistors, resistors, diodes, and capacitors, all interconnected to perform specific electronic functions. The integrated circuitry is contained in an extremely miniature solid-state monolithic chip and encapsulated in a plastic housing. A number of external prongs are present, including those for applying power-supply potentials and for signal input and output routing. It is significant that the external prongs have a bulk thousands of times greater than the electronic components and circuits within the integrated chip.

Integrated circuits are often used to make up a *module* containing external components of a size or characteristic not lending itself to integration. The module thus forms a part of a unified and complete system. Thus, computers, television systems, and so on, may have a number of integrated-circuit units as well as modules present. The basic internal structure, component formation, and other pertinent data are contained in subsequent sections of this chapter.

Integrated circuits fall into several categories relative to the type of circuitry contained within the chip. Some special-purpose ICs contain discrete devices such as transistors, diodes, and thyristors, such as the SCRs, SCSs, and others detailed in Sec. 2-41. The primary categories, however, are those covered in the remaining paragraphs of this section.

Linear ICs contain RF and IF amplifiers, audio amplifiers, operational and differential amplifiers, and others handling nondigital signals.

Digital ICs are those containing various logic circuits, such as flip-flop systems, pulse counting and arithmetic sections, encoder units, and parity-check devices (see Chaps. 5 and 6).

Memory ICs are those containing storage components for use in calculators and computers. These IC types include random-access memory (RAM), read-only memory (ROM), and other similar types. Also included are code converters and registers, as well as character generators.

Interface ICs are those especially designed to interconnect and link peripheral equipment such as printers and display units with the central processor unit (CPU). Such ICs contain sensor circuits (level converters), beginning and terminating with input and output lines matching the peripheral devices to the CPU.

Microprocessor ICs are chips containing thousands of transistors and associated components capable of performing complete digital processing in calculator and computer electronics. Some data storage capability and interface sections are included. The peripheral equipment linked to the microprocessor is termed *hardware*, and the instructional material and codes associated with a particular processor is known as *software*.

Microcomputer ICs contain the basic sections making up the complete central processor unit with necessary memory, data transfer circuitry, data processors, arithmetic units, and so on. These are multiple-prong chips, described in subsequent sections of this chapter.

4-2. DIODE-TRANSISTOR IC BASIC STRUCTURES

The basic structure and formation of integrated circuitry is shown in Figure 4-1. Numerous techniques are involved in processing the components of an integrated circuit. Combinations of thermal, chemical, and optical procedures are utilized. As shown in Figure 4-1(A), the foundation slab, termed a *substrate*, usually consists of an extremely thin silicon wafer. This particular substrate slab is chemically doped to form a *p*-zone characteristic. As also shown, an *n* strip is overlaid by fusing the two together. This process involves *isolation defusion*, which forms *n* zones as shown in (B). The isolation of the *n* zones thus forms *p-n* junctions. Consequently, as shown at (C), the basic elements of a semicon-

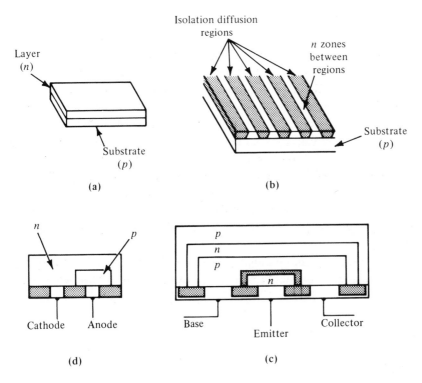

Figure 4–1 Basic IC Structure

ductor diode have been produced and appropriate terminals thus complete the diode structure.

The basic diode structure can be processed additionally to form transistors. The processes mentioned earlier may include utilization of acid for etching away portions of the structure and the employment of thermal processes and mask fabrication techniques. Photoetching procedures are used in addition to defusion techniques and vacuum-deposition procedures. Almost all of the basic electronic components needed in complete systems can be fabricated and interconnected within the microminiature IC structure. Since capacitance is always present between junctions within the basic IC chip, the *p-n* junctions are utilized as capacitors. Specific values can be obtained by design factors relating the proximity of two elements as well as mass. Although inductors present an almost insurmountable fabrication problem, the characteristics of inductance can be produced to form an equivalent inductor utilizing phase-shifting circuitry. Resistance elements present few problems.

When the component interconnections are on the same plane or surface of the IC foundation slab the structure formation is referred to as a *planer process*. Undesired elements or portions of the structure are eliminated by defusion, etching, and oxidation. During defusion, atomic structures are intermixed in precise proportions to achieve the particular operational characteristic needed. The oxidation process involves the combination of oxygen with a selected element to alter and re-form the structure as needed. By continuing the process a triode-type junction transistor is formed as shown in Figure 4–1(D). Here, an *npn*-type transistor is produced (see Chaps. 2 and 10).

4–3. FET AND COMPONENT FORMATION

As with the procedure outlined in Sec. 4–2 for diode and transistor formation, similar processes are utilized in the design of IC field-effect transistors as shown in Figure 4–2. In part (A) an *n*-type silicon substrate foundation is utilized with *p*-type defusions introduced for the production of the FET elements of *source, drain,* and *gate* (see Chaps. 2 and

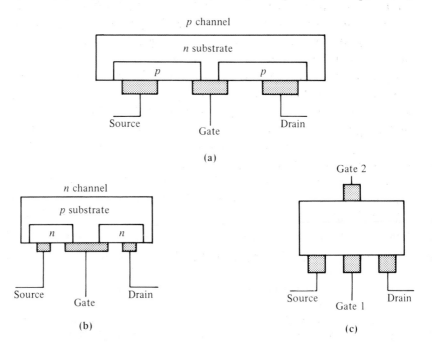

Figure 4–2 Field-Effect Transistor Formations

10). The structure is finalized by employing masking processes. An extremely thin layer of oxide is formed over the surface. Etching procedures form openings (termed *windows*) localized under the *p* regions. By utilizing a metallic evaporation process over the surface area the necessary metallic contacts are formed. For the junction field-effect transistor (JFET) the gate element is created by defusing a *p-n* junction into the channel material. Thus, as shown in (A), a *p*-channel FET is formed because of the polarity of the slab and the region that are established.

The *n*-channel type FET basic structure is shown in Figure 4–2(B). Note the polarity differences between this *n*-channel type and the *p*-channel type shown in (A). For creation of a dual-gate FET, the integrated circuit is structured to produce an additional gate element in the slab as shown in (C). The gate element (G_2) is electrically insulated from the initial (G_1) gate element. In the formation of a *p*-channel dual-gate FET there would be the same reversal of the defusion-zone polarities as was the case between the single-gate *p*-channel and *n*-channel types.

The formation of combinational components such as a diode and resistor are illustrated in Figure 4–3. As shown in (A), an *n* zone is defused into the *p*-type substrate to form the diode. The resistor is created by the defusion of a *p* zone into the *n* zone. Thus, the diode and resistor are combined in this chip element. As mentioned in Sec. 4–2, a capacitor can be included in the chip by taking advantage of the capacitance existing between two elements. To prevent conduction, reverse bias is utilized with the *p-n* junction. Generally, the value of the capacitance so formed is determined by the depletion-region gap. Of interest is the fact that the capacitance value is related to the amplitude of the applied voltage since the latter can alter the depletion region gap. Such an alteration would change the capacitance value because of the change in the dielectric constant. Thus, during design the amplitude of the applied voltage must be determined to achieve a specific capacitance value. Ranges possible are from 15 pF to over 100 pF. Varactor diodes utilized for tuning purposes in communication systems are such semiconductor units that undergo a capacitance change by altering the applied voltage (see Secs. 2–32 and 10–4).

4–4. REFERENCE SCALE OF INTEGRATED CIRCUITS

Several terms have been utilized as a general reference for the magnitude of the circuitry contained within an IC unit. Small-scale integration (SSI)

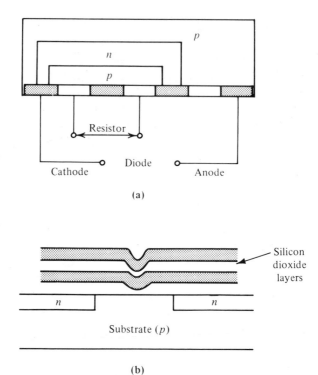

Figure 4-3 Component Formations

refers to the types generally containing linear or digital circuit sections. Such chips are usually used in association with other ICs making up the complete electronic system. Medium-scale-integration (MSI) units are types that house primary circuit combinations forming complete units used in digital watches, electronic games, smoke alarms, and similar systems. The large-scale integration (LSI) contains thousands of semiconductor transistors and components and such a single IC thus is utilized in calculators and in advanced electronic games such as chess, checkers, and backgammon.

The very-large-scale integration (VLSI) plus the very-high-speed integration (VHSI) contain transistors and associated components numbering in the hundred thousands. In addition to serving as central processing units (CPUs) they are useful in forming large-capacity memories in excess of 64 kilobits. These very-large-scale types are the vital cores of sophisticated electronic systems such as computers with extensive self-contained storage, capable of complex processes, utilizing speech synthesis when required, and capable of initiating visual display and character recognition.

The VHSI units provide for extremely high-speed digital data handling, gating, and signal routing. A capability of 1 megabit or more of data handling per second is not uncommon. Very-large-scale integration techniques involve the formation of higher packing within the chip during formation. The process involves the building up of the vertical structure of the semiconductor as shown in Figure 4–3(B). A p-type substrate is doped with n-type atomic impurities plus silicon dioxide layers. With this process components such as resistors can overlay other semiconductor units. [On occasion, polarity signs may be used with the p and n designations. When a plus sign follows a zone designation such as $n+$, it indicates an area of heavy doping with atomic impurities. The minus sign $(n-)$ refers to areas with light-percentage doping.]

4–5. HOUSING AND SYMBOLS

Since integrated-circuit units have such a wide range of internal components and circuitry, there is a corresponding difference in the number of external connectors found in commercial units. Some ICs may have only a few prongs such as shown in Figure 4–4(A) or a number of prongs as in (B). In (C) is shown a top view of a typical IC. Often the prong-numbering sequence origin is identified by either a notch, as shown, or a colored dot. Some ICs are connected to other external circuitry by being plugged into matching sockets. Others are set into prepunched holes in a printed-circuit board with the prongs soldered to appropriate circuit interconnecting wiring.

The integrated-circuit unit may be represented in several ways in the schematic for the particular electronic system in which it is used. On occasion the rectangular form is used as shown in Figure 4–4(D). Here a communications detector and output amplifier system is incorporated within the chip. The input signal is applied to the detector via IC terminal 1 and the output is obtained from terminal 5. Terminal 7 is utilized for positive voltage application while terminal 4 receives the negative voltage potential. Pin 2 connects to the volume control. Other IC representation of this type involving logic circuits are shown in Figure 6–11.

The IC may also be represented in triangular form as shown in Figure 4–4(E). In such illustrations it is common practice to depict only those terminals that are connected to internal components. Thus, for the

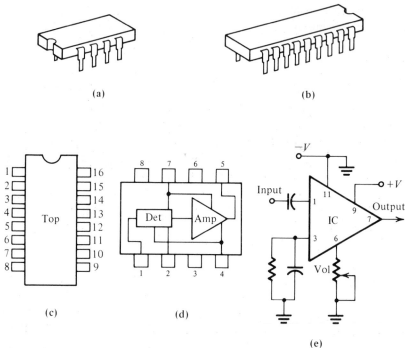

Figure 4–4 IC Housing and Symbols

IC shown in (E) there are no connections to terminals 2, 4, 5, 8, 10, and 12. Since this triangle represents an amplifier, a volume control is connected to terminal 6 and ground as shown. The capacitor–resistor network from terminal 3 to ground represents the emitter to ground network for the input transistor. The positive potential is applied to terminal 9 and the negative potential (at ground) is applied to terminal 11. The output is obtained from terminal 7 as shown.

4–6. T²L CIRCUITRY

A typical example of multiemitter transistors fabricated into integrated circuits is shown in Figure 4–5(A). Such a device provides for multiple-signal input for simplification of logic gate circuits and for decreased time in switching. Such units may have only two emitters, whereas some have three or more as needed. The unit is an *npn* transistor having the advantage of operating at low power levels in digital logic circuitry.

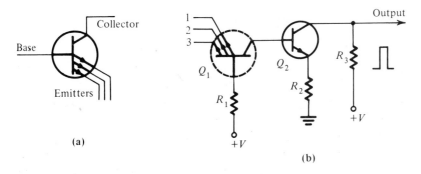

Figure 4–5 T²L Circuitry

The three-emitter transistor (Q_1) is shown in Figure 4–5(B), where it is used in conjunction with a conventional three-element transistor (Q_2) to form a *nand* gate. Such a circuit is also termed a *transistor-transistor logic* unit, designated by the letters TTL or T²L. Transistor Q_1 requires a negative emitter with respect to the base for establishing forward bias. Thus, the application of negative pulses to the input emitter sections is needed for conduction. The collector of Q_1 is directly coupled to the base terminal of Q_2 as shown. When three negative pulses appear at the input of Q_1 the resultant forward bias causes a current flow in the base and collector sections of Q_1. The in-phase change in potential at the Q_1 collector also appears at the base terminal of Q_2. The negative-polarity voltage change at Q_2 decreases the forward bias and hence the conduction for Q_2 drops. The conduction decline decreases the voltage drop across R_2. The resultant current decrease through R_3 represents a potential change in the positive direction as shown.

The T²L circuitry accomplishes logic processes utilizing a minimum of components. Switching response is very rapid because the time-delay characteristics during signal processing are negligible. As the number of emitters is increased to handle more input signals, the circuit efficiency may decline. A multiple array of emitters may also cause a rise in solid-state interelement noise generation.

4–7. N-MOS AND P-MOS

The metallic-oxide semiconductor field-effect transistors (MOSFETs) are widely used in integrated-circuit design practices because of the particular advantages they offer during the fabrication process. Often the utilization of *npn* and *pnp* bipolar transistors in LSI circuitry necessitates several diffusion processes. In addition, the chip size is reduced considerably when the semiconductor components can be packed densely during formation. For the bipolar units electrical isolation from the common substrate has hampered dense-packing processes. For the MOS devices a single diffusion is often the only requirement and since the structure is basically a self-isolating type, dense packing is expedited. The latter process not only reduces IC size but also lowers internal capacitances that interfere with rapid switching. Switching speeds are also improved because the dense packing permits the fabrication of a greater number of transistors and components within a given chip, thus shortening the interconnecting linkages between them.

The designations of N-MOS and P-MOS identify the basic structure of the MOSFET. When *n*-type doping is used for the source and drain elements with a *p*-type channel separation an N-MOS formation results. Here a positive potential is needed at the gate to permit conduction between drain and source. For the P-MOS unit the source and drain undergo a *p*-type doping with the channel between them an *n*-type. Now a negative potential at the gate permits conduction. The N-MOS unit has superior switching chracteristics because virtually all conduction is by electron movement in contrast to the P-MOS, where the majority carriers consist of holes which do not move as readily through the semiconductor structure.

4–8. C-MOS ICs

A useful and widely used circuit incorporated into the ICs is the *complementary metallic-oxide semiconductor,* termed the C-MOS. The basic circuit is shown in Figure 4–6(A), where two MOSFETs are combined, one a *p*-channel type and the other an *n*-channel type. The system is characterized by extremely low operational currents, high efficiency, and its usefulness in both linear and digital-logic systems. Since the *p*-channel and *n*-channel units are in parallel, the operational characteristics involve opposite-polarity signals. Consequently, if the *n*-channel transistor is gated into conduction the *p*-channel unit is nonconducting. In the absence of input signals, the C-MOS system consumes virtually no electric power. Complex logic-circuit arrays utilizing C-MOS sections with over 100 gating sections utilize less than 0.1 mW of electric energy.

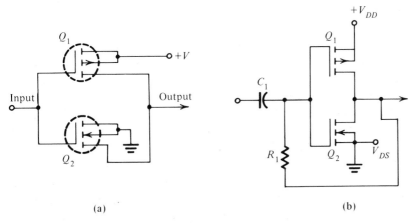

Figure 4–6   C-MOS Circuit Formation

Power consumption is related to the repetition rate of the input pulses. As the frequency is raised and the duration of the pulses as well as the time interval between them are shortened, the average power rises slightly. For gating frequencies as high as 10 kHz the C-MOS circuit still dissipates less than 1 μW for either gate of the dual-gate system.

A C-MOS system with external components is illustrated in Figure 4–6(B). The input signal may be applied via capacitor C_1 and resistor R_1 may be present during linear-circuit operation for stabilizing circuit bias. Essentially, R_1 forms a feedback path that tends to stabilize any bias drift left at the output. This circuit can be utilized for signal amplification or generation. In the latter instance a piezoquartz crystal is often placed in shunt with R_1 to improve frequency stability.

The circuits involving C-MOS design are noted for exceptional signal-transfer characteristics and operational capabilities extending well into the megahertz region. They have found wide applications in communications and instrumentation circuits as well as in digital-logic systems.

4–9. I²L CIRCUITRY

A specially designed circuit widely used in bipolar large-scale integration (LSI) is that termed *integrated-injection logic*. The symbol is I²L and the circuit is characterized by design simplicity (minimum number of components), low power consumption, and high efficiency. The I²L circuit is also useful for the storage of binary signals. The versatility of the I²L includes its usage in low-cost ICs for electronic watches, digital voltmeter applications, logic arrays, and digital-logic processing in calculators. The system is also applicable to linear circuitry in communications systems.

The basic circuit representing integrated-injection logic is shown in Figure 4–7(A). A signal inversion occurs between the base input and the multicollector *npn* transistor. The intertwined circles (in series from the base terminal to ground) signify a constant-current source for the base–emitter terminals, as described more fully later in this section.

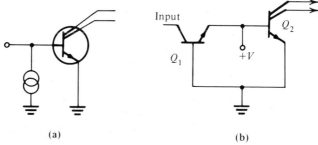

(a)   (b)

Figure 4–7   I²L Circuit Formation

The fundamental I²L design for gating purposes utilizes dual transistors in complementary formation. The multicollector transistor Q_2 provides for a signal inversion as well as amplification. As shown, there is an absence of circuit components such as resistors, capacitors, and inductors. The *pnp* transistor Q_1 combines the input terminal (emitter) with the current-source unit. The latter is one version of the circuitry represented by the overlapping circles in (A). Resistive components may be utilized here also as dictated by design requirements (see Sec. 2–22 and Figure 2–17).

4–10. SCHOTTKY-CLAMPED I²L

A special *np* junction forming a diode has been widely used with gating circuitry. The special unit is termed a *Schottky diode* and it is capable of switching function in time intervals much shorter than those obtained by conventional junction diodes. The Schottky diodes also have a lower internal resistance and hence also have a decreased voltage drop across them compared to conventional diode types. The latter characteristic decreases power losses.

A typical Schottky-diode application is shown in Figure 4–8. Here four diodes are employed to clamp the output signal amplitude from an I^2L gate system. These special diodes limit the swing of signal amplitudes of logic gate sections and hence reduce switching delays encountered with excessive signal swing levels. By using Schottky diodes the switching speeds can be increased over six times the speed encountered if the I^2L circuit is not clamped. For the system illustrated in Figure 4–8, the signal-swing amplitudes can be confined to a clamp level less than one-half of the prevailing peaks for such a circuit.

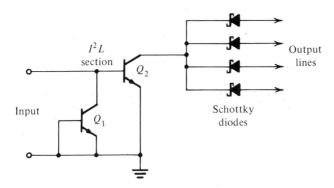

Figure 4–8 I^2L with Schottky Clamp

4–11. DCTL *NOR* CIRCUITRY

In direct-coupled circuitry successive stages are connected sequentially without intervening resistors, capacitors, or inductors. Thus, reactive losses are minimized, a higher signal-frequency response is possible, and circuit design is more simple. Consequently, fabrication techniques in IC processing are expedited. In digital systems the term *direct-coupled logic* (DCL) applies, although on occasion the term is expanded to *direct-coupled transistor logic* (DCTL).

A typical example of the utilization of direct coupling in IC practices is the *nor* circuitry, shown in Figure 4–9. As illustrated in the schematic drawing, transistors Q_1 and Q_2 are in parallel and form a *nor* circuit with dual inputs. The output represents a negated signal and this is applied to the base input terminals of both Q_3 and Q_4. Since the output from the latter two transistors is obtained from the collector circuitry the resultant phase inversion causes the output signal to revert back to

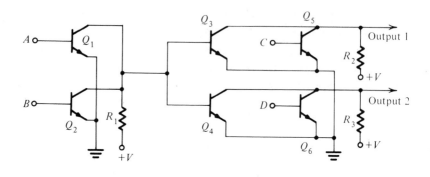

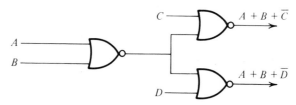

Figure 4-9 DCTL *nor* Circuitry

the same polarity at the input. In addition, independent inputs are available at the base terminals of transistors Q_5 and Q_6. Since the output from these two transistors is also obtained from the collector circuitry, the resultant phase inversion produces a negated output for either the C input or the D input.

The symbolic representation of the DCTL *nor* system is also shown in Figure 4-9. Note that the A and B inputs are applied to a single *nor* circuit, the output of which is applied simultaneously to two additional *nor* circuits. The original A+B input from the first *nor* circuit becomes $\overline{A+B}$. When the latter expression is applied to the input of another *nor* circuit, the output reverts back to the original expression of A+B. For the C and D inputs the resultant *nor* inversion produces $\overline{C}$ as well as $\overline{D}$.

4-12. MD-MOS ICs

The fabrication in IC structure of multidrain metallic-oxide semiconductors (MD-MOS) permits the packaging of high-speed logic gates in a configuration generally comparable to integrated injection logic (I²L). The MD-MOS system lends itself readily to computer-aided design (CAD) and has also been utilized for other purposes, such as the nucleus of speech synthesizer units (see Sec. 11–12).

Multidrain MOS circuitry can be considered akin to the integrated-injection logic system except for the use of MOSFETs. The basic fabrication structure is shown in Figure 4–10(A). A *p*-type substrate is utilized with multiple drain segments present by creation of the *n*-zone areas. An *n*-channel logic gate of polysilicon is utilized over a thin oxide layer, with the common gate serving as the input line. The *n*-channel logic gate and multiple drain elements are associated with the depletion-mode *n*-channel transistor. As shown at (B), the *n*-channel transistor has a base input terminal also linked to the base input of Q_2. The circuitry inherently utilizes more power than the I²L sections since it has a static characteristic. The extremely narrow polysilicon gate creates a capacitance between it and the source terminal which is over twice that encountered in the I²L. Constant improvements have resulted in increasingly wider applications for this device.

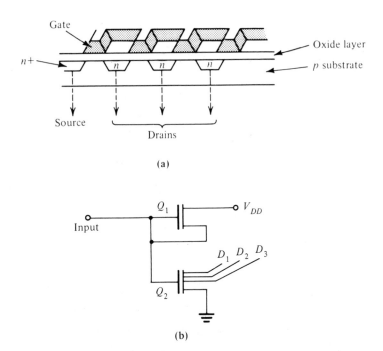

(a)

(b)

Figure 4–10 MD-MOS Fabrication and Basic Circuit

4–13. V-MOS FACTORS

In IC technology MOSFET units in large-scale integrated circuits originally were planar (two-dimensional). A later fabrication procedure created a vertical dimension to the basic IC chip by positioning the drain and gate elements above the source element rather than adjacent to them. The unit formed by this process has been termed V-MOS. The result has been a semiconductor producing gating speeds in excess of those possible by I^2L systems. The V-MOS units have also found application in a variety of digital storage systems such as static random-access memory (SRAM) units with an access time below 100 ns. In addition, erasable programmable read-only memory (EPROM) and read-only memory (ROM) sections may be fabricated readily.

The basic structure of the V-MOS is shown in Figure 4–11. Utilizing an *n* substrate, the V-MOS *n*-channel transistor is formed by employing the slopes of a groove as shown. The groove structure is created by anisotropically etching it into the surface of the silicon substrate. The active channel is in the slope area of the V-groove. The latter is within the epitaxial layer and consists of a *p*-type layer of less than 1 μm covered by a lightly doped *p* layer. The channel is formed on the slopes of the groove with the source in the body of the silicon. The drain is the upper-layer *n*-type area.

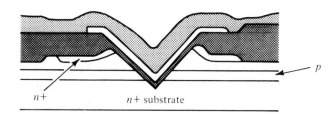

p

$n+$ $n+$ substrate

Figure 4–11   V-MOS Basic Structure

4–14. D-MOS STRUCTURES

The process involving double diffusion in forming a MOSFET in ICs produces what is termed a D-MOS unit. Such a device minimizes some voltage-gradient problems experienced with the V-MOS. As shown in

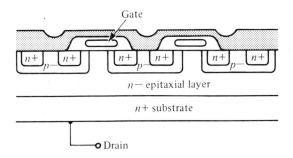

Figure 4–12 D-MOS Structure

Figure 4–12, an *n*-type epitaxial layer is grown on an *n*+ substrate slab. Next the *p*— areas are diffused and within them *n*+ regions are formed as shown. Silicon gates are structured within silicon dioxide layers, after which the source and gate terminals are added by metallization processes forming an array of *p* and *n* regions that create the channels. The term "D-MOS" has other designations also, including "Z-MOS" and "T-MOS."

4–15. SILICON ON SAPPHIRE

The term describing the silicon-on-sapphire fabrication process is designated as SOS. The process improves the metal-gate performance of the MOS. The SOS, using vertical junctions, have decreased areas and hence lower structural capacitances than component formation fabricated in bulk silicon. Consequently, the capacitances, such as those between substrate and conductors that would slow down switching speeds, are reduced significantly.

These units also have low-power dissipation advantages, particularly when the formation consists of C-MOS on sapphire. The substrate in the SOS devices is a single crystal (synthetic sapphire). The initial process consists of producing an epitaxial growth on the sapphire substrate. The layer is doped with an *n*-type infusion. Etching and defusion processes are used to build up the structure. Masking and etching procedures are applied to the silicon sections to produce contact openings. The conductor pattern formation is achieved after depositing a thin aluminum film by the evaporation process.

4–16. H-MOS TYPES

High-performance MOSFETs are designated as H-MOS units. In instances where the H-MOS units are also high-density types utilizing the C-MOS devices, the designation HD-CMOS applies. The H-MOS devices exhibit rapid switching characteristics because of their particular structure. Maximum threshold configurations are achieved by utilizing thicker field oxide. The use of an on-chip negative bias for the substrate reduces capacitances at the junctions. The formation of thin oxides and decreased channel widths helps improve gating and switching speeds.

Interconnection resistances that tend to impede conduction have been reduced by utilization of deeper phosphorus diffusion than used in other structures prior to the advent of the H-MOS type. These phosphorus diffusions under the contact area plus utilization of doped polysilicon elements contribute to the resistance reduction.

Gating and switching delays are reduced additionally by virtually exact self-alignment of the gate section with the drain–source areas. The H-MOS devices also permit the formation of computer-storage memories in excess of 250 kilobits. The unit is sufficiently versatile in its application to permit usage in various areas of electronics.

4–17. LINEAR-CIRCUIT ICs

The linear circuits described in Chap. 2 are also incorporated in ICs as well as digital circuitry. Generally, direct-coupling circuits are preferred to minimize the number. The direct-coupled Class B amplifier shown in Figure 4–13 is a typical example. Here Q_1 represents the preamplifier and Q_2 plus Q_3 provide the phase inversion process for application to the output transistors Q_4 and Q_5. The latter comprise the complementary-symmetry type of output. Such circuits are usually modified so that they require only a minimum of supply potential for operation. In many instances bipolar transistors are preferred over the field-effect type in the design of low-voltage linear ICs. Often, however, the FET threshold potential may be equal to that of the bipolar units and hence offer no advantages. Also, the FET transconductance is less than the bipolar units and a specific drain-current change may require a gate-source change equal to the base–emitter voltage of the bipolar transistors. Thus, there would be no particular advantage for the FET usage. There are in-

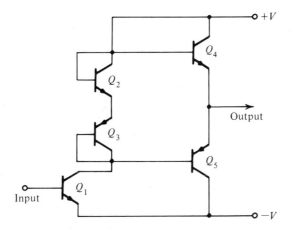

Figure 4–13   Direct-Coupled Class B Amplifier

stances, however, where the FET may be utilized in such applications as operational amplifiers (see Sec. 2–21).

4–18. RTL AND ECL CIRCUITS

Basic transistor-circuit logic is used to form gating and switching functions and one of the earliest types is resistor–transistor logic (RTL). The two-transistor type shown in Figure 4–14(A) represents one of the first such types incorporated into integrated circuitry. For the circuit shown the digital-logic *nor* function is obtained. Transistors Q_1 and Q_2 receive the A+B inputs with series resistors R_1 and R_2. Resistor R_3 is the collector resistor across which the output signal develops. Standard values for this circuit are 450 Ω for R_1 and R_2 and 640 Ω for R_3. With the collectors in parallel, an input signal applied to either gate terminal produces an output signal. Since there is a phase inversion for a common-emitter circuit, the *nor* function is obtained (see Secs. 2–2 and 6–6).

Although the RTL circuit has been superseded by more sophisticated circuits with improved switching characteristics, it is still found in existing equipment. The more modern versions include the I²L (Sec. 4–9), the DCTL (Sec. 4–11), and others described in this chapter. When resistors are utilized they combine with circuit capacitances to introduce time-constant delays. Also, if gating circuitry involves a saturation mode,

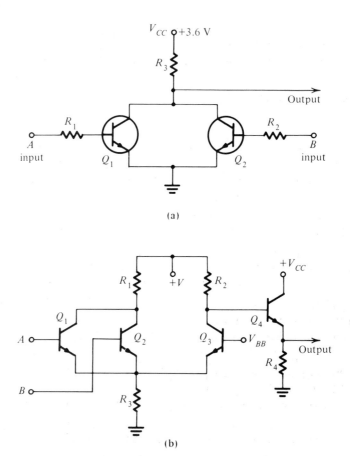

Figure 4–14 RTL and ECL Circuits

the turn-off gating time interval is increased. Hence, of particular advantage was the design of emitter-coupled logic (ECL).

The basic circuit of an emitter-coupled logic system is shown in Figure 4–14(B). In this circuit switching time is reduced because the gating principle does not depend on current amplitude, but rather on the direction of the current. For the circuit shown, a common-emitter configuration prevails for transistors Q_1, Q_2, and Q_3. An A or B input is provided at the gate terminals of Q_1 and Q_2. The operating mode is established by the collector potentials (V_{cc} and V_{BB}). The signal appearing at the base of Q_4 will not undergo phase inversion at the emitter output, thus retaining the *or* function. This circuit can, of course, be adapted for the *nor* function if needed.

5 Digital - System Codes

5–1. BASIC BINARY CODE

In digital logic circuitry forming computers, microprocessors, calculators, and pulse-code modulation systems (see Sec. 8–12) the arithmetic processes are limited to two numerals, 1 and 0. The 1 value is assigned to a specific amplitude or polarity as opposed to the 0 for a different amplitude or polarity. As an alternative the 1 and 0 states can be assigned to the conduction and nonconduction aspects of circuits. All these methods provide for a degree of precision and accuracy that could not be achieved by utilizing selected areas of pulse amplitudes or widths to represent numerals from 1 to 9. Thus, the utilization of 1 and 0 involves base 2 arithmetic rather than the more familiar base 10 (decimal) system. The base 2 process is a *binary* type and has full capability regarding numerical values, multiplication, division, subtraction, addition of numbers, and the performance of other mathematical processes.

In the base 2 binary system the *power value* increases progressively for digits to the left of the decimal point. Each successive digit to the left of the decimal point doubles in value. (The number of zeros preceding a numeral such as 001 or 00010 does not add to the total value but represents primarily the scope of the number of digits utilized for the expression.) In binary, 0001 represents the base 10 value 1 and 0010 represents the base 10 value 2. Similarly, 0100 has the value 4, 10000 has the value 8, and so on. The number 1001 equals 9, 1010 equals 10, and so on. The power relationships of base 2 binary and their place values are:

etc.	10	9	8	7	6	5	4	3	2	1	*Place*
←	2^9	2^8	2^7	2^6	2^5	2^4	2^3	2^2	2^1	2^0	*Power*
	512	256	128	64	32	16	8	4	2	1	*Value*

The power relationships given above permit ascertaining the value of any combination of 0's and 1's in a binary expression. The example 1001 given above equals 9 because the right digit has a value of 1 and the left digit, being in fourth place, has a value of 8. Thus, 1001 combines the 8 with the 1 for a value of 9. Similarly, 10110 has a value of 22, since the second-place numeral at the right has a value of 2, the third a value of 4, and the fifth a value of 16, for a total of 22. Table 5–1 lists binary numbers with their base 10 equivalent to a value of 16.

TABLE 5–1. Decimal–Binary Comparison

Decimal	Binary Representation	Decimal	Binary Representation
0	0 0 0 0 0	9	0 1 0 0 1
1	0 0 0 0 1	10	0 1 0 1 0
2	0 0 0 1 0	11	0 1 0 1 1
3	0 0 0 1 1	12	0 1 1 0 0
4	0 0 1 0 0	13	0 1 1 0 1
5	0 0 1 0 1	14	0 1 1 1 0
6	0 0 1 1 0	15	0 1 1 1 1
7	0 0 1 1 1	16	1 0 0 0 0
8	0 1 0 0 0		

Table 5–1 is easily expanded by observing the sequential grouping of the 1's and 0's. Note that down the rightmost column the 0's and 1's alternate, and this particular sequence remains the same regardless of how high the count is extended. In the second vertical column from the right two 0's alternate with two 1's successively. For the third column four 0's alternate with four 1's. The fourth column from the right alternates eight 0's with eight 1's successively regardless of the magnitude of the final number. The fifth column alternates sixteen 0's with sixteen 1's. For a six-column expression, the sixth from the right would alternate thirty-two 1's and 0's, and so on.

Table 5–2 lists other number systems and gives the respective radix for each.

TABLE 5–2. Various Number Systems

Number System	Base of Radix	Number System	Base of Radix
Binary	Two	Sextodecimal	Sixteen
Ternary	Three	Septendecimal	Seventeen
Quaternary	Four	Octodenary	Eighteen
Quinary	Five	Novendenary	Nineteen
Senary	Six	Vicenary	Twenty
Septenary	Seven	Tricenary	Thirty
Octonary (or octal)	Eight	Quadragenary	Forty
Novenary	Nine	Quinquagenary	Fifty
Decimal	Ten	Sexagenary	Sixty
Undecimal	Eleven	Septuagenary	Seventy
Duodecimal	Twelve	Octogenary	Eighty
Terdenary	Thirteen	Nonagenary	Ninety
Quaterdenary	Fourteen	Centenary	Hundred
Quindenary	Fifteen		

The binary representation for any base 10 number can be found by repeated division by 2. If, for instance, the binary number for 695 is desired, the number is repeatedly divided by 2 and each remainder set down at the right. After the final division that yields a whole number quotient, the remainders are written out starting from the bottom. The bottom numeral becomes the leftmost bit of the binary group that results. In the following process we obtain the binary number 1010110111:

			Remainder
$\dfrac{695}{2}$	$=$	347	1
$\dfrac{347}{2}$	$=$	173	1
$\dfrac{173}{2}$	$=$	86	1
$\dfrac{86}{2}$	$=$	43	0
$\dfrac{43}{2}$	$=$	21	1

				Remainder
$\dfrac{21}{2}$	=	10		1
$\dfrac{10}{2}$	=	5		0
$\dfrac{5}{2}$	=	2		1
$\dfrac{2}{2}$	=	1		0
$\dfrac{1}{2}$	=	0		1

5–2. BINARY-CODED DECIMAL

On many occasions it is convenient to code each decimal number in terms of its binary equivalent in a system referred to as binary-coded decimal. This procedure makes a convenient reference for numbers in decade counters since it indicates the true count. For instance, if 46 is written in pure binary notation, it is 101110. In a decade counter sequence where groups of four stages attain 9 as the highest count, the value 46 has the following notation: 0100 0110, thus giving a binary representation to the individual numbers. Four binary bits (0's or 1's) are employed to represent each decimal digit for uniformity with the 4 bits required to represent the highest number of a group (9), which is the binary 1001. Thus, the number 267 would be represented as 0010   0110 0111.

In coding binary numbers into individual groups of 4 bits to represent decimal values, the first nine digits would, of course, be in pure binary form. After the ninth numeral, the binary-coded notation converts to separate 4-bit groups, as shown in Table 5–3.

5–3. HEXADECIMAL CODE

In the binary-coded decimal system described in Sec. 5–2 the highest numerical value of a group of 4 bits is 9, but four 1's (1111) would have a base 10 count of 16. Hence, there are six unused values remaining in the

TABLE 5–3. Binary-Coded Decimal

Decimal Number	Binary-Coded	Decimal Number	Binary-Coded
01	0001	10	0001 0000
02	0010	11	0001 0001
03	0011	12	0001 0010
04	0100	13	0001 0011
05	0101	etc.	
06	0110	201	0010 0000 0001
07	0111	202	0010 0000 0010
08	1000	etc.	
09	1001	457	0100 0101 0111
		458	0100 0101 1000

4-bit group of the binary-coded decimal. These additional values are sometimes assigned alphabetical designations for expanding the total number identifications available when assigning memory (storage) locations (also known as addresses). Thus, 1010 represents the letter A, 1011 represents B, 1100 = C, 1101 = D, 1110 = E, and 1111 = F. Thus, an address identified as 1100 0110 1001 is C — 69; an address 1110 0101 0110 is E — 56. These binary representations are now alphanumerical. Hexadecimal, binary, and decimal values are compared in Table 5–4.

TABLE 5–4. Hexadecimal Code

Decimal Value	Alphanumeric Hexadecimal	Binary Code	Decimal Value	Alphanumeric Hexadecimal	Binary Code
0	0	0000	8	8	1000
1	1	0001	9	9	1001
2	2	0010	10	A	1010
3	3	0011	11	B	1011
4	4	0100	12	C	1100
5	5	0101	13	D	1101
6	6	0110	14	E	1110
7	7	0111	15	F	1111

5–4. OCTAL NOTATION

The octal notation system has been widely used for special purposes. It expedites converting binary representation to their decimal equivalent as well as the conversion of base 10 numbers to binary. In octal notation a

binary number, regardless of length, is separated into individual groups
each containing 3 bits, such as 001 or 111. Hence, a binary number such
as 11010011 is written in octal notation as 011 010 011. Since only
three digits comprise a group, the highest numerical value of a group is
7. Consequently, the octal system has a base (radix) of 8 and each 3-bit
group in conventional place sequence from right to left increases by a
power of 8. Each power of 8 that a group or triad place represents can
be designated, as is done for the binary powers illustrated in Sec. 5–1.
The octal-power values are:

7th	6th	5th	4th	3rd	2nd	1st	*Place*
000	000	000	000	000	000	000	*(Triad Group)*
8^6	8^5	8^4	8^3	8^2	8^1	8^0	*Power*
262,144	32,768	4096	512	64	8	1	*Value*

As an example, the binary number 1010110111 has a decimal value
of 695. The octal expression would be 001 010 110 111. Thus, the octal
representation can be specified as 1267. Table 5–5 shows the octal and
binary form for representative decimal sequences.

TABLE 5–5. Octal Notation

Decimal Sequence	Octal Sequence	Binary Form	Decimal Sequence	Octal Sequence	Binary Form
0	00	000 000	11	13	001 011
1	01	000 001	12	14	001 100
2	02	000 010	13	15	001 101
3	03	000 011	14	16	001 110
4	04	000 100	15	17	001 111
5	05	000 101	16	20	010 000
6	06	000 110		etc.	
7	07	000 111	242	362	011 110 010
8	10	001 000	243	363	011 110 011
9	11	001 001	244	364	011 110 100
10	12	001 010		etc.	

The octal system can also be utilized to ascertain the binary number of a decimal number. This is done by dividing successively by 8 and
writing down the remainder. The latter represents the octal number,
which then permits us to write the binary equivalent. As an example, the

decimal value of 695 was mentioned earlier. To find the octal number, the following division-by-8 sequence is performed:

				Remainder
$\dfrac{695}{8}$	$=$	86	$=$	7
$\dfrac{86}{8}$	$=$	10	$=$	6
$\dfrac{10}{8}$	$=$	1	$=$	2
$\dfrac{1}{8}$	$=$	0	$=$	1

Thus, when the remainder is written down, starting from the bottom, we obtain the number 1267, which is the octal representation. This gives us 001 010 110 111, which, when bunched together, gives us the binary number 1010110111.

5–5. GRAY CODE

In industrial electronics and computational systems it is often necessary to convert an analog function to a digital equivalent. When a physical change (such as a shaft rotation or a lever movement) must be converted to an equivalent numerical value (such as binary) an analog–digital conversion is indicated. The latter information can then be applied to a computer for computational purposes. The procedure is utilized in satellite guidance and tracking systems as well as industrial processes involving computer control of machine tools, fabrication control, and so on.

When small variables are coded by conversion into a number system it is preferable that only a one-digit change occurs during a numerical procession to minimize errors. In binary several digits may change; for instance, from 3 to 4 involves a 3-bit change (011 to 100). A code that has only one digit changing for each numerical increase is highly desirable and such a code is the one invented by Frank Gray and named the *Gray code*. This code is often termed a *minimum-error* code. It has also been referred to as the *cyclic code* or the *reflected binary*. Table 5–6 lists the Gray code sequence up to the decimal 18 equivalent as well as the pure binary equivalent.

TABLE 5–6. Gray Code

Decimal Sequence	Basic Binary	Gray Code	Decimal Sequence	Basic Binary	Gray Code
0	0000	0000	10	1010	1111
1	0001	0001	11	1011	1110
2	0010	0011	12	1100	1010
3	0011	0010	13	1101	1011
4	0100	0110	14	1110	1001
5	0101	0111	15	1111	1000
6	0110	0101	16	10000	11000
7	0111	0100	17	10001	11001
8	1000	1100	18	10010	11011
9	1001	1101			

A specific technique is utilized to form the Gray code numbers. Initially, the binary number is set down as the addend. Then it is again set down as the augend but indexed to the right by one place, dropping the digit that extends beyond the addend. The two numbers are then added *without carry*. As an example, assume that the binary number 6 (110) is to be converted to the Gray code. The following process applies:

$$
\begin{array}{ll}
110 & \text{(6)} \\
+\,11 & \text{(6 indexed)} \\
\hline
101 & \text{(Gray code 6)}
\end{array}
$$

5–6. EXCESS-THREE CODE

A variation of the binary-coded decimal system described in Sec. 5–2 has been devised to simplify the subtraction process in digital computers. This code is termed the *excess-three* code and Table 5–7 illustrates representations up to the decimal equivalent of 21.

Note that each excess-three number has been raised in value by three in relation to the decimal equivalent. Note from Table 5–7 that the excess-three code numbers for the decimal values 0 and 9 are symbolic

TABLE 5–7. Excess-Three Code

Decimal Sequence	Excess-Three Code	Decimal Sequence	Excess-Three Code
0	0011	12	0100 0101
1	0100	13	0100 0110
2	0101	14	0100 0111
3	0110	15	0100 1000
4	0111	16	0100 1001
5	1000	17	0100 1010
6	1001	18	0100 1011
7	1010	19	0100 1100
8	1011	20	0101 0011
9	1100	21	0101 0100
10	0100 0011		etc.
11	0100 0100		

opposites: 0011 and 1100. Similarly, the numbers 3 and 6 are symbolic opposites, as are 2 and 7, and so on. Such complementing features permit simplified subtraction involving 9's. Any number subtracted from 9 is found by interchanging the 0's and 1's in the number to be subtracted. (If, for instance, 2 is to be subtracted from 9 the excess-three number 0101 is inverted to product 1010. The latter has a decimal value of 7 in the excess-three code.)

5–7. BIQUINARY CODE

Earlier digital computers often utilized a system referred to as the *biquinary code* to reduce the number of counter circuits needed for decimal-coded binary. It is still used in some visual display circuitry. In this code, dual groups of bits are used, with one group holding the two bits representing the *bi*-portion, and the other group containing 5 bits representing the *quinary*. The latter uses only a single digit but moves it progressively to the left as 00001, 00010, and so on. The maximum quinary number is attained at the count of 01 10000, as shown in Table 5–8. After that the sequence is repeated except that the 2-bit bi-part now becomes 10 and identifies the number of times the five steps (0 through 4) occur in the quinary part.

TABLE 5–8. Biquinary Code

Decimal Sequence	Biquinary Code	Decimal Sequence	Biquinary Code
0	01 00001	5	10 00001
1	01 00010	6	10 00010
2	01 00100	7	10 00100
3	01 01000	8	10 01000
4	01 10000	9	10 10000

5–8. THE 7, 4, 2, 1 CODE

A special code referred to as the 7, 4, 2, 1 type had been utilized in early computer types for conservation of electric energy. The design of the code minimized the number of 1's in the code group and thus reduced the signal energy required. In this code the binary numbers up to the count of 9 contain only two 1's in any group. In this 7, 4, 2, 1 system the fourth-place digit has a value of 7 as shown in Table 5–9 in contrast to pure binary, where the fourth-place digit has a value of 8. (The binary system is basically an 8, 4, 2, 1 system.)

TABLE 5–9. The 7, 4, 2, 1 Code

Decimal Sequence	7, 4, 2, 1 Code	Decimal Sequence	7, 4, 2, 1 Code
0	0000	5	0101
1	0001	6	0110
2	0010	7	1000
3	0011	8	1001
4	0100	9	1010

5–9. ERROR-DETECTION CODES

Several special codes are available for digital computer systems for error-detecting purposes. They are particularly useful for error sensing in peripheral equipment such as tape storage, punch cards, disk memory, and typewriter linkages. One system is to utilize only two digits plus three zeros for numbers from 0 to 9, as shown in Table 5–10. By maintaining the number of bits that represent 1's at a minimum the possibility for error is minimized. On readout, any number containing only one zero, or more than two, is *incorrect*.

TABLE 5–10. Error-Detection Code

Decimal Sequence	Error Code	Decimal Sequence	Error Code
0	00110	5	10010
1	00011	6	01010
2	01100	7	10100
3	10001	8	01001
4	11000	9	00101

The code shown in Table 5–10 is sometimes referred to as *two-out-of-five* code because only two of the five bits are 1's. The sequence shown in Table 5–10 is arbitrary and various combinations of three 0's and two 1's can be used as desired.

Parity codes are also utilized for error detection. Parity (the quality of being equal) can be designed to show either an even number of digits or an odd number. An additional digit is utilized to achieve the required parity and such a parity digit may be either a 0 or a 1. Table 5–11 illustrates the even-parity code system. In this group, all digits in the binary representation plus the parity digit produces an even number of 1's. As

TABLE 5–11. Even-Parity Code

Decimal Sequence	Parity Digit	Binary Number
1	1	0001
2	1	0010
3	0	0011
4	1	0100
5	0	0101
6	0	0110
7	1	0111
8	1	1000
9	0	1001

shown, when the number of digits in the binary number is already even, the parity digit is 0. Errors are instantly detected because they alter the parity of a given number. Thus, if an even-parity group of numbers is processed and an odd-parity number is displayed, an error is indicated.

Table 5–12 illustrates the odd-parity code group. Here, a parity digit is utilized to form an odd number with the binary number. If the binary number already contains an odd digit grouping, the parity digit is zero, as shown.

TABLE 5–12. Odd-Parity Code

Decimal Sequence	Parity Digit	Binary Number
1	0	0001
2	0	0010
3	1	0011
4	0	0100
5	1	0101
6	1	0110
7	0	0111
8	0	1000
9	1	1001

5–10. GRAY-TO-BINARY CODE CONVERSION

The Gray code can be converted to its equivalent pure binary value in digital systems. A conversion system using a series of half-adders is shown in Figure 5–1. The half adders perform the logic *exclusive-or* function described in Sec. 6–12. A half-adder performs the addition of binary number $1+1$ *without carry*. Thus, when only a single digit appears at the input a 1 is produced at the output. For a digit input at each input line, however, a zero output results. As an example, assume that the Gray code number is 111011. The latter is applied as a *parallel* input, that is, all the bits of the number are applied simultaneously to the input, with the leftmost number applied to the uppermost half-adder as shown. The binary output is 101101, setting down the sequence of numbers from top to bottom in left-to-right formation. As many half-adders as needed can be utilized to handle the number of bits employed in a code grouping.

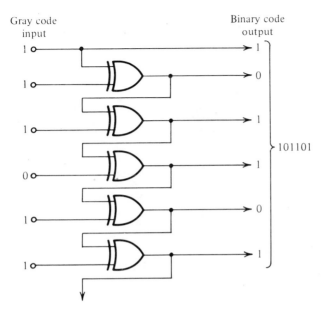

Figure 5-1   Gray Code-to-Binary Code Converter

5-11. BINARY ENCODER DISK

A widely used method for converting an analog function (such as a shaft rotation) into a digital representation is by using an encoder disk such as that shown in Figure 5–2. This disk is attached to a shaft and as rotation occurs successive binary representations are available. The disk contains alternate transparent segments or holes (light areas in Figure 5–2). A light source can be used with a pickup device as shown in Figure 5–3(A). For any specific disk position, certain segments through which light passes produce a specific binary number. An alternative method is shown in (B) using wire feeler brushes that penetrate the holes and permit current flow for number-sensing purposes. Disks in which the segments are printed-circuit types are also utilized.

For Figure 5–2 a pure binary output number is obtained as the disk rotates. At the vertical segment identified as the start of rotation, no holes are present and the output is read as 0000. (For higher binary

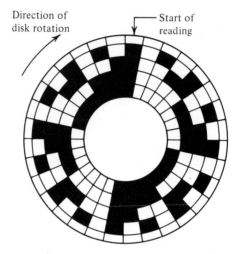

Figure 5–2 Encoder for Analog-to-Digital Binary

numbers, an increased disk diameter is utilized to accommodate additional segments.) When the disk moves for one segment clockwise, the binary number 0001 is sensed (reading from the inside of the disk toward the perimeter). For another one-segment rotation, the number 0010 is sensed, and so on for complete rotation. For a 180° rotation a maximum count of 15 is obtained for the disk shown. Additional rotation begins the count over again starting at 0000. Each ring can be extended to contain more segments as needed.

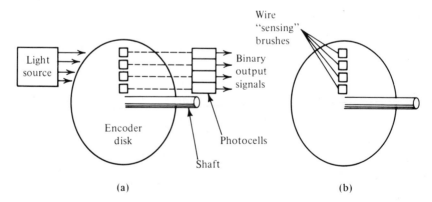

Figure 5–3 Encoder Sensing Systems

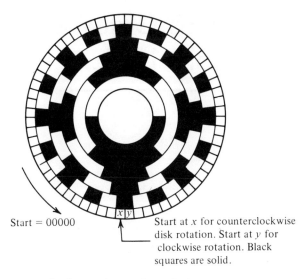

Start = 00000   *x* *y*   Start at *x* for counterclockwise
disk rotation. Start at *y* for
clockwise rotation. Black
squares are solid.

Figure 5–4   Encoder for Analog-to-Gray Code

5–12. GRAY ENCODER DISK

An encoder disk producing a five-place Gray code representation is shown in Figure 5–4. The sensing processes can again be as shown in Figure 5–3. For the disk in Figure 5–4 the starting position consists of a series of solid segments; hence, the number represented is 00000. As the disk rotates for one segment clockwise, the number 00001 will be read, starting from the innermost segment and reading toward the perimeter of the disk. Successive one-segment rotations produce the Gray code sequence of 0001, 0011, 0010, and so on, as shown in Table 5–6. After this particular disk has rotated 180°, the output Gray code numbers are successively repeated.

6 Switches, Gates, and Symbolic Logic

6-1. DIGITAL-LOGIC *OR* CIRCUIT

In digital electronic systems a group of logic circuits is extensively employed in various combinations to attain necessary switching and gating functions in such devices as calculators, computers, control systems, and other digital units. One such circuit is the logic-*or* illustrated in both schematic and symbol forms in Figure 6–1. Here there are three inputs provided, designated as A, B, and C. A two-input system (or a four or five) could, of course, also be used. For the circuit shown, the three inputs are applied to respective diodes and to the base element of an *npn* transistor. The output is obtained from the emitter resistor in typical emitter-follower fashion as described more fully in Sec. 2–6.

For conduction the potential at the base element of the transistor must be positive with respect to the emitter. Thus, positive-polarity pulses are used for this circuit. Obviously, a positive pulse applied to any (or all) inputs would cause transistor conduction and produce an output. Hence, this circuit is termed an *or* circuit because an input at A *or* B *or* C, *or* all three, will produce an output. For a *pnp* transistor, negative pulses would be used at the input to cause conduction.

The *or* logic function is identified by using the plus (+) mathematical symbol as in A+B, A+B+C+D, and so on. The plus sign used in this manner is known as the *logic connective* and it does not indicate an additive process, only an *or* function. Several other type *or* circuits can

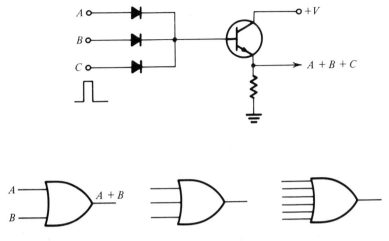

Figure 6–1   Logic *or* Circuit and Symbols

be formed, although all function in the same logic manner. Series resistors could replace the diodes shown, or several transistors could be used with separate base-terminal inputs, but sharing the same emitter load resistor for the output line. In all instances the standard symbol is as shown in Figure 6–1, the only differences being in the number of input lines shown.

The logic connective is also used when the binary 1 and 0 numerals are used, as $1+0 = 1$ to show the logic-*or* process. The letters identify the input lines and are used to show the resultant output expressions, but the individual inputs receive only the 0 and 1 representations of the binary system in digital logic systems.

6–2. LOGIC *OR* TRUTH TABLES

A listing of input and output values for a given logic function forms what is termed a *truth table*. For the three-input *or* circuit of Figure 6–1, the truth table is given in Table 6–1. The horizontal row of 0's under the alphabetical designations represents the status of the system during the absence of any input signals representative of logic 1. Every possible combination of input signals is shown in Table 6–1.

TABLE 6-1. Three-Input *or* Circuit

A	+	B	+	C	Output
0		0		0	0
0		0		1	1
1		0		0	1
0		1		0	1
1		1		0	1
0		1		1	1
1		0		1	1
1		1		1	1

Thus, Table 6-1 shows that an output logic 1 is obtained in every instance that a logic 1 is applied to one or more of the input lines. For more input lines, the table would become increasingly longer to accommodate all the variations of logic 0 and logic 1 input combinations.

6-3. LOGIC *AND* GATES

As with the *or* circuit discussed in Sec. 6-1, the *and* circuit shown in Figure 6-2 may have more than two input terminals. Such logic circuits can be formed by diodes as well as junction or field-effect transistors, but the basic circuit shown in Figure 6-2 serves to illustrate the principles involved. The transistors are in series, where the collector of Q_2 is connected to the emitter of Q_1. For conduction to occur, the input signal must provide for a forward bias and hence should be positive at the base terminal. If a positive pulse is applied to the A terminal Q_1 could conduct but is unable to do so because of the series circuit and the nonconducting Q_2. Similarly, an input at the B terminal alone will not cause conduction. When both inputs have a positive pulse applied, both transistors conduct and hence a positive signal appears at the output terminal from the emitter of Q_2. Consequently, the logic for such a circuit is A *and* B produces an output, but not A alone or B alone. Thus, such a circuit is essentially a *coincidence gate* since all inputs must occur coincidentally to obtain an output.

For the *or* circuit covered in Sec. 6-1 the logical connective was the arithmetic + sign. The logical connective for the *and* circuit is the

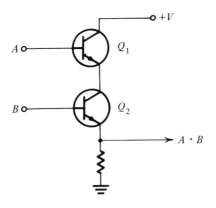

Figure 6–2 Logic *and* Circuit and Symbols

multiplication sign and hence can take the form A × B, or the placing together of letters in algebraic form as AB, or use of the raised dot as A·B. The symbols for the *and* circuit are also shown in Figure 6–2, where multiple input lines are indicated. Thus, for a four-input *and* circuit the logic is ABCD. (The logical connectives do not represent an arithmetical multiplication, only a signal coincidence input representation.)

6–4. LOGIC *AND* TRUTH TABLES

As with the truth tables for the *or* circuit discussed in Sec. 6–2, similar tables can be used to illustrate the logic function of the *and* circuits. For a three-input *and* circuit, the truth table is given in Table 6–2. As with Table 6–1, the horizontal row of 0's under the alphabetical designations represents the status during the absence of any input signals. Every possible combination of input signals is shown in Table 6–2.

TABLE 6–2. Three-Input *and* Circuit

A	B	C	Output
0	0	0	0
0	0	1	0
1	0	0	0
0	1	0	0
1	1	0	0
0	1	1	0
1	0	1	0
1	1	1	1

Thus, Table 6–2 shows that an output logic 1 is obtained only when every input terminal of the *and* circuit has a logic 1 applied to it in coincidence. For more input lines, the truth table is expanded to accommodate all the variations of logic 0 and logic 1 input combinations.

6–5. PHASE-INVERTING *NOT* LOGIC

Another logic function in digital systems is that termed *not* logic. Essentially, this relates to the phase inversion process, where the input and output signals are 180° out of phase (see Secs. 2–2 and 2–3). The basic function is illustrated in Figure 6–3. In (A) is shown the conventional triangle symbol for an amplifier. Here a positive pulse or other type of

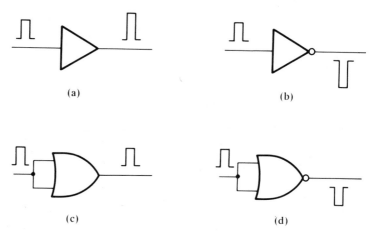

(a)   (b)

(c)   (d)

Figure 6–3 Formation of *not* Logic

signal at the input produces an in-phase amplified output signal (see also Secs. 2–6 and 2–7). For the amplifier in (A), a negative-polarity input signal would produce a negative-signal output. For the common-emitter circuits, there is a phase inversion as shown in (B). Here a positive input signal produces a negative-polarity output signal. For a negative-polarity input, a positive signal output would be obtained. This phase-inverting system is identified by using a small circle as shown. This circuit is termed a *not* circuit because the output phase *does not* follow that of the input.

In Figure 6–3(C) is shown an *or* circuit with the inputs shorted together to form a single input terminal. Thus, we have a nonamplifying circuit with identical-polarity input and output signals. In (D) is shown the inverting or *not*-circuit version, wherein the output signal is 180° out of phase with the input. This *not* logic is applicable to both the *or* and *and* circuits, as discussed in subsequent sections of this chapter.

6–6. *NOR* FUNCTION

Various examples of utilizing the *not* logic (covered in Sec. 6–5) with *or* circuits are shown in Figure 6–4. When the *not* logic is applied to the *or* circuit, it forms a *not-or* (also termed *nor*) system. Thus, as shown in Figure 6–4, a two-input *or* circuit forms the logic $A + B$. When we have an inversion in polarity at the output we obtain a negated $A + B$ and the negation is identified with an overbar: $\overline{A + B}$. Similarly a three-input circuit with negation gives us: $\overline{A + B + C}$. The amplifier symbol with negation shown in Figure 6–3(B) could also be used to form a *nor* function. Thus, as shown in Figure 6–4, the two input *or* circuit is followed by a *not* circuit to produce the negated output. Double negation reverts the negated expression to its original form as shown in the fifth example in Figure 6–4. Combinations can also be utilized for more than one output, as shown in the last example in Figure 6–4. Here the output provides us with $\overline{A + B}$ as well as $A + B$.

6–7. LOGIC *NOR* TRUTH TABLES

The truth table for the three-input *nor* circuit shown in the third example of Figure 6–4 is given in Table 6–3. As with earlier tables in this chapter, the horizontal row of 0's under the alphabetical designations

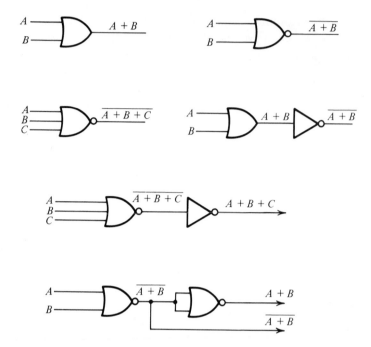

Figure 6–4   Logic *nor* Examples

represents an absence of input signals. Below the row of 0's is every possible combination of input signals.

TABLE 6–3. Three-Input *nor* Circuit

$\underline{A}$ +	$\underline{B}$ +	$\underline{C}$	*Output*
0	0	0	1
0	0	1	0
1	0	0	0
0	1	0	0
1	1	0	0
0	1	1	0
1	0	1	0
1	1	1	0

Note that Table 6–3 has an output sequence opposite to that of the table for the *or* circuit (Table 6–1). Thus, the *nor* logic provides for a logic 0 output in every instance that a logic 1 is applied to one or more of the input lines. As with other systems described herein, the truth table is expanded to accommodate all the variations of logic 0 and logic 1 combinations for tables having four, five, or more inputs.

6-8. *NAND* FUNCTION

When the *not* function described in Sec. 6–6 is utilized in conjunction with the *and* gate covered in Sec. 6–3, the logic *not-and* (also termed *nand*) is formed. The applicable logic in symbolic form is illustrated in Figure 6–5. When the *and* function AB is negated by the *not* function, the output expression is shown with an overbar as $\overline{AB}$. Similarly, as shown by the third example, a three-input *nand* circuit produces $\overline{ABC}$. The negation can also be performed by the *not* logic discussed in Sec. 6–5 and shown in the fourth example of Figure 6–5. The fifth example shows a three-input system using double negation for producing an output expression ABC, and an additional output line obtained from the *nand* circuit to obtain $\overline{ABC}$.

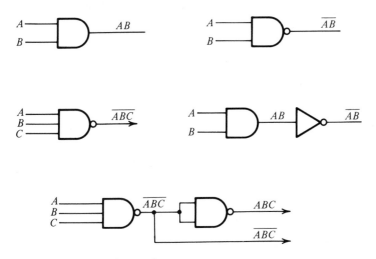

Figure 6–5 Logic *nand* Examples

6-9. LOGIC *NAND* TRUTH TABLES

As with Table 6–3 the truth table for a three-input *and* circuit has an output logic that is opposite to that given in Table 6–2. Thus, the logic sequence for a *nand* circuit follows the progression shown in Table 6–4. Note that no output is obtained when full coincidence prevails.

TABLE 6–4. Three-Input *nand* Circuit

A	B	C	Output
0	0	0	1
0	0	1	1
1	0	0	1
0	1	0	1
1	1	0	1
0	1	1	1
1	0	1	1
1	1	1	0

6–10. VARIOUS GATES AND COMBINATIONS

The *and* and *nand* circuits can be utilized for gating-in or gating-out purposes by taking advantage of the necessity for coincidence in producing an output. Typical examples of the gating function are shown in Figure 6–6. In a two-input *and* circuit, either input terminal can be used as the gating line. For the *and* system shown in Figure 6–6(A) the lower line constitutes the gating input. Note that the upper input line has a pulse train applied to it. For each group of four pulses applied to the upper line, three pulses are applied to the gating input as shown. Since coincidence occurs for only the first, third, and fourth pulses of the input train in the upper line, the output pulses consist of the initial pulse followed by a blank interval and two final pulses as shown. Negative pulses are shown for the example in (A), although positive pulses could also be used with identical gating results.

Instead of pulses, dc could also be used for gating purposes by applying a dc burst for the time interval wherein a section of a pulse train is to be obtained at the output. Long-duration pulses could also be used as shown in (B). Here, coincidence prevails for the two initial pulses of the input train but not for the third pulse. Consequently, the output waveform is as shown in Figure 6–6(B). Again, opposite polarity pulses can be utilized, as was shown at (A) without disturbing the logic gating functions illustrated. If *nand* circuits were used at (A) and (B) instead of *and*, the output pulses would have a polarity opposite to that shown for each circuit.

Negations could also be indicated at the input to a *nand* gate, as shown at (C). For a dual negated input, the output expression is $\bar{A} \cdot \bar{B}$.

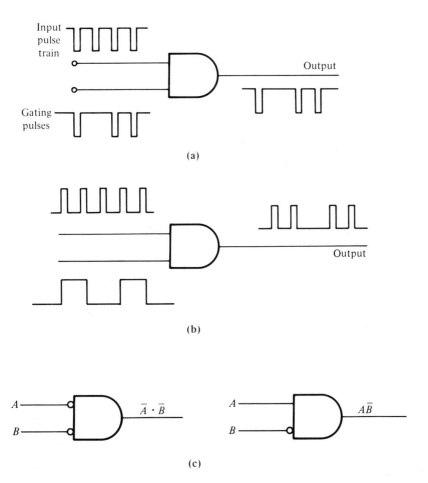

Figure 6–6 Gating Examples

Note that the *logical connective is not negated* in this instance. Negation of the logical connective converts its function. Negating a logical *and* multiplication connective converts it to a logical *or* connective ($+$). This factor is expanded in Sec. 6–11. For the second example in Figure 6–6(C) only one input is negated, producing an output expression of $A\overline{B}$. This gate is sometimes termed an *inhibitor*, since the negated B input has an inhibiting effect on the logic.

Gating combinations employing the *or* and *and* functions are illustrated in Figure 6–7. The first example shows an *or* circuit that transfers the A input directly to the output. The B and C inputs can appear at the

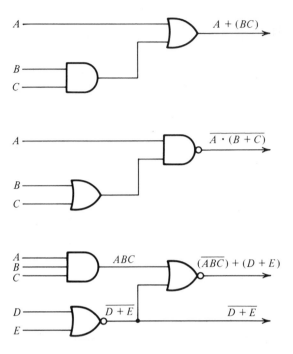

Figure 6–7   Gate Combinations

output only if they occur in coincidence. Hence, the output expression is A, or the combination of B and C, or both as shown. For the second example, the A input must have coincidence before an output is obtained; hence, the A input must be accompanied by either the B, the C, or both. Since the output is negated the expression becomes A·(B+C). For the last example, an *and* circuit is used with two *nor* circuits. Since ABC in coincidence is produced from the *and* circuit it could pass through the *or* circuit alone and undergo inversion to form $\overline{ABC}$. The D or E inputs to the first *nor* gate form an independent output, but the expression is also applied to the second *nor* circuit, which converts the negated expression back to its original form. Thus, one output is obtained having the logic $(\overline{ABC})+(D+E)$ and another with the logic $\overline{D+E}$.

6–11. DE MORGAN'S THEOREM

The negation factor in digital logic (Sec. 6–4) creates conditions involving duality. When a negated logic expression involves an *and* circuit such as $\overline{A \cdot B}$ the logic connective is also negated, and hence the multiplication

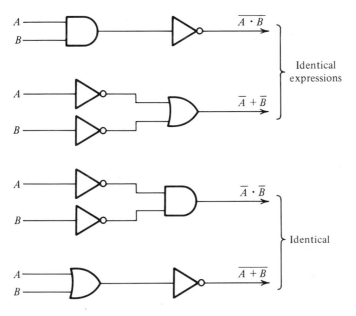

Figure 6–8   De Morgan's Theorem Logic

logical connective for *and* becomes an *or* logical connection $(+)$. Thus, the expression $\overline{A \cdot B}$ is equivalent to $\overline{A} + \overline{B}$. Similarly, if a negation of *or* logic is involved, such as $\overline{A + B}$ the *or* logical connective inverts to an *and* logical connective and the expression becomes $\overline{A} \cdot \overline{B}$. These similarities and comparisons involve De Morgan's theorem and are illustrated in Figure 6–8. In the upper illustration the output from an *and* gate is negated and the resultant expression is identical to the expression obtained when the A and B inputs to an *or* circuit are negated initially, as shown by the second example. Similarly, if the A and B input to an *and* circuit are negated, the resultant expression is identical to that obtained when the output from an *or* circuit is negated.

6–12. *EXCLUSIVE OR* AND *NOR* GATES

Another logic gate useful in digital application is the *exclusive or* circuit. As shown in Figure 6–9, the basic *or* circuit symbol is utilized with an additional curved line at the input section. Either *or* or *nor* logic can be utilized. The logic for the *exclusive or* circuit is that an output is produced for an input at either A or B, but not both. Thus, the circuit is

Figure 6–9 Exclusive *or* and *nor* Symbols

useful in the formation of logic circuit combinations for binary addition, since it follows the logic of $1+1=0$, carry 1 (see Sec. 5–1). Instead of using the *or*-logic connective ($+$), the symbol $\oplus$ is commonly employed. The second example in Figure 6–9 shows the *exclusive nor* symbol and here the output expression is $\overline{A \oplus B}$.

6–13. *EXCLUSIVE OR* LOGIC AND APPLICATIONS

Tables 6–5 and 6–6 indicate the output logic for the *exclusive or* and the *exclusive nor* logic discussed in Sec. 6–12. Note that for Table 6–5 the *exclusive or* function provides an output only for a single input to either A or B. For the *exclusive nor* function given in Table 6–6, negated outputs appear for an input to either A or B, but not both.

TABLE 6–5	TABLE 6–6
$A \oplus B$	$\overline{A \oplus B}$
0 0 = 0	0 0 = 1
0 1 = 1	0 1 = 0
1 0 = 1	1 0 = 0
1 1 = 0	1 1 = 1

One application for the *exclusive or* circuit is illustrated in Figure 6–1, where a series of such circuits is utilized to convert the Gray code to the binary code. Another application is shown in Figure 6–10, where the *exclusive or* circuit forms a comparator that provides a logic output when all inputs have a logic 1 applied, *or* if all inputs are in the logic 0 state. For Figure 6–10, an eight-input system is shown using four *exclusive nor* circuits. The output lines of the four independent gates are joined together to form one output section at the unit termed a *wired and* gate. The latter represents a connection formed of several outputs,

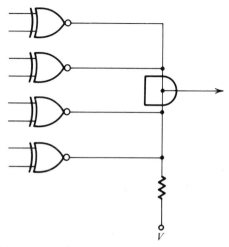

Figure 6–10 Eight-Bit-Input Comparator

which produce the *output and-gate* function, referenced by the special symbol indicated in Figure 6–10.

For the system shown in Figure 6–10 an 8-bit group applied to the input is compared for equality and an output is obtained only if such a quality exists. If any one of the inputs to the *exclusive nor* circuits is logic 0, there is no output. The latter indicates inequality. Additional *exclusive nor* circuits can be added to the system as needed.

6–14. IC GATE PACKAGES

Numerous combinations of *and, or, nor, nand,* and *exclusive or* logic circuits are combined in integrated-circuit packages to serve specific needs. Typical examples are illustrated in Figure 6–11 to show the method of depicting the logic involved and the IC pin connections utilized. Commercial IC logic sections may, of course, utilize many more logic gates in a single IC chip. Some packages may contain all similar-type gates or extensive gating-tree formation of the type illustrated in Figure 6–16.

In (A) is shown a dual-gate formation with three inputs to an *and* circuit, the output of which is fed to one input of an *or* circuit as shown. A three-gate package is illustrated in (B), where a dual-input *nand* circuit has its output connected to the inputs of two *or* circuits as shown. Additional inputs are available for the *or* circuits. For the circuit shown

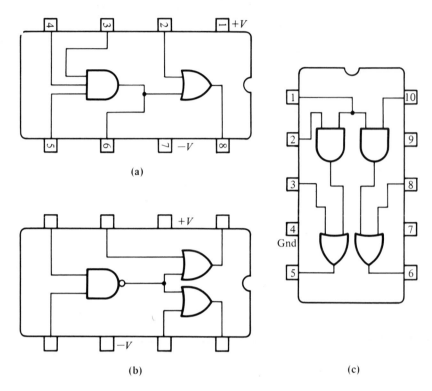

(a)

(b)   (c)

Figure 6-11 IC Gate Packages

in Figure 6-11(C), combinations of *and* and *nor* circuits are utilized. In addition to a common *and*-circuit input from IC terminal 1, individual *and* logic inputs are available at pins 2 and 10. Similarly, additional *or*-gate inputs are available at pins 3 and 8. The output lines from the *or* circuits are available at pins 5 and 6.

6-15. BASIC FLIP-FLOP SECTIONS

The flip-flop circuit is an important unit in digital systems because of its switchable dual-state characteristics. The basic flip-flop circuit is illustrated in Figure 6-12. As shown, two transistors are utilized, designated as Q_1 and Q_2. Note the symmetrical circuit configuration having identical base, emitter, and collector components as well as similar input and output sections. In contrast to the relaxation-type oscillators, such as the multivibrator and blocking oscillator (see Secs. 2-33 and 2-34), the flip-

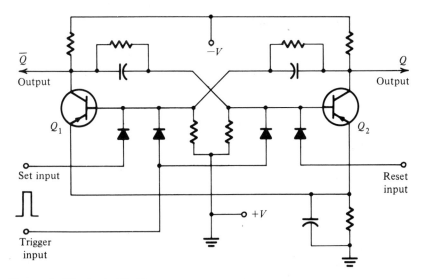

Figure 6–12   Basic Flip-Flop

flop circuit is not a free-running oscillator. Thus, it does not provide for a continuous output signal, but produces an output only when an input signal of proper polarity and amplitude is applied. For the circuit shown in Figure 6–12, three input lines are present: the *set*, the *trigger*, and the *reset*. Two output terminals are present, and when an input signal is applied, the output line designated as $\overline{Q}$ produces a logic 0 and the Q output produces a logic 1. Thus, one steady-state logic representation has been achieved by the flip-flop circuit and it remains in this state until another input signal is applied. For a new input signal, logic 0 appears at the Q output and a logic 1 at the $\overline{Q}$ output.

For the circuit shown in Figure 6–12, logic 1 is represented by a positive-polarity pulse. For utilization of a negative-polarity pulse for logic 1, the transistors would be replaced by *npn* types and the diodes and voltage polarities reversed. The input line for the set function is effective only when Q_1 is in the conducting state, at which time the positive-pulse potential at the transistor base terminal overcomes the forward bias and causes this transistor to go into a nonconducting state. Once this transistor is in the latter state, an additional positive-polarity input pulse applied to the set line would be ineffectual. Since Q_2 conducts when Q_1 is nonconducting, a positive pulse at the reset line would retrigger the flip-flop to its original state. Diodes in the base-terminal lines provide for a unidirectional positive-pulse signal path. The trigger input is attached to both base-terminal lines and hence is capable of changing the state of the flip-flop circuit for each pulse entered.

The pulse applied to the set input at Q_1 that causes this transistor to become nonconductive causes the voltage drop across the Q_1 collector resistor to decrease to zero and hence the collector becomes negative and equal to the battery potential. The latter is held at the base terminal of Q_2 by the coupling network of resistor and capacitor. The negative potential appearing at the base of Q_2 forms the forward bias (negative at the base compared to the positive emitter). Now Q_2 conducts and the voltage drop across its collector resistor rises and hence represents a positive-polarity change. This potential, coupled to the base terminal of Q_1, maintains the latter in its nonconducting state. Now, a reset pulse input to Q_2 reverses the status of Q_1 and Q_2, causing the latter to become nonconducting and Q_1 conducting.

The flip-flop unit can be designed around logic-*or* and logic-*nor* sections, as shown in Figure 6–13. For the *nor* circuits, connections are as shown in (A). Here the reset terminal is applied to one *nor* circuit and the set terminal to the other. The output from each *nor* circuit is also fed back to the input of the other *nor* as shown. When the flip-flop is in the state producing a logic 1 at the Q output, the logic 0 appears at the $\overline{Q}$ output. In this state the application of a signal to the S terminal will be

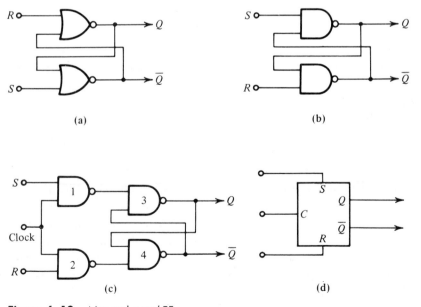

(a) (b)

(c) (d)

Figure 6–13 *Nor* and *nand* FF

inverted and represent a logic 0 at the *nor* output line, thus initiating no change since the circuit is already in the set mode. Also, with a set line input the logic 0 is also fed to the input of the upper *nor* circuit and is inverted at the output to form a logic 1. Thus, it is evident that once the circuit is in the set condition, another input signal applied to the set terminal will cause no change. To obtain the change of state a reset input is required.

When a signal is applied to the R input, the output at the Q line is negated and produces a logic 0 that is also fed to one of the S terminal inputs. At the latter *nor*-circuit output a logic 1 is produced and thus the state of the flip-flop is changed. Now an input applied to the S line is required to change the state again. A similar circuit is shown in Figure 6–13(B), where two *nand* circuits are used. For either *nand* gate signal coincidence must prevail at the inputs to obtain an output. This *nand*-type flip-flop is combined with other circuitry for obtaining specific digital functions. A typical example is that shown at (C), where a clocked input line is added to the system by employing two additional *nand* gates.

Clock pulses are precisely timed signals obtained from frequency-controlled generators as discussed in Sec. 6–17. The clock pulse system thus generates the fundamental train of pulses utilized throughout a particular digital system. For the flip-flop system shown in (C), the clock pulses with their fixed repetition rate are applied to the clock input line and hence are present at each initial *nand* gate (1 and 2) as shown. The continuous input train places each initial *nand* gate in readiness for coinciding signals applied to the S or R input line. For an S input, for instance, the coincidence obtained with a clock pulse produces a negated output at *nand* gate 1. The negated output appears at the input to *nand* gate 3. The logic 0 output from *nand* gate 4 also appears at *nand* gate 3 to provide for coincidence. The logic 0 input signals at *nand* gate 3 are inverted to produce a logic 1 output.

The flip-flop is sometimes represented by a rectangular symbol as shown in Figure 6–13(D), instead of using the logic symbols. The three input lines are the set, clock pulse, and reset modes. Sometimes the clock pulse input is designated as CP.

6–16. J-K SYSTEMS AND SYMBOLS

A flip-flop system of special design is that termed the J-K flip-flop. The letters J and K are used to designate the two particular input lines for this special flip-flop system. A typical example is shown in Figure 6–

14(A) utilizing two additional *and* circuits for feeding the J and K inputs to the clocked R-S flip-flop representing the type illustrated in Figure 6–13. As shown, the Q and $\overline{Q}$ output lines are also fed back to the inputs of the two *and* circuits. If the J-K flip-flop is in the logic 1 state, logic 0 appears at the $\overline{Q}$ output. This logic 0 also appears at the input coinciding with the J line and thus inhibiting an input to the set (S) line. When a logic 1 signal is applied to the K and CP inputs, the reset function is initiated. The K input produces an output since a logic 1 is fed back from the Q output to the K *and* circuit. When a logic 1 is applied to inputs J, CP, and K simultaneously, a trigger function is obtained just as for the trigger input of the flip-flop shown in Figure 6–12. Thus, such coinciding inputs trigger the J-K flip-flop system consecutively into its set and reset modes.

Another J-K flip-flop system is shown in Figure 6–14(B). Here four *nand* gates, having five inputs, are utilized. As with the system shown in (A), feedback lines are used to obtain the desired logic functions. If the system shown in (B) is in the set state, the Q output pro-

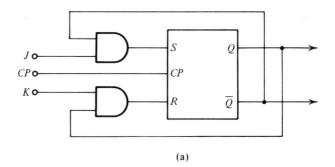

(a)

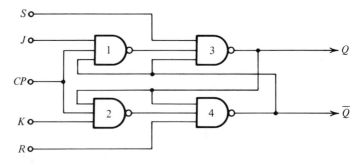

Figure 6–14 Basic J-K Flip-Flops

duces a logic 1 and the $\overline{Q}$ a logic 0, as with the other flip-flop systems. Note that the logic 0 on the $\overline{Q}$ line is fed back to the input of the three-input J *nand* gate identified as No. 1. Because this logic 0 inhibits coincidence at the J input, *nand* gate 1 remains closed.

The flip-flop representations illustrated in Figures 6–13 and 6–14 are conventional system representations. The discrete circuitry includes numerous additional components often necessary to assure stable operation and prevent such undesired effects as *race around*. The latter effect (produced by inherent signal-delay circuit characteristics) causes a flip-flop to cycle more than once for a single input reset pulse. The logic symbols in Figures 6–13 and 6–14 show the interconnections for the logic gates and thus illustrate the logic functions to be performed. Obviously, supporting circuitry such as power supplies, interfacing, and other sections not performing logic functions are included.

6–17. CLOCK PULSE SYSTEMS

The circuit referred to as *the clock* in digital systems originates precisely timed pulse signals for use through a particular system. The clock is essentially a feedback oscillator utilizing a quartz crystal for frequency-control purposes, as shown in Figure 6–15(A). The conventional amplifier represented by the triangle symbol has the output line coupled to the crystal using resistor R_2. The crystal unit forms a feedback loop to the input of the amplifier for sustaining oscillations. Essentially, the crystal forms a closed loop that feeds back a specific portion of the output signal in proper phase for regenerative purposes.

Another clock system is shown in Figure 6–15(B). Here a dual output is obtained, each producing a series of pulses at a repetition rate one-half that of the train produced by the clock pulse generator. Note that the output train from logic gate 2 is displaced with respect to the pulse output from gate 1. Thus, this system is also termed a *phased clock system*. As shown in Figure 6–15(B), the clock pulse generator output is applied to the CP input of a J-K flip-flop. The output line from the clock also branches to one input of logic gate 1 and one input of logic gate 2. The Q and $\overline{Q}$ outputs are applied to gate 1 and gate 2, respectively. Because the outputs from the flip-flops are logic 1 and logic 0, these outputs alternately establish coincidence at the inputs to the *and* circuit. The pulse counter applied to the Q output measures the repetition rate.

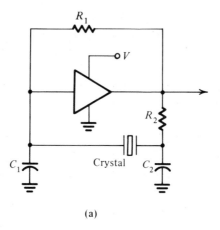

(a)

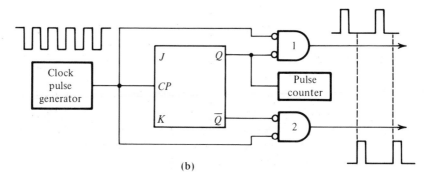

(b)

Figure 6–15 Clock Pulse Systems

By appropriate selection of signal inputs to J, K, or both, the output pulse timing and quantity can be regulated as desired (see Sec. 6–16).

When an output clock pulse is applied to the CP input, the initiation of a set condition produces a logic 1 from the Q output. For negative-polarity clock pulses, coincidence prevails at logic gate 1 and an inverted signal (now positive) appears at the output. For the next clocked pulse at CP, the output from the Q line becomes positive and does not provide for a coincidence, but the $\overline{Q}$ line is now negative to produce coincidence at logic gate 2. Thus, the two sets of output pulses alternate in time. This system could, of course, be designed so that the clock applies positive pulses to the J-K input when negative-polarity output pulses are required.

6–18. GATING TREE

When successive logic circuits have several outputs supplied to other logic gates, as shown in Figure 6–16, a configuration termed a *gating tree* is formed. Thus, the three *or* circuits shown could have their inputs supplied to another *or* circuit with three inputs, for a single output. For the system shown, however, the flip-flop circuits have the Q and $\overline{Q}$ outputs applied to individual *and* circuits that, in turn, feed an *or* circuit. Coincidence prevails only if a pulse is applied either to the *complementary* gate line or the *true* gate line. Thus, if a pulse is applied to the complementary gate line to provide for coincidence with the $\overline{Q}$ output, the *or* circuits would provide for a complement binary reading, that is, the inverse of the binary number. Similarly, if a pulse is applied to a true gate line to coincide with the Q output pulse polarity, the true binary representation would be obtained.

As an example, assume that the three flip-flops contain the binary number 101. A pulse applied to the true gate line would find coincidence for the first and third flip-flop stages. However, since the second flip-flop represents logic symbol 0, the Q line does not provide for coincidence with the true gate line pulse and hence there is no output from the second *or* circuit. Since the complement gate input is not applied, no $\overline{Q}$ lines are coincident. Hence, the output reading from the *or* circuits is 101. If a complement gate pulse is applied, however, coincidence occurs

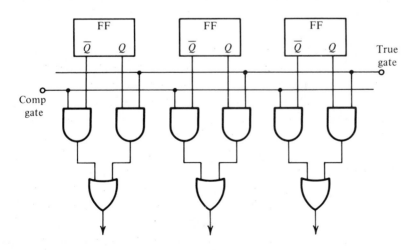

Figure 6–16   Gating Tree

only for the $\overline{Q}$ output line of the second flip-flop. Thus, the output number would be 010, the complement of 101.

6-19. SINGLE-SHOT MULTIVIBRATOR

The single-shot multivibrator is one of several special-purpose units utilized in digital electronics. Although termed a *multivibrator,* it is not a free-running signal generator as is the case for the unit described in Sec. 2–33. Instead, the single-shot type produces an output signal only when a signal is injected into its input terminal, as with the flip-flop circuit discussed in Sec. 6–15. The basic circuit for the single-shot unit is shown in Figure 6–17. This device is sometimes referred to as a *start–stop* multivibrator. The latter term defines its basic characteristics as a monostable multivibrator as opposed to the astable types of relaxation oscillators discussed in Secs. 2–33 and 2–34.

For the circuit shown in Figure 6–17, a positive input pulse is required. For a negative-polarity input signal the transistors would be changed to *pnp* types and the voltage-supply polarities reversed. When the positive pulse is applied to the trigger input lines, the base terminal of Q_2 now conducts and the consequent current flow through collector resistor R_4 produces a voltage drop that decreases the collector potential

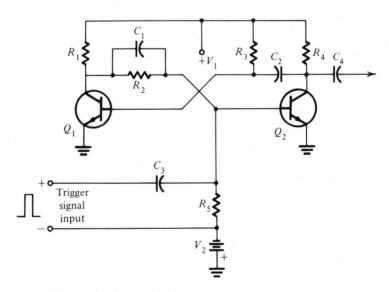

Figure 6–17 Single-Shot Multivibrator

toward the ground-level state (negative with respect to the collector). The voltage change that occurs at the collector of Q_2 is coupled via C_2 to the base terminal of transistor Q_1. Thus, the forward bias for Q_1 is reduced sufficiently to cause nonconduction. Now the voltage drop across R_1 decreases, causing the collector potential of Q_1 to rise, hence augmenting the potential applied by the input signal. Thus, within a short time interval Q_1 conduction is cut off while Q_2 conducts fully.

Since the input pulse that initiates the conduction cycles is of short duration the forward bias established at Q_2 is removed when the input pulse amplitude drops to zero. Now capacitor C_2 changes to its original charge level, permitting Q_1 to resume conduction. Thus, the original state is again obtained. In the absence of an input trigger, the voltage supply V_2 holds Q_2 in its nonconducting state because of the reverse bias potentials applied. During the momentary conduction of Q_2 an output pulse is produced (via C_4) that has a fixed duration as determined by the selection of components during design. Thus, when such a fixed-duration pulse is required it can be procured from the multivibrator for a wide latitude of input pulse characteristics.

6-20. SCHMITT TRIGGER

The Schmitt trigger is another special circuit used in digital electronics in addition to the flip-flop system covered in Sec. 6–15 and the single-shot multivibrator discussed in Sec. 6–19. The Schmitt trigger is useful because its switching sensitivity is related to the *amplitude* of the input pulse. Hence, this trigger system is useful for reshaping pulse or square-wave signals when the latter undergo distortion in their travel through specific sections. The circuit is also useful for the attenuation of noise signals. If the latter are present between the pulses of a pulse train or appear as transient overshoots, the signal group can be applied to the Schmitt trigger and a pure distortionless output waveform produced having the same repetition rate.

The basic Schmitt trigger circuit is shown in Figure 6–18. As with multivibrator circuits, two transistors are utilized. A positive input pulse is needed for the circuit shown, although the selection of *pnp* transistors and a reversal of supply potential polarities can be used for negative input signals. As with the one-shot multivibrator discussed in Sec. 6–19, the Schmitt trigger remains in a stable state when no input signal is present. Since no forward bias is present for Q_1 this transistor does not

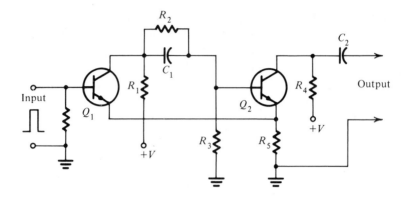

Figure 6–18 Schmitt Trigger

conduct. For Q_2, however, the voltage drop across R_3 supplies the necessary forward bias for conduction.

When a positive-polarity input pulse is applied to the Schmitt trigger as shown in Figure 6–18, the base terminal of Q_1 attains a positive amplitude that is sufficiently high to overcome the reverse bias existing between the base and emitter. (The latter has a positive potential applied to it because it taps R_5.) When Q_1 conducts, the collector resistor R_1 develops a voltage drop across it that causes the potential at the collector to decrease. The drop in collector potential is felt at the base of Q_2 and causes a decrease in forward bias, reducing reduction for Q_2. The process is rapid and continues until Q_2 no longer conducts and Q_1 conducts fully. At the time that Q_2 goes into nonconduction, the collector potential rises as the voltage drop across R_4 declines. This amplitude change of collector potential thus produces an output signal.

When the input pulse amplitude drops to zero the Schmitt trigger circuit rapidly changes to its original state wherein transistor Q_2 conducts again. The interval required for Q_2 to revert to its conducting state determines the duration of the output pulse. The duration of conduction as well as the amplitude change in the collector circuit is established by selection of specific component values. Thus, when the input pulse has reached an amplitude sufficient to trigger the Schmitt circuit, an output pulse is produced that is uneffected by any additional input pulse amplitude change (such as a transient or for any other changes below the trigger amplitude).

7 Various Tables and Miscellaneous Data

7-1. DECIBEL RATIOS

A description of decibels is given in Sec. 1–7. Table 7–1 lists the decibel comparisons of voltage, current, and power ratios for decibel values ranging from 0.5 to 30. As explained in Sec. 1–7, the decibel system is basically a *comparison* of voltage, current, or power values and is related to discrete quantities only by providing for a direct reference level. A doubling of power (power ratio equals 2) provides a 3-dB reference regardless of the respective amounts of the two powers forming the ratio. Thus, a ratio of 4 W to 2 W = 3 dB, as does a ratio of 1000 W/500 W. For voltage ratios as well as current ratios a doubling (where the ratio is 2) produces 6 dB, as shown in Table 7–1.

7-2. PREFIXES AND THEIR SYMBOLS

Various prefixes relating to the powers of 10 have been standardized for convenience in expressing electric and electronic quantities. Table 7–2 lists representative prefixes plus their letter symbols and values ranging from 1×10^{-18} to 1×10^{12}. Note that the letter symbols are all lower-case except for the last three, involving *mega, giga,* and *tera.* Relating these to electric–electronic quantities permits us to write kilovolts as kV, megavolts as MV, milliamperes as mA, microamperes as μA, picofarad as pF, and so on. Utilization of the standard prefixes and letter symbols shown in Table 7–2 avoids the confusion resulting from usage of words such as trillion, billion, and so on, which have different numerical values in various countries, as shown in Sec. 7–3.

TABLE 7–1. Decibel Comparisons of E, I, and P Ratios

Decibel	Current or Voltage Ratio	Power Ratio
0.5	1.06	
1	1.12	1.26
1.5	1.19	
2	1.26	1.58
2.5	1.33	
3	1.41	2
3.5	1.49	
4	1.58	2.5
4.5	1.67	
5	1.78	3.16
5.5	1.89	
6	2	3.98
6.5	2.1	
7	2.24	5
7.5	2.35	
8	2.5	6.31
9	2.82	7.94
10	3.16	10
11	3.55	12.6
12	3.98	15.8
13	4.47	20
14	5	25
15	5.62	31.6
16	6.31	39.8
17	7.08	50.1
18	7.94	63.1
19	8.91	79.4
20	10	100
25	17.8	316
30	31.6	1000

TABLE 7–2. Standard Prefixes and Letter Symbols

Prefix	Symbol	Value	Submultiples and Multiples
atto	a		1×10^{-18}
femto	f		1×10^{-15}
pico	p	one-millionth millionth	1×10^{-12}
nano	n	1000 of a millionth	1×10^{-9}
micro	μ	one-millionth	1×10^{-6}
milli	m	one-thousandth	1×10^{-3}
centi	c	one-hundredth	1×10^{-2}
deci	d	one-tenth	1×10^{-1}
deca	da	ten	1×10^{1}
hecto	h	one hundred	1×10^{2}
kilo	k	one thousand	1×10^{3}
mega	M	one million	1×10^{6}
giga	G	one-thousand million	1×10^{9}
tera	T	one-million million	1×10^{12}

7–3. SYSTEM DIFFERENCES

Table 7–3 shows the system differences in various countries. As indicated, a billion represents 1000 million in the United States and France, but in Great Britain or Germany a billion equals a million millions. A giga equals a standard 1000 millions even though it may be referred to as a billion in the United States or in France but not in Great Britain or Germany. Thus, the standard prefixes refer to specific quantities even though *atto* is referred to as a quintillionth in the United States but would be referred to as a trillionth in Great Britain.

TABLE 7–3. System Differences

Designation	U.S. and French	Power	British and German	Power
million	1000 thousands	10^{6}	1000 thousands	10^{6}
milliard	1000 millions	10^{9}	1000 millions	10^{9}
billion	1000 millions	10^{9}	1 million millions	10^{12}
trillion	1000 billions (a million millions)	10^{12}	1 million billions	10^{18}
quadrillion	1000 trillions	10^{15}	1 million trillions	10^{24}
quintillion	1000 quadrillions	10^{18}	1 million quadrillions	10^{30}

7–4. TIME CONSTANTS

The time-constant characteristics of resistance and capacitance or inductance are covered in Sec. 1–9. A convenient time-constant listing for quick reference is given in Table 7–4 from values of 0.001 through 5 as shown.

TABLE 7–4. Time Constants

Time Constant	Percentage of Capacitor Discharge Voltage or Charge Current; also Percentage of Inductor Charge Voltage or Discharge Current	Percentage of Capacitor Charge Voltage or Percentage of Inductor Charge Current
0.001	99.9	0.1
0.002	99.8	0.2
0.003	99.7	0.3
0.004	99.6	0.4
0.005	99.5	0.5
0.006	99.4	0.6
0.007	99.3	0.7
0.008	99.2	0.8
0.009	99.1	0.9
0.01	99	1
0.02	98	2
0.03	97	3
0.04	96	4
0.05	95	5
0.06	94	6
0.07	93	7
0.08	92	8
0.09	91	9
0.10	90	10
0.15	86	14
0.20	82	18
0.25	78	22
0.30	74	26
0.35	70	30
0.40	67	33
0.45	64	36
0.5	61	39

TABLE 7–4. *continued*

Time Constant	Percentage of Capacitor Discharge Voltage or Charge Current; also Percentage of Inductor Charge Voltage or Discharge Current	Percentage of Capacitor Charge Voltage or Percentage of Inductor Charge Current
0.6	55	45
0.7	50	50
0.8	45	55
0.9	40	60
1	37	63
2	14	86
3	5	95
4	2	98
5	0.7	99.3

7–5. POWERS OF 2

A listing of the successive doubling of numerical values is shown in Table 7–5. It indicates the progression of place values for powers of 2 (binary numbers) (see also Sec. 5–1). Table 7–5 thus illustrates successive values, such as binary $0001 = 1$, $0010 = 2$, $0100 = 4$, $1000 = 8$, and so on.

TABLE 7–5. Powers of 2

n	2^n	n	2^n
1	2	21	2,097,152
2	4	22	4,194,304
3	8	23	8,388,608
4	16	24	16,777,216
5	32	25	33,554,432
6	64	26	67,108,864
7	128	27	134,217,728
8	256	28	268,435,456
9	512	29	536,870,912
10	1,024	30	1,073,741,824
11	2,048	31	2,147,483,648

TABLE 7–5. *continued*

n	2^n	n	2^n
12	4,096	32	4,294,967,296
13	8,192	33	8,589,934,592
14	16,384	34	17,179,869,184
15	32,768	35	34,359,738,368
16	65,536	36	68,719,476,736
17	131,072	37	137,438,953,472
18	262,144	38	274,877,906,944
19	524,288	39	549,755,813,888
20	1,048,576	40	1,099,511,627,776

7–6. MUSICAL-TONE FREQUENCIES

The progressive frequency of musical tones (in hertz) is shown in Table 7–6. Twelve notes are shown, from C to B, as the fundamental lowest tones shown in the table. Progressive octaves for each tone are

TABLE 7–6. Frequencies of Musical Tones: Progressive Octaves

C	$C^\#$	D	$D^\#$	E	F
0032.703	0034.648	0036.708	0038.891	0041.203	0043.654
0065.406	0069.296	0073.416	0077.782	0082.407	0087.307
0130.813	0138.591	0146.832	0155.563	0164.814	0174.614
0261.626	0277.183	0293.665	0311.127	0329.628	0349.228
0523.251	0554.365	0587.330	0622.254	0659.255	0698.456
1046.502	1108.731	1174.659	1244.508	1318.510	1396.913
2093.005	2217.461	2349.318	2489.016	2637.021	2793.826
4186.009	4434.922	4698.636	4978.032	5274.042	5587.652

$F^\#$	G	$G^\#$	A	$A^\#$	B
0046.249	0048.999	0051.913	0055.000	0058.270	0061.735
0092.499	0097.999	0103.830	0110.000	0116.540	0123.470
0184.997	0195.998	0207.652	0220.000	0233.082	0246.942
0369.994	0391.955	0415.305	0440.000	0466.164	0493.883
0739.989	0783.991	0830.609	0880.000	0932.328	0987.767
1479.978	1567.982	1661.219	1760.000	1864.655	1975.533
2959.955	3135.964	3322.438	3520.000	3729.310	3951.066
5919.910	6271.928	6644.876	7040.000	7458.620	7902.132

given below the alphabetical designations. Thus, the musical tone A at 440 Hz becomes 880 Hz for the same tone at an octave higher. For an octave lower, the frequency would be 220 Hz, and so on.

7-7. BESSEL FUNCTIONS

The Bessel functions shown in Table 7–7 are of importance in frequency-modulation communication systems. The table shows the relationship of a number of significant sidebands generated during the modulation process as determined by the modulation index (see Secs. 8–3 and 8–4). The modulation index (m) is found by dividing the frequency deviation of the carrier by the frequency of the modulating signal. Only a specific number of sidebands are considered significant in relation to the amplitude. Hence, Table 7–7 has blank sections wherein sideband amplitudes are no longer relevant. For an unmodulated waveform the carrier amplitude is 1.0, although the algebraic addition of the amplitudes of carriers and sidebands for various values of the modulation index does not produce 1.0 as the sum because *vector* addition is necessary when ac waveforms are involved.

TABLE 7–7. Bessel Functions

Modulation Index, m	Carrier Amplitude, $J_0(x)$	$J_1(x)$	$J_2(x)$	$J_3(x)$	$J_4(x)$	$J_5(x)$	$J_6(x)$	$J_7(x)$	$J_8(x)$	$J_9(x)$
0	1.000									
0.01	1.000	0.005								
0.02	0.999	0.010								
0.05	0.999	0.025								
0.1	0.998	0.050								
0.2	0.990	0.100								
0.5	0.938	0.242	0.310							
1.0	0.765	0.440	0.115	0.003						
2.0	0.224	0.577	0.353	0.129	0.034					
3.0	−0.260	0.339	0.486	0.309	0.132	0.043	0.012			
4.0	−0.397	−0.066	0.364	0.430	0.281	0.132	0.049	0.015		
5.0	−0.178	−0.328	0.047	0.365	0.391	0.261	0.131	0.053	0.018	
6.0	0.151	−0.277	−0.243	0.115	0.358	0.362	0.246	0.130	0.057	0.021

7–8. FREQUENCIES FOR *LC* PRODUCTS

When the reactances of capacitance and inductance are equal, the opposing characteristics of each cancels the net reactance and the state known as *resonance* has been achieved. Hence, the only opposition to ac energy is resistance. The resonance is achieved only for a specific frequency since either an increase or decrease of frequency alters both capacitive reactance X_C and inductive reactance X_L (see Sec. 1–6). At resonance the product of *LC* is a constant for a given frequency. Thus, respective values of inductance and capacitance can change, but resonance kept at a certain frequency (the inductance value can be increased, for instance, as the capacitance value is decreased). As long as the product is not altered, the same frequency prevails. Table 7–8 lists resonant frequencies in kilohertz and wavelength in meters for various *LC* products ranging from 1 meter to 1000 meters and for frequencies from 300 MHz to 300 kHz.

TABLE 7–8. Resonant Frequency or Wavelength for a Given *LC* Product

Wavelength (meters)	Frequency (kHz)	$L \times C$ $(L = \mu H)$ $(C = \mu F)$	Wavelength (meters)	Frequency (kHz)	$L \times C$ $(L = \mu H)$ $(C = \mu F)$
1	300,000	0.0000003	110	2,727	0.00341
2	150,000	0.0000111	120	2,500	0.00405
3	100,000	0.0000018	130	2,308	0.00476
4	75,000	0.0000045	140	2,143	0.00552
5	60,000	0.0000057	150	2,000	0.00633
6	50,000	0.0000101	160	1,875	0.00721
7	42,900	0.0000138	170	1,764	0.00813
8	37,500	0.0000180	180	1,667	0.00912
9	33,333	0.0000228	190	1,579	0.01015
10	30,000	0.0000282	200	1,500	0.01126
20	15,000	0.0001129	210	1,429	0.01241
30	10,000	0.0002530	220	1,364	0.01362
40	7,500	0.0004500	230	1,304	0.01489
50	6,000	0.0007040	240	1,250	0.01621
60	5,000	0.0010140	250	1,200	0.01759
70	4,290	0.0013780	260	1,154	0.01903
80	3,750	0.0018010	270	1,111	0.0205
90	3,333	0.0022800	280	1,071	0.0221
100	3,000	0.00282			

TABLE 7–8. *continued*

Wavelength (meters)	Frequency (kHz)	$L \times C$ $(L = \mu H)$ $(C = \mu F)$	Wavelength (meters)	Frequency (kHz)	$L \times C$ $(L = \mu H)$ $(C = \mu F)$
290	1,034	0.0237	570	527	0.0915
300	1,000	0.0253	575	522	0.0931
310	968	0.0270	580	517	0.0947
320	938	0.0288	585	513	0.0963
330	909	0.0306	590	509	0.0980
340	883	0.0325	595	504	0.0996
350	857	0.0345	600	500	0.1013
360	834	0.0365	605	496	0.1030
370	811	0.0385	610	492	0.1047
380	790	0.0406	615	488	0.1065
390	769	0.0428	620	484	0.1082
400	750	0.0450	625	480	0.1100
410	732	0.0473	630	476	0.1117
420	715	0.0496	635	472	0.1135
430	698	0.0520	640	469	0.1153
440	682	0.0545	645	465	0.1171
450	667	0.0570	650	462	0.1189
460	652	0.0596	655	458	0.1208
470	639	0.0622	660	455	0.1226
480	625	0.0649	665	451	0.1245
490	612	0.0676	670	448	0.1264
500	600	0.0704	675	444	0.1283
505	594	0.0718	680	441	0.1302
510	588	0.0732	685	438	0.1321
515	583	0.0747	690	435	0.1340
520	577	0.0761	695	432	0.1360
525	572	0.0776	700	429	0.1379
530	566	0.0791	705	426	0.1399
535	561	0.0806	710	423	0.1419
540	556	0.0821	715	420	0.1439
545	551	0.0836	720	417	0.1459
550	546	0.0852	725	414	0.1479
555	541	0.0867	730	411	0.1500
560	536	0.0883	735	408	0.1521
565	531	0.0899	740	405	0.1541

TABLE 7–8. *continued*

Wavelength (meters)	Frequency (kHz)	$L \times C$ $(L = \mu H)$ $(C = \mu F)$	Wavelength (meters)	Frequency (kHz)	$L \times C$ $(L = \mu H)$ $(C = \mu F)$
745	403	0.1562	875	343	0.216
750	400	0.1583	880	341	0.218
755	397	0.1604			
			885	339	0.220
760	395	0.1626	890	337	0.223
765	392	0.1647	895	335	0.225
770	390	0.1669	900	333	0.228
775	387	0.1690	905	331	0.231
780	385	0.1712			
			910	330	0.233
785	382	0.1734	915	328	0.236
790	380	0.1756	920	326	0.238
795	377	0.1779	925	324	0.241
800	375	0.1801	930	323	0.243
805	373	0.1824			
			935	321	0.246
810	370	0.1847	940	319	0.249
815	368	0.1870	945	317	0.251
820	366	0.1893	950	316	0.254
825	364	0.1916	955	314	0.257
830	361	0.1939			
			960	313	0.259
835	359	0.1962	965	311	0.262
840	357	0.1986	970	309	0.265
845	355	0.201	975	308	0.268
850	353	0.203	980	306	0.270
855	351	0.206			
			985	305	0.273
860	349	0.208	990	303	0.276
865	347	0.211	995	302	0.279
870	345	0.213	1000	300	0.282

7–9. METERS–KILOHERTZ CONVERSION

As indicated in Sec. 7–8, waveforms of a specific frequency have a fixed wavelength in meters when propagated into free space (see Sec. 1–14). Table 7–9 lists conversions showing the relationships between the frequency in kilohertz and the wavelength in meters.

TABLE 7–9. Conversion Table: Kilohertz to Meters (or Meters to Kilohertz)[a]

kHz (meters)	meters kHz	kHz or m	m or kHz	kHz or m	m or kHz
10	29,982.0	360	832.8	710	422.3
20	14,991.0	370	810.3	720	416.4
30	9,994.0	380	789.0	730	410.7
40	7,496.0	390	768.8	740	405.2
50	5,996.0	400	749.6	750	399.8
60	4,997.0	410	731.3	760	394.5
70	4,283.0	420	713.9	770	389.4
80	3,748.0	430	697.3	780	384.4
90	3,331.0	440	681.4	790	379.5
100	2,998.0	450	666.3	800	374.8
110	2,726.0	460	651.8	810	370.2
120	2,499.0	470	637.9	820	365.6
130	2,306.0	480	624.6	830	361.2
140	2,142.0	490	611.9	840	356.9
150	1,999.0	500	599.6	850	352.7
160	1,874.0	510	587.9	860	348.6
170	1,764.0	520	576.6	870	344.6
180	1,666.0	530	565.7	880	340.7
190	1,578.0	540	555.2	890	336.9
200	1,499.0	550	545.1	900	333.1
210	1,428.0	560	535.4	910	329.5
220	1,363.0	570	526.0	920	325.9
230	1,304.0	580	516.9	930	322.4
240	1,249.0	590	508.2	940	319.0
250	1,199.0	600	499.7	950	315.6
260	1,153.0	610	491.5	960	312.3
270	1,110.0	620	483.6	970	309.1
280	1,071.0	630	475.9	980	303.9
290	1,034.0	640	468.5	990	302.8
300	999.4	650	461.3	1000	299.8
310	967.2	660	454.3		
320	967.9	670	447.5		
330	908.6	680	440.9		
340	881.8	690	434.5		
350	856.6	700	428.3		

[a] Higher values can be obtained by shifting the decimal point. For every zero added to the first column, the decimal place in the second column is moved one place to the *left*. Thus, where 190 kHz = 1578 m, for instance, 1900 kHz would be 157 m, or 19,000 kHz = 15.78 m. Similarly, 10,000 kHz = 29.98 m.

7–10. CONVERSIONS INVOLVING LENGTH

The relationships between measurements of length involving inches, feet, and miles as opposed to meters, centimeters, and kilometers are listed in Table 7–10 (see Sec. 7–12). Reference should also be made to Table 7–11 for velocity and speed relationships.

TABLE 7–10. Conversion Factors Involving Length

Multiply Number of	by	To Obtain Number of
inches	2.540	centimeters
inches	0.02540	meters
feet	30.48	centimeters
feet	0.3048	meters
miles	5280.0	feet
miles	1.6093	kilometers
miles	1609.3	meters
centimeters	0.3937	inches
centimeters	0.01	meters
centimeters	10.0	millimeters
meters	100.0	centimeters
meters	3.2808	feet
meters	39.37	inches
meters	1000.0	kilometers
microns	10^{-6}	meters
microns	10^{-4}	centimeters
millimicrons	10^{-7}	centimeters
angstroms	10^{-10}	meters
angstroms	10^{-8}	centimeters

7–11. SPEED OR VELOCITY CONVERSIONS

Conversion factors relating to speed and velocity are given in Table 7–11. Reference should also be made to Table 7–10 and Sec. 7–12.

7–12. WEIGHTS AND MEASURES

Table 7–12 includes the differences in unit values for certain weights, as well as metric equivalents. The table also includes circular and cubic measurement values as well as dry and linear units.

TABLE 7–11. Conversion Factors Involving Velocity or Speed

Multiply Number of	By	To Obtain Number of
feet/second	1.097	kilometers/hour
feet/second	0.6818	miles/hour
feet/second	0.01136	miles/minute
centimeters/second	1.969	feet/minute
centimeters/second	0.036	kilometers/hour
centimeters/second	0.02237	miles/hour
miles/hour	44.70	centimeters/second
miles/hour	88.0	feet/minute
miles/hour	1.467	feet/second
miles/hour	26.82	meters/minute

TABLE 7–12. Weights and Measures

Apothecaries' Weight

20 grains = 1 scruple

3 scruples = 1 dram = 60 grains

8 drams = 1 ounce = 24 scruples = 480 grains

12 ounces = 1 pound = 96 drams = 288 scruples = 5760 grains

Avoirdupois Weight

27 11/32 grains = 1 dram

16 drams = 1 ounce = 437½ grains

16 ounces = 1 pound = 256 drams = 7000 grains

100 pounds = 1 hundredweight = 1600 ounces

20 hundredweight = 1 short ton = 2000 pounds

112 pounds = 1 long hundredweight

20 long hundredweight = 1 long ton = 2240 pounds

Metric Equivalents

1 gram = 0.03527 ounce

1 ounce = 28.35 grams

1 kilogram = 2.2046 pounds

1 pound = 0.4536 kilogram

1 metric ton = 0.98421 English ton

1 English ton = 1.016 metric ton

TABLE 7–12. *continued*

Troy Weight

(Used for gold, silver, and jewels)
24 grains = 1 pennyweight
20 pennyweights = 1 ounce = 480 grains
12 ounces = 1 pound = 240 pennyweights = 5760 grains

Circular Measure

60 seconds (″) = 1 minute (′)
60 minutes = 1 degree (°)
90 degrees = 1 quadrant
4 quadrants = 1 circle of circumference

Cubic Measure

1728 cubic inches = 1 cubic foot
27 cubic feet = 1 cubic yard
128 cubic feet = 1 cord (wood)
40 cubic feet = 1 ton (shipping)
2150.42 cubic inches = 1 standard bushel
231 cubic inches = 1 standard gallon (U.S.)

Dry Measure

2 pints = 1 quart
8 quarts = 1 peck = 16 pints
4 pecks = 1 bushel = 32 quarts = 64 pints
105 quarts = 1 barrel = 7056 cubic inches

Linear Measure

12 inches = 1 foot
3 feet = 1 yard = 36 inches
5½ yards = 1 rod = 16½ feet
40 rods = 1 furlong = 220 yards = 660 feet = ⅛ mile
8 furlongs = 1 statute mile = 1760 yards = 5280 feet
3 miles = 1 league = 5280 yards = 15,840 feet

TABLE 7–12. *continued*

Metric Equivalents

1 centimeter = 0.3937 inch
1 inch = 2.54 centimeters
1 decimeter = 3.937 inches = 0.328 foot
1 foot = 3.048 decimeters
1 meter = 39.37 inches = 1.0936 yards
1 yard = 0.9144 meter
1 dekameter = 1.9884 rods
1 rod = 0.5029 dekameter
1 kilometer = 0.62137 mile
1 mile = 1.6093 kilometers

Liquid Measure

4 gills = 1 pint
2 pints = 1 quart = 8 gills
4 quarts = 1 gallon = 8 pints
31½ gallons = 1 barrel = 126 quarts
2 barrels = 1 hogshead = 63 gallons = 252 quarts

Square Measure

144 square inches = 1 square foot
9 square feet = 1 square yard = 1296 square inches
30¼ square yards = 1 square rod = 272¼ square feet
160 square rods = 1 acre = 4840 square yards
640 acres = 1 square mile = 3,097,600 square yards

Metric Equivalents

1 square centimeter = 0.1550 square inch
1 square inch = 6.452 square centimeters
1 square decimeter = 0.1076 square foot
1 square foot = 9.2903 square decimeters
1 square meter = 1.196 square yards
1 square yard = 0.8361 meter
1 acre = 4047 square meters
1 square kilometer = 0.386 square mile
1 square mile = 2.59 square kilometers

7–13. DIELECTRIC CONSTANTS

The dielectric constants for various materials is important in electronics since utilization of such materials in capacitor or other components has a significant bearing on characteristics. The dielectric constant has for its symbol k. For air, the dielectric constant is considered to be 1, while all other materials have a higher k value. The word *constant* in relation to dielectrics is misleading because the k value may vary in some materials for temperature changes, frequency differences, and a change of the applied voltage, and so on. Table 7–13 lists approximate k values for a number of materials.

TABLE 7–13. Dielectric Constants of Various Materials

Air	1.0	Nylon	3.00
Aluminum silicate	5.3 to 5.5	Paper	1.5 to 3
Bakelite	3.7	Paraffin	2 to 3
Beeswax (yellow)	2.7	Polyethylene	2.2
Butyl rubber	2.4	Polystyrene	2.5
Formica XX	4.00	Porcelain	5 to 7
Glass	4 to 10	Quartz	3.7 to 4.5
Gutta-percha	2.6	Steatite	5.3 to 6.5
Halowax oil	4.8	Teflon	2.1
Kel-F	2.6	Tenite	2.9 to 4.5
Lucite	2.8	Vaseline	2.16
Mica	4 to 8	Water (distilled)	76.7 to 78.2
Micarta 254	3.4 to 5.4	Wood	1.2 to 2.1

7–14. MATHEMATICAL SYMBOLS AND CONSTANTS

Various mathematical symbols and basic constants are given in Table 7–14. Common practice in expressing quantities in mathematical equations or references is the usage of a, b, and c for known quantities, and x, y, and z for unknowns. Relationships to electricity and electronics are indicated in Chap. 1.

TABLE 7-14. Mathematical Symbols

$\times$ or $\cdot$	Multiplied by
$\div$ or :	Divided by
$+$	Positive. Plus. Add
$-$	Negative. Minus. Subtract
$\pm$	Positive or negative. Plus or minus
$\mp$	Negative or positive. Minus or plus
$=$ or ::	Equals
$\equiv$	Identity
$=$	Is approximately equal to
$\neq$	Does not equal
$>$	Greater than
$>>$	Is much greater than
$<$	Less than
$<<$	Is much less than
$\geq$	Greater than or equal to
$\leq$	Less than or equal to
$\therefore$	Therefore
$\angle$	Angle
$\triangle$	Increment or decrement
$\perp$	Perpendicular to
$\|$	Parallel to
$\|n\|$	Absolute value of n
$\sqrt{}$	Square root
$\sqrt[3]{}$	Cube root

$\pi = 3.14$

$2\pi = 6.28$

$(2\pi)^2 = 39.5$ (All are

$4\pi = 12.6$ rounded off)

$\pi^2 = 9.87$

$\dfrac{\pi}{2} = 1.57$

$\dfrac{1}{\pi} = 0.318$

$\dfrac{1}{2\pi} = 0.159$

$\dfrac{1}{\pi^2} = 0.101$

$\dfrac{1}{\sqrt{\pi}} = 0.564$

$\sqrt{\pi} = 1.77$

$\dfrac{\pi}{2} = 1.25$

$\sqrt{2} = 1.41$

$\sqrt{3} = 1.73$

$\dfrac{1}{\sqrt{2}} = 0.707$

$\dfrac{1}{\sqrt{3}} = 0.577$

$\log\pi = 0.497$

$\log\dfrac{\pi}{2} = 0.196$

$\log\pi^2 = 0.994$

$\log\sqrt{\pi} = 0.248$

Base of natural logs $\epsilon = 2.718$

1 radian $= 180°\ /\pi = 57.3°$

$360° = 2\pi$ radians

TABLE 7–15. Greek Alphabet

Capital Letter	Lowercase	Name	Commonly Designates
A	α	Alpha	Angles, attenuation constant, transistor characteristics
B	β	Beta	Angles, coefficients, transistor characteristics
Γ	γ	Gamma	Propagation constant
Δ	δ	Delta	Increment or decrement of a quantity (capital or lowercase), angles
E	ϵ	Epsilon	Base of natural logarithms (2.71828), electric intensity
Z	ζ	Zeta	Coordinates, coefficients
H	η	Eta	Efficiency, surface charge density, hysteresis, coordinates
Θ	θ	Theta	Phase angle
I	ι	Iota	Unit vector
K	κ	Kappa	Coupling coefficient, susceptibility
Λ	λ	Lambda	Wavelength, attenuation constant
M	μ	Mu	Permeability, amplification factor (tubes)
N	ν	Nu	Reluctivity, frequency
Ξ	ξ	Xi	Coordinates
O	o	Omicron	
Π	π	Pi	3.1416
P	ρ	Rho	Resistivity, coordinates
Σ	σ	Sigma	Summation (cap), complex propagation constant, leakage coefficient
T	τ	Tau	Time constant, time-phase displacement, transmission factor
Υ	υ	Upsilon	
Φ	ϕ	Phi	Angles, magnetic flux, scalar potential (cap)
X	χ	Chi	Electric susceptibility
Ψ	ψ	Psi	Dielectric flux, phase difference, coordinates
Ω	ω	Omega	Resistance in ohms (capital), angular velocity ($6.28f$) (lowercase)

7-15. GREEK ALPHABET

Both capital and lowercase letters of the Greek alphabet are extensively used in electronics as well as in related mathematics for designating quantities and identifying specific units. Thus, the lowercase Greek letter μ (mu) denotes *micro* and is used as a prefix for microfarads, as 0.002 μF. Similarly, the lowercase letter ω (omega) is utilized to identify angular velocity (6.28f). The capital letter Ω indicates ohms, while π (lowercase pi) denotes 3.1416, and so on. Table 7-15 lists the complete Greek alphabet plus common designations that apply.

7-16. SOUND FREQUENCIES AND LEVELS

Typical frequency ranges for various sound levels are given in Table 7-16. The approximate range in hertz is shown. The approximate levels of various sounds utilizing decibel (dB) comparisons is shown in Table 7-17 (see Secs. 1-7 and 1-8).

TABLE 7-16. Typical Frequency Range of Various Sounds

Type of Sound	Approximate Frequency Span (Hz)
Desirable range for good speech intelligibility	300 to 4,000
Audibility range (normal hearing, young person)	16 to 20,000
Piano	26 to 4,000
Baritone	100 to 375
Tenor	125 to 475
Soprano	225 to 675
Cello	64 to 650
Violin	192 to 3,000
Piccolo	512 to 4,600
Harmonics of sound	32 to 20,000

TABLE 7–17. Sound Levels

Type of Sound	Relative Intensity (dB)
Reference level	0
Threshold of average hearing	10
Soft whisper; faint rustle of leaves	20
Normal whisper; average sound in home	30
Faint speech; softly playing radio	40
Muted string instrument; softly spoken words (at a distance of 3 ft)	50
Normal conversational level; radio at average loudness	60
Group conversation; orchestra slightly below average volume	70
Average orchestral volume; very loud radio	80
Loud orchestra volume; brass band	90
Noise of low-flying airplane; noisy machine shop	100
Roar of overhead jet-propelled plane; loud brass band close by	110
Nearby airplane roar; beginning of hearing discomfort	120
Threshold of pain from abnormally loud sounds	130

7–17. EFFECTS OF FREQUENCY ON L, C, AND R

As mentioned in Sec. 7–8, a change of frequency of the electric energy applied to circuits containing L, C, and R alters reactance. Since impedance (Z) is a combination of reactance and resistance, there is also a corresponding impedance change. Table 7–18 lists the effects of circuitry containing L, C, and R either in single units or in combination.

7–18. RESISTOR COLOR CODES

The ohmic value of resistors is indicated by imprinting colored bands on the resistor casing. For resistors of the molded composition type shown in Figure 7–1, the color coding is read from left to right from the end wherein the color bands are grouped. Generally, there are four color

TABLE 7–18. Effects of Frequency on *L-C-R* Circuits

Component	Effect of Frequency	
	Increase	*Decrease*
Resistance (R)	None	None
Capacitance (C)	None	None
Capacitive reactance (X_C)	Lowers X_C	Raises X_C
Inductance (L)	None	None
Inductive reactance (X_L)	Raises X_L	Lowers X_L
Series capacitor–resistor combination (Z)	Lowers Z	Raises Z
Series inductance–resistor combination (Z)	Raises Z	Lowers Z
Parallel capacitor–resistor combination (Z)	Lowers Z	Raises Z
Parallel inductance–resistor combination (Z)	Raises Z	Lowers Z
Series resonance (Z)	Raises Z	Raises Z
Parallel resonance (Z)	Lowers Z	Lowers Z

bands used on the carbon-composition resistors and five bands for the film type. In both instances the last color band refers to the tolerance that applies to the ohmic value indicated. Thus, if a resistor is rated at 500 Ω and had a tolerance of 10%, its actual value could range from 450

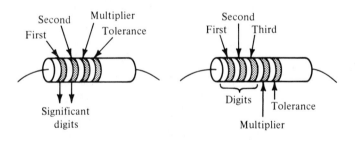

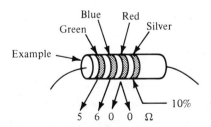

Figure 7–1   Resistor Color Codes

to 550 Ω. Table 7–19 gives the color-coded values and tolerances apply-ing to the types of resistors shown in Figure 7–1. The letters GMV indi-cates *guaranteed minimum value*. Also, if a value is marked (*alt.*) it indicates *alternate*. Generally, in modern practice, a value may be marked (*pref.*) for *preferred*.

TABLE 7–19. Ohmic Values of Color Bands

Color	Digit	Multiplier	Carbon ± Tolerance	Film-Type Tolerance
Black	0	1	20%	0
Brown	1	10	1%	1%
Red	2	100	2%	2%
Orange	3	1,000	3%	
Yellow	4	10,000	GMV	
Green	5	100,000	5%(alt.)	0.5%
Blue	6	1,000,000	6%	0.25%
Violet	7	10,000,000	12.5%	0.1%
Gray	8	0.01 (alt.)	30%	0.05%
White	9	0.1 (alt.)	10%(alt.)	
Silver		0.01 (pref.)	10%(pref.)	10%
Gold		0.1 (pref.)	5%(pref.)	5%
No color			20%	

7–19. CAPACITOR COLOR CODES

The capacitance value of capacitors is indicated by imprinting colored bands on the capacitor casing. As with the resistors discussed in Sec. 7–18, the colored bands indicate unit values and certain tolerances plus other factors. For the tubular-type capacitors shown in Figure 7–2 the leads may consist of *axial* types connected through the ends, or *radial* types connected at right angles to the capacitor length. Again, as with resistors, the identification starts at the end of the capacitor, where the color bands are grouped.

Unit values obtained from the digit color bands are in picofarads (pF). Besides the digit bands, a temperature-coefficient band and a toler-ance band are also used. The temperature coefficient of ceramic capaci-tors is given in *parts per million per degree* Celsius (ppm/°C). A letter N precedes the value to indicate a negative-temperature coefficient (a capaci-tance decrease for an increase in operating temperature). A P designation

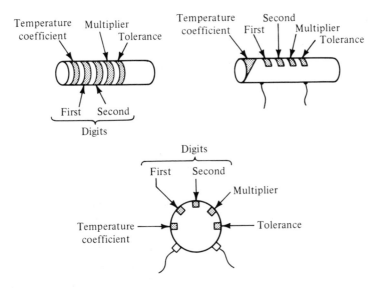

Figure 7–2 Color Codes for ac/dc Capacitors

indicates a positive-temperature coefficient and a *NPO* designation indicates a negative–positive–zero coefficient. The NPO-rated capacitors are stable units having negligible temperature effects on capacitance values.

As shown in Figure 7–2, five identification markings are used for such capacitors. The first band indicate *temperature coefficient* and the next two bands indicate the *significant digits.* Often axial-type capacitors have a wider first band to identify the initial coating. For the five-dot disk types shown, the lower left dot is the temperature coefficient and the other dots (in clockwise sequence) are coded the same as the axial or radial types. The button-silver mica, the button ceramic, and the feed-through capacitors are shown in Figure 7–3. The related color coding for all the capacitors discussed in this section is given in Table 7–20.

The extended-range temperature coefficient ceramic capacitors and the molded mica types are shown in Figure 7–4. For the extended-range capacitors the first color area identifies the temperature coefficient as with the five-dot types. The second color area, however, represents the temperature-coefficient *multiplier.* For the flat rectangular-shaped molded mica (extensively used at one time) an arrow is imprinted on the flat face to indicate the color-coding sequence direction. The lower left-hand color dot identifies a specific type for clarification of the particular capacitor according to the manufacturer's specifications regarding temperature coefficient, *Q* factor, and related characteristics.

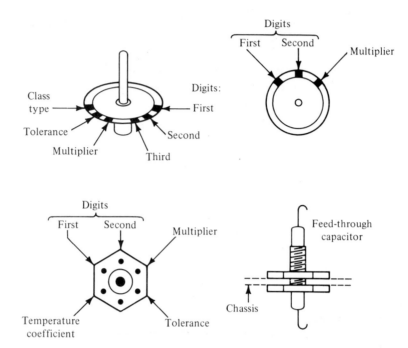

Figure 7–3 Mica and Ceramic Capacitors (Button and Feed-Through)

TABLE 7–20. Picofarad Values of Color Bands

Color	Digit	Multiplier	10 pF or less	Over 10 pF	5-dot Temp. Coeff. TC	Extended Range Significant Digits	Extended Range Multiplier
Black	0	1	2.0 pF	20%	NP0	0.0	−1
Brown	1	10	0.1 pF	1%	N033		−10
Red	2	100		2%	N075	1.0	−100
Orange	3	1000		3%	N150	1.5	−1000
Yellow	4	10,000			N220	2.2	−10,000
Green	5		0.5 pF	5%	N330	3.3	+1
Blue	6				N470	4.7	+10
Violet	7				N750	7.5	+100
Gray	8	0.01 (alt.)	0.25 pF		a	b	+1000
White	9	0.1 (alt.)	1.0 pF	10%	c		+10,000
Silver		0.01 (pref.)					
Gold		0.1 (pref.)					

[a] General-purpose types with a TC ranging from P150 to N1500.
[b] Coupling, decoupling, and general bypass types with a TC ranging from P100 to N750.
[c] If the first band (TC) is black, the range is N1000 to N5000.

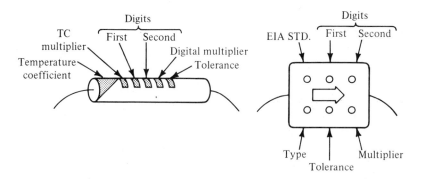

Figure 7–4   Temperature Coefficient and Mica Types

7–20. MKS AND CGS UNIT SYSTEMS

Standard units and symbols used in various branches of science have undergone significant changes over the years in an effort to make them universally standard for simplification purposes. Early systems included the mks (*meter-kilogram-second*) and the cgs (*centimeter-gram-second*). These two systems, although still found in literature, have been superseded by the *International System of Units* (SI) described and listed in Sec. 7–21. Table 7–21 on page 208 lists the quantities and symbols for basic units in both the mks and cgs systems.

7–21. SI UNIT SYSTEM

The *International System of Units* has the official abbreviation of *SI* and represents the modernized version of the metric system. Adopted by international agreement, it is the basis for all measurements throughout the world and integrates such measurements for science, industry, and commerce. Throughout this system only one unit is used for a particular quantity, whether thermal, electrical, or mechanical. The system can be considered an *absolute one*, using absolute units for simplicity in engineering practices.

In the SI system the unit of force is defined by the acceleration of mass (kg·m/s²) and is unrelated to gravity. The SI system was devised with a foundation of six base units: *length, mass, time, temperature, electric current*, and *luminous intensity*. Four of these units are independent: *length, mass, time*, and *temperature*, while the other two require usage of

TABLE 7–21. Comparisons between *mks* and *cgs*

Quantity	Symbol	mks Unit	cgs Unit
Capacitance	C	farad	farad
Conductance	G	mho	mho
Current	I	ampere	ampere
Electric charge	Q	coulomb	coulomb
Electric potential	$V(E)$	volt	volt
Flux density	B	weber/square meter	gauss
Force	F	newton	dyne
Inductance	L	henry	henry
Length	l	meter (m)	centimeter (cm)
Magnetic field intensity	H	ampere-turn/meter	oersted
Magnetic flux	ϕ	weber	maxwell
Magnetization	M	weber/square meter	
Magnetomotive force	mmf	ampere-turn	gilbert
Mass	m	kilogram	gram
Permeability	μ	henry/meter	gauss/oersted
Permeance	P	weber/amp-turn	maxwell/gilbert
Power	$\mathscr{P}$	watt	watt
Resistance	R	ohm	ohm
Reluctance	$\mathscr{R}$	amp-turn/weber	gilbert/maxwell
Time	t	second	second
Energy–work	$W(J)$	joule	joule

other units for definition. Two supplementary units are also used: the *radian* (for measurement of plane angles) and the *steradian* (for measurement of solid angles). These are supplemental because they are not based on physical standards but on mathematical concepts. The standards for the six base units are defined by international agreement. The prototype for mass is the only basic unit still defined by a rigid physical device. As an example, the *kilogram* is a cylinder of platinum–iridium alloy housed at the International Bureau of Weights and Measures in France with a duplicate in the National Bureau of Standards in the United States.

The *meter* is a specific wavelength in a vacuum of the orange-red line of the spectrum of krypton 86. The *time second* is defined as the duration of specific periods of radiation corresponding to the transition between two levels of cesium 133. For temperature, the *degree Kelvin* is established as 1/273.16 of the thermodynamic temperature of the triple point of water (the latter is approximately 32.02°F). The *ampere* of *current* is that amount flowing into infinitely long parallel wires (in vacuum) separated by 1 meter and producing a force of 2×10^{-7} neutrons per meter of length between the wires. The *candella* (luminous intensity) is the intensity of 1/600,000 square meter of a perfect radiator at the freezing temperature of platinum, 2024 K.

Table 7–22 lists the basic units in the SI system as well as the supplementary and derived units. The latter are produced without having to use conversion factors. As an example, a force of 1 N acting for a length of 1 m produces 1 J of energy. If such a force is maintained for 1 s, the power is 1 W.

TABLE 7–22. SI Units and Symbols

Quantity	Symbol	SI Unit	Derivation
Base Units			
Length	m	meter	
Mass	kg	kilogram	
Time	s	second	
Temperature	K	degree Kelvin	
Electric current	A	ampere	
Luminous intensity	cd	candela	
Supplementary Units			
Plane angle	rad	radian	
Solid angle	sr	steradian	
Derived Units			
Area	m^2	square meter	
Acceleration	m/s^2	meter per second squared	
Angular acceleration	rad/s^2	radian per second squared	
Angular velocity	rad/s	radian per second	
Conductance	S	siemens	A/V
Density	kg/m^3	kilogram per cubic meter	
Electric capacitance	F	farad	A·s/V
Electric charge	C	coulomb	A·s
Electric field strength	V/m	volt per meter	

TABLE 7–22. *continued*

Quantity	Symbol	SI Unit	Derivation
Electric resistance	Ω	ohm	V/A
Energy, work, quantity of heat	J	joule	N·m
Flux of light	lm	lumen	cd·sr
Force	N	newton	kg·m/s^2
Frequency	Hz	hertz	s^{-1}
Illumination	lx	lux	lm/m^2
Inductance	H	henry	V·s/A
Luminance	cd/m^2	candela per square meter	
Magnetic field strength	A/m	ampere per meter	
Magnetic flux	Wb	weber	V·s
Magnetic flux density	T	tesla	Wb/m^2
Magnetomotive force	A	ampere	
Power	W	watt	J/s
Pressure	N/m^2	newton per square meter	
Velocity	m/s	meter per second	
Voltage, potential difference, electromotive force	V	volt	W/A
Volume	m^3	cubic meter	

7–22. PUBLIC-ENTERTAINMENT BROADCAST ALLOCATIONS

Amplitude-modulated radio stations broadcasting public entertainment transmit at specific frequencies within the range 550 to 1600 kHz. The bandwidth per station is nominally 10 kHz, although this span varies depending on interference factors. The preferred intermediate frequency (IF) is 455 kHz.

Frequency-modulated radio stations broadcasting public entertainment transmit at specific frequencies within a range extending from 88 to 108 MHz. Each station is allocated a 200-kHz bandwidth. The preferred intermediate frequency (IF) is 10.7 MHz. Television stations broadcasting public entertainment (both VHF and UHF) transmit at specific frequencies as shown in Tables 7–23 and 7–24. Each station utilizes a

6-MHz total bandwidth, including video and audio. The video portion uses amplitude modulation and the audio-portion frequency modulation (see also Chaps. 8 and 11). Preferred intermediate frequencies (IF) are 45.75 MHz for the picture carrier and 41.25 MHz for the sound carrier. Both picture and sound IF signals are heterodyned in the receiver for the production of a final sound IF of 4.5 MHz.

TABLE 7–23. VHF Television Station Allocations (U.S.)

Channel Number	Frequency (MHz)	Video Carrier	Sound Carrier
1	Not used		
2	54–60	55.25	59.75
3	60–66	61.25	65.75
4	66–72	67.25	71.75
5	76–82	77.25	81.75
6	82–88	83.25	87.75
	FM band (88 to 108 MHz)		
7	174–180	175.25	179.75
8	180–186	181.25	185.75
9	186–192	187.25	191.75
10	192–198	193.25	197.75
11	198–204	199.25	203.75
12	204–210	205.25	209.75
13	210–216	211.25	215.75

TABLE 7–24. UHF Television Station Allocations (U.S.)

Channel Number	Frequency Range (MHz)	Picture Carrier (MHZ)	Sound Carrier (MHz)
14	470–476	471.25	475.75
15	476–482	477.25	481.75
16	482–488	483.25	487.75
17	488–494	489.25	493.75
18	494–500	495.25	499.75
19	500–506	501.25	505.75
20	506–512	507.25	511.75
21	512–518	513.25	517.75
22	518–524	519.25	523.75
23	524–530	525.25	529.75

TABLE 7–24. *continued*

Channel Number	Frequency Range (MHz)	Picture Carrier (MHZ)	Sound Carrier (MHz)
24	530–536	531.25	535.75
25	536–542	537.25	541.75
26	542–548	543.25	547.75
27	548–554	549.25	553.75
28	554–560	555.25	559.75
29	560–566	561.25	565.75
30	566–572	567.25	571.75
31	572–578	573.25	577.75
32	578–584	579.25	583.75
33	584–590	585.25	589.75
34	590–596	591.25	595.75
35	596–602	597.25	601.75
36	602–608	603.25	607.75
37	608–614	609.25	613.75
38	614–620	615.25	619.75
39	620–626	621.25	625.75
40	626–632	627.25	631.75
41	632–638	633.25	637.75
42	638–644	639.25	643.75
43	644–650	645.25	649.75
44	650–656	651.25	655.75
45	656–662	657.25	661.75
46	662–668	663.25	667.75
47	668–674	669.25	673.75
48	674–680	675.25	679.75
49	680–686	681.25	685.75
50	686–692	687.25	691.75
51	692–698	693.25	697.75
52	698–704	699.25	703.75
53	704–710	705.25	709.75
54	710–716	711.25	715.75
55	716–722	717.25	721.75
56	722–728	723.25	727.75
57	728–734	729.25	733.75
58	734–740	735.25	739.75
59	740–746	741.25	745.75
60	746–752	747.25	751.75
61	752–758	753.25	757.75
62	758–764	759.25	763.75

TABLE 7–24. *continued*

Channel Number	Frequency Range (MHz)	Picture Carrier (MHZ)	Sound Carrier (MHz)
63	764–770	765.25	769.75
64	770–776	771.25	775.75
65	776–782	777.25	781.75
66	782–788	783.25	787.75
67	788–794	789.25	793.75
68	794–800	795.25	799.75
69	800–806	801.25	805.75
70	806–812	807.25	811.75
71	812–818	813.25	817.75
72	818–824	819.25	823.75
73	824–830	825.25	829.75
74	830–836	831.25	835.75
75	836–842	837.25	841.75
76	842–848	843.25	847.75
77	848–854	849.25	853.75
78	854–860	855.25	859.75
79	860–866	861.25	865.75
80	866–872	867.25	871.75
81	872–878	873.25	877.75
82	878–884	879.25	883.75
83	884–890	885.25	889.75

7–23. MISCELLANEOUS BROADCAST ALLOCATIONS

Tables 7–25 through 7–29 indicate frequency allocations for citizens' band, amateur, general frequency designation, military designations, and the International Morse Code. Additional data are given in Chaps. 8 and 11 regarding modulation types and general characteristics.

The citizens' band (CB) radio station listing in Table 7–25 shows the 40 channels allocated between 26.965 and 27.405 MHz. Note that Channel 22 is followed by 24, and 25 precedes 23. This procedure keeps the frequency change at a progressive sequency as it rises. Manufacturered CB units, however, indicate a proper sequence on tuning dials. The channel number designations have been omitted from the rules by the FCC and channel identification is solely by the designated center frequency. The altered sequence in Table 7–25 occurred because the prior station allocations were changed by the addition of two channels between the previous 22 and 23. The EIA suggested the new channels be designated as 24 and 25, with a sequence as shown in the table.

TABLE 7–25. Citizens' Band Listing

Channel	Frequency (MHz)	Channel	Frequency (MHz)
1	26.965	21	27.215
2	26.975	22	27.225
3	26.985	24	27.235
4	27.005	25	27.245
5	27.015	23	27.255
6	27.025	26	27.265
7	27.035	27	27.275
8	27.055	28	27.285
9	27.065	29	27.295
10	27.075	30	27.305
11	27.085	31	27.315
12	27.105	32	27.325
13	27.115	33	27.335
14	27.125	34	27.345
15	27.135	35	27.355
16	27.155	36	27.365
17	27.165	37	27.375
18	27.175	38	27.385
19	27.185	39	27.395
20	27.205	40	27.405

TABLE 7–26. Amateur-Radio Bands

160-meter band	1.8	to	2.0 MHz
80-meter band	3.5	to	4.0 MHz
40-meter band	7.0	to	7.3 MHz
20-meter band	14.0	to	14.35 MHz
15-meter band	21.0	to	21.45 MHz
10-meter band	28.0	to	29.7 MHz
6-meter band	50.0	to	54.0 MHz
2-meter band	144.0	to	148.0 MHz

TABLE 7–27. General Frequency Designations

VLF	(very low frequencies)	3 Hz to	30	kHz
LF	(low frequencies)	30 kHz to	300	kHz
MF	(medium frequencies)	300 kHz to	3	MHz
HF	(high frequencies)	3 MHz to	30	MHz
VHF	(very high frequencies)	30 MHz to	300	MHz
UHF	(ultrahigh frequencies)	300 MHz to	3000	MHz
SHF	(superhigh frequencies)	3 GHz to	30	GHz
EHF	(extra-high frequencies)	30 GHz to	300	GHz

TABLE 7–28. Military Frequency Designations

P band	225 MHz to	390	MHz
L band	390 MHz to	1,550	MHz
S band	1,550 MHz to	5,200	MHz
X band	5,200 MHz to	10,900	MHz
K band	10,900 MHz to	36,000	MHz
Q band	36 GHz to	46	GHz
V band	46 GHz to	56	GHz

TABLE 7–29. International Morse Code

A . –	N – .	1 . – – – –
B – . . .	O – – –	2 . . – – –
C – . – .	P . – – .	3 . . . – –
D – . .	Q – – . –	4 . . . . –
E .	R . – .	5 . . . . .
F . . – .	S . . .	6 – . . . .
G – – .	T –	7 – – . . .
H	U . . –	8 – – – . .
I . .	V . . . –	9 – – – – .
J . – – –	W . – –	0 – – – – –
K – . –	X – . . –	
L . – . .	Y – . – –	
M – –	Z – – . .	

Period (.)	. – . – . –
Comma (,)	– – . . – –
Interrogation (?)	. . – – . .

TABLE 7–29. *continued*

Quotation mark (")	. – . . – .
Colon (:)	– – – . . .
Semicolon (;)	– . – . – .
Parenthesis ()	– . – – . –

Zero (0) is often transmitted as a long dash. The following letter combinations are transmitted without any space between:

Wait sign (AS)	. – . . .
Double dash (break)	– . . . –
Error (erase sign)	. . . .
Fraction bar (/)	– . . – .
End of message (AR)	. – . – .
End of transmission (SK)	. . . – . –
International distress signal (SOS)	. . . – – – . . .

7–24. TELEVISION TECHNICAL STANDARDS

Table 7–30 lists the most common television technical standards of today.

TABLE 7–30. Television Technical Standards

Function	Data
One horizontal sweep cycle (start of one horizontal line trace to start of next)	63.5 μs
Horizontal blanking interval	10.16 to 11.4 μs
Horizontal trace (without blanking time)	53.34 μs
One frame	33,334 μs
One field	16,667 μs
Horizontal sync pulse duration	5.08 to 5.68 μs
Vertical sync pulse interval (total of six vertical blocks)	190.5 μs
Vertical blanking interval	833 to 1300 μs for each field
Vertical scan frequency (B/W)	60 Hz
Verical scan frequency (color)	59.94 Hz
Horizontal scan frequency (B/W)	15,750 Hz
Horizontal scan frequency (color)	15,734.264 Hz
Total frequency span for an individual station (B/W or color)	6 MHz

TABLE 7–30. *continued*

Function	Data
Picture carrier is nominally above the lower end of the channel (B/W or color)	1.25 MHz
Aspect ratio of B/W or color picture (picture width versus height)	4.3
Scan lines per frame (B/W or color)	525 (interlaced)
Scan lines per field (B/W or color)	262.5
The frequency-modulated sound carrier is above the picture-carrier frequency (B/W or color)	4.5 MHz
Maximum deviation of sound carrier each side of center frequency	25 kHz
The effective radiated power of the audio expressed as the percent of the peak power of the picture-signal carrier	50 to 70
Color-picture carrier frequency	3.579 MHz (3.58 MHz)
Transmitted burst signal sync	Eight cycles minimum
Brightness (luminance) portion of color transmission, symbol Y	0.59 green, 0.30 red, 0.11 blue
I (in-phase) signal combines portions of B-Y and R-Y	-0.27B less the Y signal, and 0.74R less the Y
The Q (quadrature) signal combines portions of B-Y and R-Y	0.41B less the Y, and 0.48R less the Y
Blue signal combines portions of Y, Q, and I	(Y plus $1.72Q$) less 1.11 of I
Green signal combines portions of Y, Q, and I	(Y less $0.64Q$) less 0.28 of I
Red signal combines portions of Y, Q, and I	(Y plus $0.63Q$) pluse 0.96 of I

8 Transmission Principles

8–1. AMPLITUDE MODULATION

In the broadcasting of audio, video, or other information signals, the transmitted RF signal is modified so that the information signals can be reformed at the receiver. The RF signal is termed the *carrier* and the low-frequency signals modify (*modulate*) the RF carrier. There are several modulation methods as described in this chapter. One of these is *amplitude modulation* and the basic principle is illustrated in Figure 8–1. As with other modulation methods, the carrier modification process produces additional signals termed *sidebands*, which accompany the transmitted carrier to form a composite signal. The circuitry illustrated in Figure 8–1 consists of push-pull Class C RF amplifiers and push-pull modulators. Single-ended stages can also be used.

The modulator output is applied across a transformer primary (L_4 and L_5) and appears in the secondary winding (L_6). The latter is in series with the power-supply feedline to the center tap RF transformer consisting of L_1 and L_2. When there is no modulator signal the carrier output at L_3 has a constant amplitude as shown. When the modulator transistors Q_3 and Q_4 process an audio or video signal, an amplified version appears across transformer windings L_4 and L_5, and hence across L_6 secondary. If the modulating signal consisted of a pure sine wave as shown, a positive alternation across the secondary winding L_6 produces a peak positive voltage that aids the power-supply potential. Consequently, the voltage applied to the collectors of Q_1 and Q_2 increases over that which normally prevails. The potential increase causes a corresponding rise in the ampli-

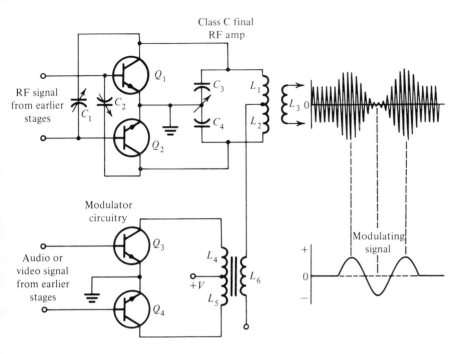

Figure 8–1   Amplitude Modulation

tude of the RF carrier output as shown. When the modulating signal appearing across L_6 changes to a negative alternation, it opposes the power-supply potential and consequently the Class C amplifier amplitude also drops. Now, the power output of the carrier declines and the amplitude can drop almost to zero as shown. For a positive alternation the carrier again increases as shown.

   With circuitry having a fairly constant resistive value, carrier power varies as the square of the applied voltage. Since full modulation causes a carrier amplitude increase and proportionate decrease as illustrated, the peak output power of the carrier reaches a value that is quadruple that of the unmodulated RF carrier. Hence, for full modulation, the carrier signal amplitude varies between almost zero and twice the amplitude of the unmodulated carrier. The average Q_1 and Q_2 collector-current flow from the power supply remains constant because successive collector-current increases are balanced by proportionate decreases. For AM, full modulation is defined as 100% modulation and represents the conditions where the modulator output power is one-half the Class C input power from the dc supply system. (Class C input power is defined as the product of the collector's direct current and voltage.)

If too great a modulating signal is utilized, the condition of the modulated carrier deteriorates because the overmodulation causes the carrier to drop to zero periodically as shown in Figure 8–2(A). Such modulation causes distortion when demodulated. When the modulator output power drops substantially, the change in carrier signal amplitude is affected to a lesser degree as shown in (B). Thus, the modulation is less than 100%.

8–2. SIDEBAND FACTORS

An RF carrier signal consisting of pure sine waves has only a single frequency. For any waveform distortion, additional signals are generated having frequencies above and below the fundamental carrier frequencies (see Secs. 8–1 and 11–1). The nature and number of sidebands that are produced, however, are related to the type of modulation employed (AM, FM, etc.) as well as the frequency of the modulating signal. For

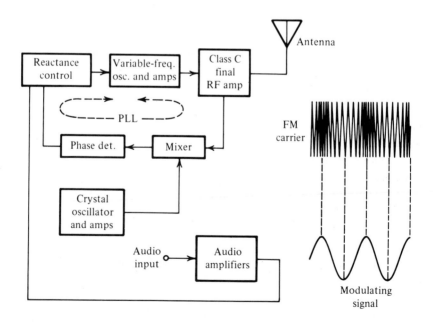

Figure 8–2 Percentages and Sidebands

amplitude modulation two sidebands are produced for each single-frequency signal as shown in Figure 8–2(C) and (D). Hence, if the RF carrier frequency is 2000 kHz and the modulating signal is 500 Hz, one sideband occurs 500 Hz above the carrier frequency and hence would be 2000.5 kHz. The second sideband would be 500 Hz below the carrier frequency and hence would be 1999.5 kHz. If the carrier were modulated by a signal of 1 kHz, the upper sideband would have a frequency of 2001 kHz and the lower 1999 kHz. If both the 500-Hz and the 1-kHz signals were simultaneously used for modulation purposes, there would be four sidebands present in addition to the carrier signal. For AM, the variations in the carrier amplitude during modulation represents the composite carrier signal and therefore includes the carrier plus the sidebands. During AM, the amplitude of the basic carrier (single frequency) *does not vary*. The power of the sideband signals, however, changes in proportion to the amplitude variations of the modulating signals. If the sideband signals were removed from the modulated carrier shown in Figure 8–1, the basic carrier would have a constant amplitude in similar fashion to the two sidebands illustrated in Figure 8–2(C) and (D).

For the frequency-modulation process discussed in Sec. 8–3, many more sidebands are produced for a given modulating signal than is the case for AM. The sideband factors relating to frequency modulation are covered in Sec. 8–4. All the sidebands are not always transmitted when it is desired to save spectrum space. Filter networks can be utilized to suppress one of the sidebands in AM. Reception is still possible at the receiver when only one sideband accompanies the carrier, although signal strength would be somewhat lower than when the full complement of sidebands is present. Such transmission using a single sideband is designated as SSB. The designations LSB (lower sideband) and USB (upper sideband) are also used on occasion. Single-sideband transmission is popular with citizens'-band radio as well as many commercial transmitters for interference reduction and spectrum space conservation. In television transmission (public entertainment) most of the lower sidebands are eliminated and during color transmission the color carrier is also suppressed. In the latter instance it is necessary to generate the missing carrier at the receiver for demodulation processes (see Secs. 8–5 and 11–9). Obviously, the modulation process increases the necessary bandwidth for the transmitted signal to accommodate the additional sidebands. A nominal bandpass utilized in public-entertainment AM is 10 kHz. Since many more sidebands are generated for FM, public-entertainment FM has a 200-kHz allocation for each FM station.

8-3. FREQUENCY MODULATION

During frequency modulation, the audio-modulating signal is made to shift the RF carrier signal in frequency. Thus the unmodulated-signal frequency (also termed resting frequency) is shifted above and below at a rate identical to the modulating-signal frequency. Hence, if a 600-Hz audio signal modulates the FM carrier, the latter deviates from its resting frequency 600 times per second (both above and below the carrier resting frequency). The degree by which the carrier shifts in frequency from the resting point is controlled by the *amplitude* of the modulating signal. To illustrate, if the 600-Hz audio signal causes the carrier to deviate 10 kHz above and below the resting frequency, an increase in the amplitude of the audio-modulating signal may create a deviation of 18 kHz each side of the resting frequency even though the identical 600-Hz deviation rate prevails. If the audio-modulating signal is increased additionally, the deviation of the carrier may extend to 26 kHz or more each side of the resting frequency. For an 800-Hz modulating signal, the deviation would occur 800 times per second with the *extent* of the deviation again established by the amplitude of the 800-Hz signal.

There are several methods for frequency modulating a carrier and a representative system is shown in Figure 8–3 (see also Chap. 11). Here

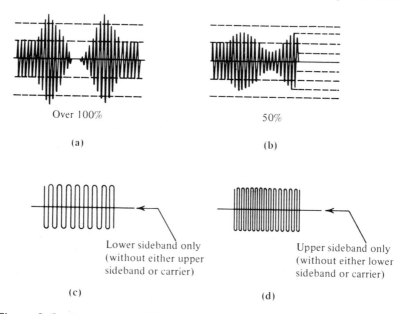

Over 100%

(a)

50%

(b)

Lower sideband only
(without either upper
sideband or carrier)

(c)

Upper sideband only
(without either lower
sideband or carrier)

(d)

Figure 8–3 Frequency Modulation

two oscillators are utilized: one, a fixed-frequency oscillator, to establish frequency stability and another, a variable-frequency oscillator, for carrier generation. After the carrier has been generated it is amplified and its frequency multiplied as required for application to the final Class C amplifier. A mixer stage samples the frequency of the signal of the Class C final amplifier and also the frequency of the signal generated by the crystal oscillator. If the carrier is at its proper resting frequency the phase detector has zero output. If, however, the Class C amplifier frequency deviates, a signal change is felt by the phase detector and a correction voltage is applied to the reactance control circuit (see Secs. 2–30 through 2–32). The result is a correction of the Class C signal frequency. The circuitry forms a continuous loop (phase-locked loop) for precise FM resting frequency control. The audio amplifier again forms a modulator that is fed to the reactance control. Audio signals cause the reactance control circuit to shift the frequency of the variable oscillator and thus the carrier as shown in Figure 8–3. For this particular system a rise in the audio amplitude causes an increase in FM carrier frequency while a decline (negative) causes a decrease in carrier frequency. The frequency-shifting process produces sideband components as discussed in Sec. 8–4 (see also Sec. 11–2).

8–4. FM SIDEBAND FACTORS

In frequency modulation, a number of sideband signals are created for each single-frequency audio signal. These sidebands are spaced apart by a frequency that coincides with that of the modulating signal. Hence, if a 900-Hz modulating signal is employed, the first two sidebands will be spaced 900 Hz from the carrier, one sideband above the resting frequency and the other sideband below. The additional sidebands would all be spaced 900 Hz from each other. Those sidebands having a frequency nearer the resting frequency of the carrier have the highest amplitude while those beyond that immediate grouping have insignificant amplitudes. Thus, only a few sidebands above and below the carrier frequency are of sufficient amplitude to be significant during detection. In public-entertainment FM (88 to 108 MHz) eight significant sidebands are created above and below the resting frequency at the time of maximum permissible modulation.

The permissible modulation factors are related to the extent of carrier deviation and audio-signal ratios. The ratio of the carrier frequency shift to the frequency of the modulating signal that causes such carrier deviation is termed the *modulation index*. The latter is designated as m_f:

$$m_f = \frac{df_c}{df_m} \tag{8-1}$$

where df_c is a given deviation in carrier frequency
df_m is the frequency of the modulating signal

The deviation ratio involves maximum values rather than the instantaneous ones utilized to solve modulation index:

$$\text{Deviation ratio} = \frac{\text{maximum frequency deviation of carrier}}{\text{highest frequency of modulation signal}} \tag{8-2}$$

For any modulation index between 1 and 10, the number of significant sidebands produced can be found by the following table:

Modulation Index	Number of Sidebands Each Side of Carrier
1	2
2	4
3	6
4	7
5	8
6	9
7	10
8	12
9	13
10	14

8-5. TELEVISION BANDPASS REQUIREMENTS

Since black-and-white television transmission preceded the advent of color television by over a decade, the transmission and reception standards in force had to accommodate the additional signals encountered in color television. The composite video signal used to amplitude-modulate the RF carrier for black-and-white television consisted of the picture signal information, the retrace blanking pulses, the sync pulses, and the equal-

izing pulses utilized for maintaining horizontal scan during vertical retrace. This composite video signal that modulates the carrier produces
numerous sideband signals that tend to bunch around the frequencies of
the harmonics of the horizontal sweep signals. In color transmission this
tendency for sideband signals to cluster around the harmonics of the
sweep signal permits the insertion of the color signals into the gaps between the sideband groups. The early standards for black-and-white did
not have provisions for accommodating the additional carrier required
for the color signals, hence the color carrier (termed the subcarrier) is
suppressed at the transmitter. Since the subcarrier's frequency determines
the exact placement of the color sidebands, the subcarrier frequency
should be an odd multiple of one-half the horizontal sweep-signal frequency for proper color sideband frequency positioning. If the color
subcarrier is too high in frequency it would encroach on the 4-MHz
span from the primary carrier. Such crowding results in restricted color
bandwidth and fine-detail attenuation. If the color subcarrier is too low
in frequency, heterodyne interference could occur between the primary
carrier and the color sidebands.

A compromise for the frequency selection of the subcarrier was
made by multiplying one-half of the horizontal sweep frequency by 455
(there are 525 scan lines per frame, or 262.5 scan lines per field (see Sec.
11–9). The conventional 15,750 Hz in black-and-white horizontal sweep
frequency is unsuitable because the desired harmonic relationship between sound carrier and the video signal cannot be maintained. Hence,
the horizontal sweep for color receivers is 15,734.264 Hz and when multiplied by 455 results in a color subcarrier frequency of 3.579545 MHz
usually designated as 3.58 MHz. The vertical scan becomes 59.95 Hz.
The color vertical and horizontal scan frequencies are sufficiently close
to those for black and white to avoid loss of synchronization when receiving a black-and-white transmission and then switching to a color
transmission.

By utilization of design factors just outlined, the bandpass of color
signals has the same total span as black and white and hence achieves
compatibility. For fine detail the video signals extend far beyond the audio range to several megacycles and hence amplitude modulation would
produce an enormous spectrum span. Consequently, lower sidebands are
suppressed and only a 1.25-MHz vestigial section remains below the picture carrier frequency as shown in Figure 8–4. The color picture-tube
screen has the same width-to-height ratio of four to three as black and
white and the vertical scan down the picture-tube face is still interlaced

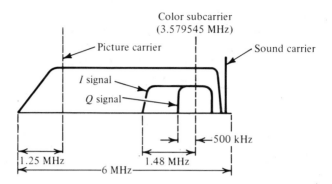

Figure 8–4 Color Television Bandpass

two to one. Similarly, the FM sound carrier for black-and-white or color video is situated 4.5 MHz above the picture carrier, with a permissible deviation of 25 kHz each side of center.

In the additive color principle that must be utilized, three primary colors are involved: red, blue, and green. Again, a compromise must be undertaken since three color signals would produce an excessive number of sidebands that cannot be accommodated in the spectrum space available. The compromise consists of using a matrix system for blending the three colors to produce two identified as the I signal (in phase) and the Q signal (quadature, or out of phase). Basically, the process is initiated in the pickup camera section as shown in Figure 8–5. Here three separate pickup camera tubes are used with a special filter system. A condenser lens picks up the televised images and the filters (consisting of dichroic mirrors) reflect light of only one color (B and C in Figure 8–5). Front-surface mirrors (identified as A and D) channel the red and blue signals to the respective cameras as shown. Thus, blue images are reflected by mirror B to the front-surface mirror D and thence to the blue pickup camera. Red images are reflected by mirror C and directed by front-surface mirror A to the red pickup camera, too. Green images transfer through the C and D mirrors and thence to the green pickup camera. The pickup camera tubes feed the signals into amplifiers, sweep circuits, and synchronization sections. From there the primary color signals are applied to a matrix network as shown. The matrix obtains a luminance signal (Y) corresponding to the black-and-white transmission. As shown, the luminance signal samples the red, green, and blue signals, to the proportions of 0.30 red, 0.59 green, and 0.11 blue. Such propor-

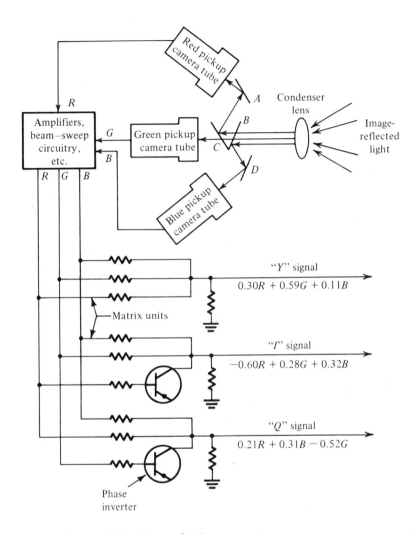

Figure 8–5 TV Color Camera Sections

tions must be used to achieve the color density as perceived by the human eye. If the luminance signal consisted of equal-amplitude red, blue, and green signals, some colors would appear to have greater intensity to the human eye than they actually possess in proportion to others.

The matrix system combines proper portions of the three primary colors for the formation of the I and Q signals (relative amplitudes are given in Table 7–30). The I and Q signals are then utilized to modulate the color subcarrier as described more fully in Chap. 11. At the receiver, a special oscillator must reproduce a suitable subcarrier to mix with the incoming sidebands for demodulation purposes. Such an oscillator, however, must be precisely synchronized with the subcarrier frequency suppressed at the transmitter. To assure frequency and phase synchronization, a minimum of eight cycles having a frequency of 3.58 MHz are transmitted in conjunction with the horizontal blanking as shown in Figure 8–6 (see also Sec. 11–8).

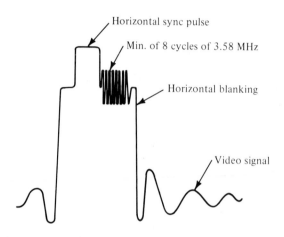

Figure 8–6 Burst Signal Mounted on Blanking

At the receiver a complex process and demodulation system must be utilized to retrieve the video signals and color information. In contrast to public-entertainment AM and FM radio where only a single intermediate frequency (IF) is encountered, dual IFs are present (picture and sound). In addition, the two IF signals are heterodyned at the video detector to produce a new sound IF signal of 4.5 MHz (see Sec. 11–9). Once the picture and sound signals have been mixed in the tuner, the resultant IF have a fixed frequency as with AM and FM receivers. Figure 8–7 is a representative breakdown of the frequency involved when Channel 9 is being received. Although other stations would have different carrier frequencies, the corresponding change of the tuner oscillator frequency still produces the same intermediate frequencies. A typical television IF bandpass for Channel 9 is shown in Figure 8–8. The dips are attenuation points for signals that may cause interference if not diminished.

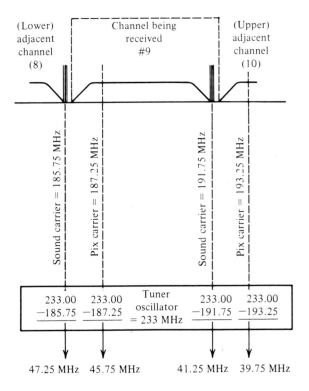

Figure 8–7 TV Signal Mixing in Tuner

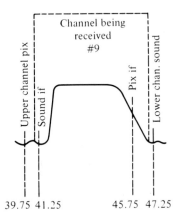

Figure 8–8 TV Response Curve for IF

8–6. COLOR PHASE FACTORS

The relative portions of luminance and color signals are given in Table 7–30. The color phase relationships are illustrated in Figure 8–9. Here, the phase differences regarding the R-Y, B-Y the I signal as well as the Q. As shown, the B-Y signals are displaced clockwise 33° from the Q signal, and the R-Y signals are displaced clockwise 33° from the I signal. Dashed lines indicate the relative phase positions and placements of the primary colors for the additive color television system. The lower section of Figure 8–9 is emphasized in the drawing in Figure 8–10. The latter illustrates how the same color signal is produced for signal voltages of either I/Q, or R-Y/B-Y. Saturated green is used as an illustrative example. If a signal amplitude of -0.52 is referenced along the $-Q$ axis and an amplitude of -0.28 is taken along the $-I$ axis as shown, a parallelogram drawn by dashed lines along the reference points gives us the vector addition of the two $-Q$ and $-I$ amplitudes. The resultant is 0.596 and indicates the amplitude of the saturated green signal. This identical green-signal amplitude is also obtained by taking the amplitude of 0.29 along the $-B$-Y axis and taking an amplitude of -0.517 on the $-R$-Y axis. Using these two points to form a parallelogram produces the same amplitude that had been obtained for the I/Q parallelogram. For any other color, identical vectors are obtained for specific values of I

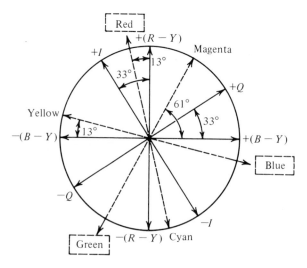

Figure 8–9 Color Television Signal Phasing

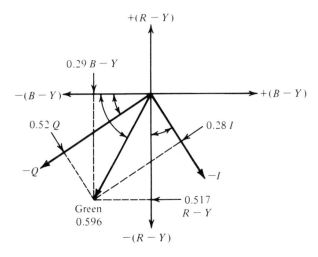

Figure 8–10 Green Signal Derivations

and Q or R-Y and B-Y. When the R-Y and B-Y signals are obtained by a matrix network as shown in Figure 2–35. In some instances the letters X and Y are arbitrarily selected to designate a particular phase relationship for a design variation utilized by a particular manufacturer. In most instances, the demodulation axes are phased 105° apart as shown in Figure 8–9.

8–7. CW AND ICW PRINCIPLES

When an RF unmodulated carrier signal is broken up so that there are short and long bursts of transmission, the process is termed the continuous-wave (CW) mode. The *continuous-wave* terminology refers to the constant or *continuous amplitude* of the RM signal. For a listing of the International Morse code, see Table 7–29. A basic method for CW is shown in Figure 8–11(A), where the emitter circuit of a crystal oscillator is opened and closed to produce the coded segments of RF signal carrier transmission. As shown, a telegraph key input line is present and if open there is no dc conduction for electron flow from emitter to collector. When the telegraph key is depressed, the emitter circuit is closed and current flow through the emitter–collector circuitry forms a segment of the carrier signal. Capacitor C_2 is for minimizing transients caused by the

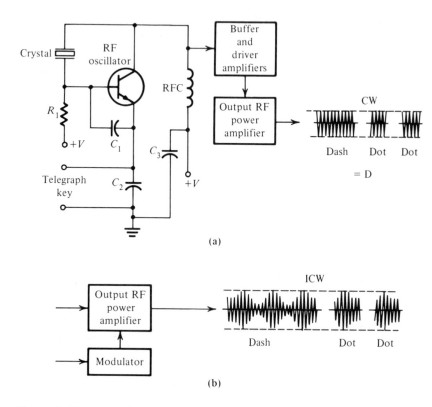

Figure 8–11 Basic CW Transmitter System

abrupt on and off switching by the telegraph key. The transistor conduction could, of course, be interrupted in the collector as well as the base circuits if desired. The coded carrier is applied to a buffer and driver RF amplifier and to an output power amplifier as shown. For the coded output illustrated, the dash–dot–dot representation indicates the Morse code letter **D**.

On occasion a *modulated* RF carrier is utilized for the production of code as shown in Figure 8–11(B). Here, an amplitude-modulated signal is broken up and again represents the letter D. Such transmission is referred to as *interrupted continuous wave* (ICW). This term denotes that the carrier no longer has a continuous amplitude but that the latter is interrupted by the increasing and decreasing levels. The ICW code transmission permits the use of a conventional receiver for reception purposes since the modulation produces a tone output from the receiver in the form of long and short durations. For CW demodulation, however, an oscillatory detector (regenerative) or a separate oscillator must be used to generate a signal in the receiver that can be mixed with the incoming CW signal for audibility. If the incoming CW signal is 2500 kHz, for instance, and the heterodyning oscillator is 2505 kHz, a 5-kHz tone is produced.

The CW signals have the advantage of narrow-band transmission since modulation and its accompanying sidebands are absent. The disadvantage is the need for a heterodyne receiver. The advantage of the ICW is the ease of reception by conventional receivers while the disadvantage is occupancy of a broader spectrum space.

8–8. PULSE-AMPLITUDE MODULATION

Pulse-amplitude modulation is one of several systems wherein the waveforms in pulse trains are modified in amplitude, width, or position to conform to the configuration of the modulating signal. In the pulse-amplitude modulation system the peak level of a pulse train is increased or decreased to conform to the modulating signal as shown in Figure 8–12.

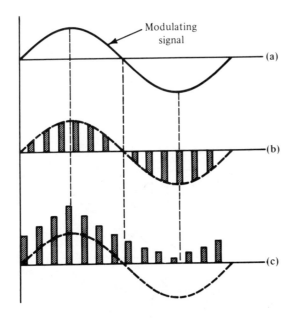

Figure 8–12 Pulse-Amplitude Modulation Process

For a sine-wave modulating signal as shown in (A), the pulse-amplitude modulation can take two forms: both positive and negative pulses can be utilized as shown in (B), or pulses of one polarity can be used as shown in (C). For the system in (A) a positive pulse peak is reached at the highest amplitude of the positive alternation of the modulating signals and a negative peak is obtained for the second alternation of the modulating signal as shown. For the unipolarity pulse train shown in (C), maximum pulse amplitude is attained at the positive peak of the modulating signal, while the lowest pulse level prevails at the negative peak of the second alternation of the modulating signal.

The pulse amplitude-modulation technique is also used in a special high-efficiency amplifier designated as Class D. With Class D amplification a high degree of efficiency is achieved and signals can be driven into higher peak-current amplitudes than are possible with conventional amplifiers such as Class A and B. A typical Class D system is shown in Figure 8–13(A) and the pulses have amplitudes related to the modulating sine-wave signal. An alternative method is to utilize the single-polarity pulses as was shown in Figure 8–12(C).

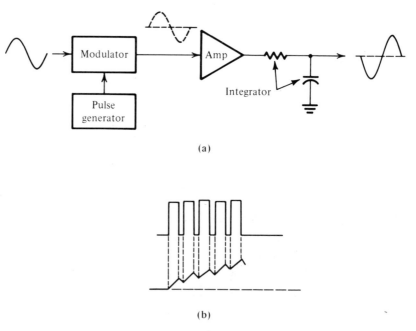

(a)

(b)

Figure 8–13   Class D Factors

For the Class D amplifying system shown in Figure 8–13, the input modulating signal is applied to a pulse modulator fed by a pulse generator. The modulator then forms an amplitude-modulated pulse train as shown. In practical applications the modulating signal would consist of complex audio waveforms. After the modulated signal is amplified it tends to have sawtooth characteristics due to the space between pulses and the amplitude-changing level of the individual pulses. Thus, an integrator section can be employed to build up a charge from pulse to pulse as shown in (B). The latter process restores the waveshape to that of the original modulating signal in all aspects except amplitude. The latter depends on the degree of amplification utilized.

The integration principle is also employed for the alternate pulse-modulation system. In the system where the pulse amplitude remains constant but the widths are varied (see Sec. 8–11) most of the circuitry is similar to that shown in Figure 8–13, although a pulse-width modulator is used.

8–9. PULSE-POSITION MODULATION

The pulse-position modulation (PPM) system modifies the pulse train as shown in Figure 8–14. This system is also referred to as *pulse-time modulation* (PTM) because a change in the modulating signal causes a corresponding change in the pulse position in time. The time change can relate to the time interval between pulses as shown or to the time a pulse appears relative to a fixed marker position. When a fixed marker pulse

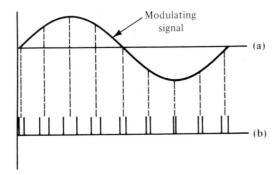

Figure 8–14   Pulse-Position Modulation Process

position is utilized, one of each pair of pulses remains in a fixed position and the other pulse shifts in relation to such a fixed position. The pulse having a fixed position can be selected to have a time relationship directly below the dashed vertical position lines shown in Figure 8–14.

8–10. PULSE-DURATION MODULATION

The pulse-duration modulation system is also known as the *pulse-width-modulation* (PWM) system. As shown in Figure 8–15, the width of each pulse of the train is gradually altered to conform to the changing amplitude of the modulating signal as shown in (A) and (B). The advantage of this system is its ability to diminish noise signals and other undesired transients. Since the pulses have a fixed amplitude, any noise signals accompanying the transmitted modulated signal can be removed by amplitude limiters or clippers in the receiver circuitry.

As with other pulse-modulation systems, pulses are selected that have very short durations so that the narrow pulses permit the use of a greater number for a given alternation of the modulating signal. The usage of very narrow pulses also permits the insertion of additional pulse transmissions into the original train. This permits the increase of information channels and aids in the reduction of spectrum space. The pulses

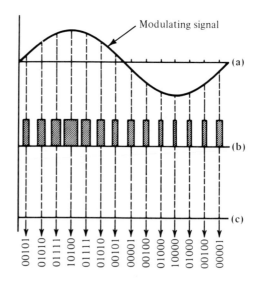

Figure 8–15 Pulse-Width and Pulse-Code Modulation Process

illustrated in Figure 8–14(B) are wider than those normally used in practical systems for convenience in depicting the pulse-duration system.

For such pulse-duration modulating systems, the process can alter either the initial edge (leading) of the pulse or the trailing edge. When the pulse train is applied to an integrator circuit, the demodulation process occurs as was shown earlier in Figure 8–13.

8–11. PULSE-CODE MODULATION

Another form of modulation involves the conversion of amplitude variations of the modulating signal to a set of pulses that, in binary form, represents a specific amplitude. The process is illustrated in Figure 8–15(C). Note that the numbers shown below the vertical dashed lines are binary representations (see Sec. 5–1). These binary numbers identify specific pulse positions. This modulation system necessitates utilization of several sequential operations. The modulating signal must be sampled at a predetermined rate and the significance of the amplitude must also be a factor in accordance with the amplitude changes of the modulating signal.

For the pulse-code-modulating system the amplitude of the pulse train is compared to a selected scale of discrete levels. Each pulse is then assigned a value corresponding to the closest indicated by the comparison process. This quantizing method yields values that are translated into a pulse code such as binary (base 2). The system has a low noise-prone characteristic as well as a minimum of signal attenuation; hence, the PCM has been found to be a valuable system and is widely used.

The number of amplitude levels that can be sampled in the PCM process for a single alternation of the modulating signal is limited by the maximum number of pulses selected for the code group. Obviously, with a selection of a three-pulse maximum, only seven amplitude variations can be referenced (001 through 111). The three-pulse selection can be expanded to eight amplitude variations by utilizing 000. For a code group employing four pulses, 16 levels can be sampled (from 000 to 1111).

8–12. TELEMETRY AND MULTIPLEXING

Telemetry is a process whereby several special modulating systems are combined into a single system for the transmission of data. Basically, the gathering of information includes the measurement and sensing of the data by transducers (speed sensors, temperature-reading devices, light-sensitive components, pressure-sensitive devices, microphones, etc.). The data sensed are analog functions that must be converted to a representative quantity that can be used for modulation purposes. The telemetry process involves *multiplexing* (usage of several frequency bands to transmit two or more information signals).

Multiplexing permits the transmission of such data as voice information, industrial-control data, space exploration information, and other similar information. Frequency-deviation multiplexing (FDM) utilizes several bands for the transmission of several modulations. Thus, a primary RF carrier is involved, with separate subcarriers that may, in turn, modulate the final carrier. Such a process is employed in public-entertainment stereo frequency-modulation transmission wherein a subcarrier is utilized for multiplexing, after which the subcarrier is suppressed. At the receiver a signal-generating oscillator must produce a subcarrier having the same frequency as the original before suppression. This generated subcarrier is then combined with the sideband signal prior to demodulation. A similar process occurs in color television transmission, where a color subcarrier is modulated to form the color signals. This subcarrier is then suppressed but the sidebands are transmitted. Again, as with stereo FM, a subcarrier coinciding in frequency with the original must be generated and combined with the sideband signal (see Secs. 8–5 and 11–8).

The frequency-division multiplexing system is widely used for expanding the signal-carrying capacities of cables or radio-linked devices in international telephone processes. This system, however, is susceptible to intermodulation distortion and the encroachment of unwanted noise signals. Consequently, the preferred systems are the pulse-modulation types described in Secs. 8–8 through 8–11.

An additional multiplexing system is the *time-division multiplexing* (TDM). This process has the capability of transmitting two or more signals at the same time because it allocates each signal a finite time interval. Instantaneous amplitudes of the signals are sampled and then transmitted in a time sequence. After the last signal has been sampled, the process is repeated. Any of the pulse-modulating systems described in Secs. 8–8 through 8–11 can be used. With a sampling rate in the range 8000 per second or higher, very little signal information is attenuated. Each channel transmission is subsequently decoded separately to obtain the equivalent of the original modulating signal data.

9 Fundamental Principles of Instrumentation

9-1. ANALOG CURRENT METERS

A common practice in the design of analog instruments is to utilize a current-reading meter as the fundamental unit for ammeters, voltmeters, ohmmeters and so on. The basic meter movement utilizes the principle invented by D'Arsonval in 1880. The basic device is illustrated in Figure 9-1(A). Here an aluminum form is utilized on which a coil is wound. The assembly is pivoted in dual jeweled bearings (sapphire) within a field generated by a permanent magnet connected to soft-iron pole pieces. The coil assembly has a pointer arm that indicates the amount of current to be read on a calibrated scale on the meter dial face. The pivot unit contains coil springs at each pivot end. These springs are wound in opposite fashion to provide a counterforce against the coil-form movement in either the right or left direction. These springs are also used as conductors for channeling the current through the coil. The current flow creates an electromagnet of the coil and the poles of the electromagnet either aid or oppose the fixed-strength fields of the permanent magnet. For a proper polarity current, the torque so developed moves the pointer toward the right to read the amount of current flow. The aluminum coil form produces damper characteristics and prevents oscillations of the pointer. Thus, it aids in bringing the pointer to a quick stop because current induced into the aluminum form establishes a counterelectromotive force.

A current-reading meter is placed *in series* with the circuit or device to be measured. An ammeter has a low internal resistance and the

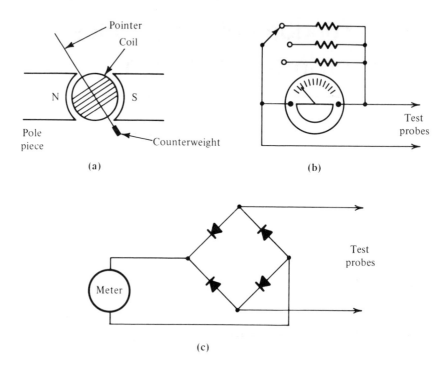

Figure 9–1 Current-Meter Factors

better-quality meter contributes only a negligible amount of resistance to the circuit under measurement. (In special meters, current measurements are made by utilizing inductive principles to eliminate the necessity for opening a circuit, as described in Sec. 9–15.) Many basic current-reading meters read fractional values because of their high sensitivity. The latter include types having a maximum meter range of 10 mA, 1 mA, 50 μA, and so on. Any of these can read higher currents by utilizing shunt resistors to bypass that amount of current above the value that would damage the meter movement. As shown in Figure 9–1(B), shunting resistors can be switched across the meter movement to provide the current-reading range desired. Additional resistors are utilized as needed. Regardless of the resistor selected, the current flow through the internal meter coil must not exceed its rating. If, for instance, the milliammeter movement had a full-scale deflection of 1 mA but a 10-mA range was needed, the shunt resistor must pass 9 mA to avoid exceeding the 1-mA rating of the meter when the maximum current is read.

The value of the required shunt resistor for a desired full-scale reading can be found by using

$$R_{\text{sh}} = \frac{R_m}{N-1} \qquad (9\text{--}1)$$

where R_{sh} is the ohmic value of the shunt resistor

R_m is the internal resistance of the meter

N is the number by which the meter scale is to be increased

Note that the N value in Eq. 9–1 is the number *by which the scale is to be increased.* Thus, if a 1-mA movement has an internal resistance of 45 Ω and the scale is to be increased for a full-scale deflection of 10 mA, the ohmic value by Eq. 9–1 for the shunt is

$$\frac{45}{10-1} = \frac{45}{9} = 5\ \Omega$$

The ammeter shown in Figure 9–1(B) is for direct current only, and polarity of the test probes must be correct to get proper direction of movement with the pointer. For alternating-current measurements the ac must be rectified by either the half-wave or full-wave principles discussed in Chap. 2. The bridge rectifier system is shown in Figure 9–1(C) for an ac ammeter [see also Sec. 2–39 and Figure 2–29(A)]. The meter is calibrated to display root-mean-square (rms) values (also termed *effective* values, as discussed in Sec. 1–13). For the rectifying-type ac meters that are to be used to read alternating current, design problems occur in areas of calibration, sensitivity, and current-carrying capacity. Hence, the rectifying-type meter design is primarily used in ac applications to construct voltmeters.

9–2. ANALOG VOLTMETERS

The analog voltmeter measures the amplitude of a voltage drop *across* a circuit component as opposed to the current-reading meter discussed in Sec. 9–1, where the meter is placed *in series* with the current flow. Since the voltmeter bridges a circuit component it should have as high an internal resistance as feasible so that it does not load down the circuit under test by introducing a shunt resistance across the component being measured.

The analog-type voltmeter utilizes a current meter as the foundation unit as shown in Figure 9–2. To increase the scale, various series resistors are utilized, depending on the variety of ranges needed. As shown for the four series resistors in Figure 9–2, a selector switch is utilized. With the switch connected to the junction of R_1 and R_2 the lowest voltage scale is obtained. When connected to the junctions of resistors R_2 and R_3 resistors R_1 and R_2 are in series, and consequently the higher resistance provides for a higher scale reading. As with the basic ammeter, the current flow through the meter movement must not exceed the rated amount. The ohmic value of the external resistance needed to achieve a specific meter range can be ascertained by using

$$R_s = R_m(N - 1) \qquad (9\text{–}2)$$

where R_s is the ohmic value of the series multiplier resistor
   R_m is the internal resistance of the meter coil
   N is the number by which the meter voltage scale is to be increased

As with the ammeter discussed in Sec. 9–1, the N factor must be properly utilized. Thus, if the meter is to read 5 V at full-scale deflection, the full-scale reading desired is divided by the voltage necessary to cause such a deflection. Assume that the basic meter movement has 100 Ω of internal resistance and that the full-scale deflection is 0.1 V. Thus, $5/0.1 = 50$ and the latter is utilized in Eq. 9–2 with the meter resistance of 100 Ω: $R_s = 100(50 - 1) = 4.9 \text{ k}\Omega$.

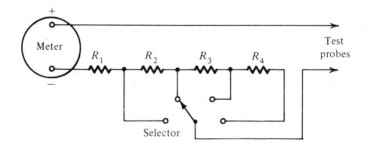

Figure 9–2   Basic Voltmeter System

As mentioned earlier in this section, the higher the voltmeter resistance, the less loading effect shunting the component across which the meter is placed. Consequently, the sensitivity of the voltmeter is rated in *ohms per volt* and the phrase denotes the ohmic value by which the multiplier resistor must be raised to increase the meter scale by 1 V. Essentially, voltmeter sensitivity represents the ratio of a multiplier resistor and the meter coil resistance to the voltage deflection of the meter. Thus, if a 50-ΩA meter movement has a sensitivity of 20 kΩ/V as compared to only 1 kΩ/V, the first would have considerably less loading effect on the circuit when used for voltage measurements.

The ohms-per-volt sensitivity can be calculated by using Eq. 9–2 initially to solve for the ohmic value of the series resistance required for a 1-V full-scale reading. Assume that R_s for a particular meter was found to be 18 kΩ. Also, for the same meter, an increase to a 2-V full-scale reading would provide a resistance of 38 kΩ. Thus, for a 1-V difference in full-scale deflection the series resistor change was from 18 kΩ to 38 kΩ, or 20,000 Ω/V (20 kΩ/V).

9–3. ANALOG OHMMETERS

The ohmic values of circuit components are measured by an ohmmeter that utilizes the basic current-reading meter as was the case for the units discussed in Secs. 9–1 and 9–2. The basic circuit and typical scale are shown in Figure 9–3. As shown in (A), two resistors can be used in a series circuit with a battery. Resistor R_1 is a current-limiting unit that establishes the range of the scale in conjunction with resistor R_2. The latter is a variable type that permits adjusting the current flow so that full-scale deflection is obtained when the test probes are shorted together. Under this condition there is a minimum of resistance at the test probes and hence the full-scale needle deflection indicates a zero point on the scale as shown at (B). The scale is nonlinear as shown, with crowding at the high-resistance reading section at the left. As with the voltmeter and ohmmeter units, the ohmmeter is usually combined with the others in a single volt-ohmmeter designated as VOM and discussed in Sec. 9–4. In some transistorized units the ohms scale can be designed to read increasing values from left to right as shown later in Figure 9–6(A).

For accurate results, the ohmic value of resistors and other circuit components should be read while one side of the measured unit is dis-

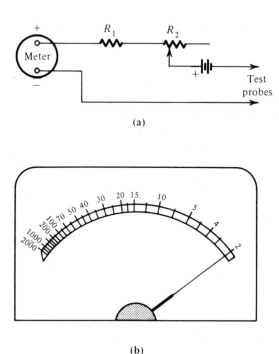

Figure 9–3 Ohmmeter Circuit and Scale

connected. (Circuit power should be off.) This procedure avoids the shunting effect of other parallel resistances. In a number of electronic circuits, resistors may have a tolerance value of 10 to 20%. Thus, at 10% a reading of 800 to 2200 Ω for a 2000-Ω resistor can often be assumed to be within the normal range. In some circuitry, however, critical tolerances are essential. Often schematics for a system will give tolerance factors. Ohmmeters are also useful for test procedures such as continuity checking. Thus, the ohmmeter will indicate the presence of short circuits, open circuits, and so on. In continuity checking it is usually unnecessary to ascertain exact ohmic values since the purpose is merely to test for continuity from one circuit to another regarding power distribution and signal handling. With continuity checking, the electric power is again disconnected from the circuits under test, as is the case with general ohmmeter reading procedures.

9–4. VOM TYPES

Although individual meters are widely used for rating current, voltage, and other amplitudes in stationery equipment, the combination of such meters in a single unit provides for a portable testing device in design, maintenance, and servicing of electronic devices. Combinational meters are sometimes referred to as volt-ohmmeters (VOM) or, when digital, as digital multimeters (DMM). With a single meter unit performing a number of tasks, the switching circuitry becomes involved. The basic design factors of the multimeters are shown in Figure 9–4, in which the voltmeter, ohmmeter, and ammeter functions are indicated. For reading ac values, rectifier systems would have to be utilized and for extended scale readings more complex circuitry would be involved.

A representative front panel of a VOM showing the variety of controls is illustrated in Figure 9–5. Although this is representative, there are numerous variations among the many manufacturers. Pushbutton selections are utilized for this meter and the one marked $+/-$ reverses the polarity input of the probes for reading negative values. As with other ohmmeters, in the $\times$ 1 position the meter scale is read directly to in-

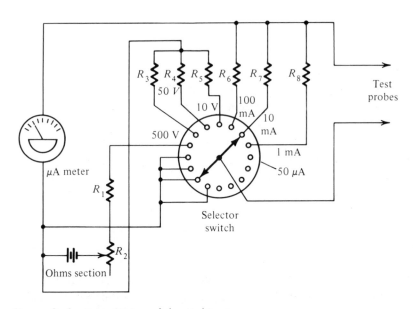

Figure 9–4 Basic Design of the Multimeter

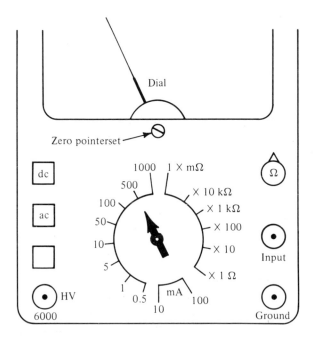

Figure 9–5   Representative VOM Controls

dicate the ohmic value being measured. Thus, for the dial shown in Figure 9–3(B) the range is from 0 Ω to approximately 2000 Ω. For higher readings, changing the selector position selects various multiplier ranges, so that if the dial is set at × 1 kΩ, each number on the dial of Figure 9–3(B) is multiplied by 1 kΩ.

Most multimeters have accessory devices for special measurement purposes. Many units have RF probes available for reading amplitudes of ac with frequency ranges into the megacycles. Similarly, high-voltage probes are available for measuring voltage amplitudes to several dozen kilovolts. Some VOM units utilize transistorized circuitry for improved sensitivity and accuracy. The field-effect transistors have been widely used to provide a high probe impedance, with some units providing as much as 15 MΩ during dc measurements. Other types include the digital units described in Sec. 9–6.

9–5. DECIBEL AND VU SCALES

A typical multimeter scale is shown in Figure 9–6(A). The two upper scales are utilized for reading ohmic values as well as for current and voltage in various ranges. The lower scale is for reading decibels (dB) (see Sec. 1–7 and Table 7–1). For the decibel dial shown in (A) the scale is read directly when measurements are made across a 600-Ω resistance. In the representation of power ratios, many meters use for a reference zero dB = 1 mW of power across a 600-Ω load. This reference then represents the 0.7746 V of ac (rms) across the 600-Ω load.

Some manufacturers use a reference based on 0 dB = 6 mW at 500 Ω, where the 0-dB point is at 1.732 V on the voltage scale. Still another reference that has been utilized is 0 dB = 6 mW across a 600-Ω

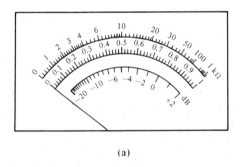

(a)

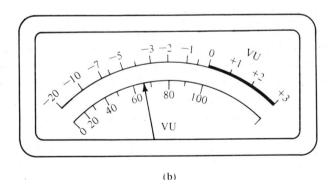

(b)

Figure 9–6 Decibel and VU Scales

load with the 0-dB point at 1.897 V. In comparing decibel differences between the signals present at the input and output of an electronic system, the ohmic values of the input and output resistances must be identical for obtaining accurate readings. Decibel measurements should be made utilizing sine-wave signals. For complex waveshapes, including composite audio types made up of multiple signal combinations (or square waves, etc.), the *volume unit* measurements are indicated.

The volume unit (VU) is useful for audio testing and measurement. Basically, the VU is a decibel-oriented unit. Cassette decks, tape recorders, and eight-track units usually contain two VU meters to indicate on-going recording levels to minimize the distortion that occurs during overload conditions. For volume-unit measurements, the zero level is assumed to represent 0.001 W across 600 Ω of impedance (Z). In equation form this is

$$VU = 30 \log_{10} P \tag{9-3}$$

The dial for a representative volume-unit meter is shown in Figure 9–6(B). Here, the upper scale ranges from -20 to $+3$ VU. The lower scale represents *percentage* of voltage, with 100% located beneath the zero in the upper scale. In many meters the numbers and scale markings to the left of the zero in the upper scale are imprinted in black and to the right of the zero in red. Normal volume level is considered to be at the zero point on the upper scale representing 100% (located at approximately 70% of full-scale deflection).

In observing readings on the VU meter it is preferable to note readings over a short time interval to check for peak excursions of the signal so that controls can be adjusted to keep the peaks below the overload point. The volume-unit meter design incorporates full-wave rectification (see Sec. 2–36). Thus, the scale indications are approximate rms values of the complex audio-signal waveform. In contrast to the use of sine-wave test signals that are maintained at a constant amplitude during measurement procedures, the volume-unit measurements involve signals of varying frequencies and amplitudes making up a *composite* signal. The VU reading is actually an arbitrary value and has no fixed value as in the case of *dBm*, which is used to designate the decibel based on zero decibel = 1 mW across a 600-Ω load.

9–6. DIGITAL METERS

Since the advent of liquid-crystal and light-emitting diode displays, digital-readout meters have come into wide use. They present a high degree of accuracy and are available for reading ac or dc, usually with selector switch convenience. Typical display types include the reading of fractional values, as shown in Figure 9–7(A). Multiple range switches as well as select switches for ac and dc are present as with transistorized multimeters. Many digital multimeters (DMMs) are designed for automatic sensing and displays of the polarity without the necessity for observing probe polarities. Thus, the probes are placed across a unit to read voltages, and the reading will show a $+$ or $-$ sign in addition to the digital display. It is not uncommon for accuracy to range from $+0.1$ to $+0.5\%$ of the reading, plus one digit.

As shown in Figure 9–7(B), hand-held digital meters equipped with a fixed probe and a flexible negative line are also available for convenience in testing and measuring electronic circuitry. For the DMM units input resistance can exceed 50 MΩ, presenting a minimum of circuit

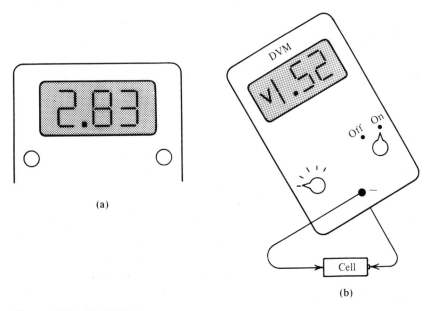

(a)

(b)

Figure 9–7 Digital Meters

loading during measurement. Since the digital meters display the reading in less than a few seconds, they provide for rapid voltage reading as compared to the analog types, where the pointer must swing from the zero position to some higher value.

9-7. BRIDGE SYSTEMS

In Figure 9–8(A) is shown the basic bridge circuit configuration. Here, there is a symmetrical arrangement of four resistors, R_1, R_2, R_s, and R_x. For finding the value of unknown units, a voltage is applied across the junctions shown, and a meter reading is obtained from across the opposite two junctions. Such a bridge circuit can also be composed of inductors, capacitors, and capacitors in conjunction with resistors in various test instruments. The basic circuit is sometimes referred to as the *Wheatstone bridge* after the English physicist who initially brought attention to the value of the balanced bridge circuit. For finding values of unknown resistance, the resistors R_1 and R_2 are usually of fixed value; R_s is a standard resistor of known value; and R_x is the unknown resistor to be measured. A galvanometer, consisting of a zero-center scale with positive and negative readings each side can be used to show a balanced bridge as well as an unbalance in either direction. A micrometer can also be used.

When the resistance bridge achieves a balanced circuit condition, there will be no potential difference across the galvanometer. Under these conditions the resistor relationships in equation form are

$$R_x = R_s \frac{R_2}{R_1} \qquad (9\text{–}4)$$

In similar fashion the utilization of inductance and capacitance can form bridge circuits for the measurement of reactance and impedance values as well as capacitance values in fractional farads and inductance values in henrys or fractional values thereof. Commercial meters have incorporated within the units standard-value components having a high degree of accuracy. Some have provisions for connecting standard values externally for comparison measurement purposes. A typical capacitance bridge is shown in Figure 9–8(B). Here, the standard ratio-arm resistors R_1 and R_2 are again used as with the resistance bridge in (A). Capacitor

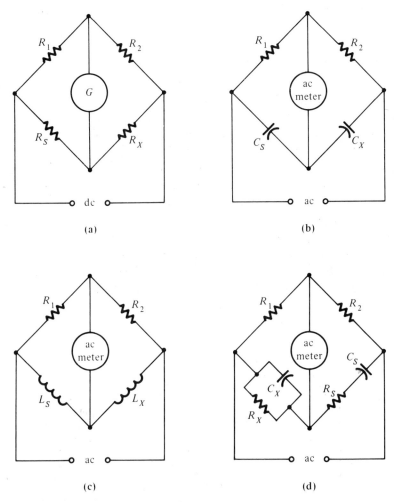

Figure 9–8 Bridge-Circuit Meter Systems

C_s is the standard-value unit and C_x is the unknown unit to be measured. For this bridge, an ac meter is required.

In equation form the capacitance value of C_x is given as

$$C_x = C_s \frac{R_1}{R_2}$$ (9–5)

Note the inverse function between the ratio-arm resistors R_1 and R_2 of Eqs. 9–4 and 9–5. This difference occurs because the reactance of a capacitor decreases for larger-value capacitors. For inductors, however, the reactance increases for higher values of inductance. Thus, for the inductance bridge circuit shown in Figure 9–8(C) the equation for finding the inductance value of L_x has the ratio arm resistors the same as for the resistance bridge given in Eq. 9–4:

$$L_x = L_s \frac{R_2}{R_1} \qquad (9\text{–}6)$$

Inductors and capacitors can be put in series for forming resonant bridge circuits. In addition, bridge circuits can also be used for signal frequency measurement. A typical type is the Wein bridge circuit shown in Figure 9–8(D). The equation that follows applies if C_x is equal to C_s, if R_x is equal to R_s, and if R_1 is half the resistance value of R_2. When these conditions prevail the frequency is found using the equation

$$f = \frac{1}{6.28 R_x C_x} \qquad (9\text{–}7)$$

9–8. SIGNAL GENERATORS

A signal generator, as the name implies, produces a signal for injection into electronic circuitry during tests, measurements, and troubleshooting. The basic signal generator is capable of supplying a sine-wave signal of variable frequency, as well as pulse signals of different repetition rates. In addition, controls are present for varying the output level, and switching from RF to AF (radio-frequency to audio-frequency ranges) as shown in Figure 9–9. The signal generator is also a useful instrument for signal-tracing purposes to localize defective or inoperative states in a successive group of circuits. The signal from the generator is injected into a circuit and its presence is verified by an oscilloscope or other sensing device in subsequent stages. Thus, the stage that does not pass the injected signal is then indicated as the defective one.

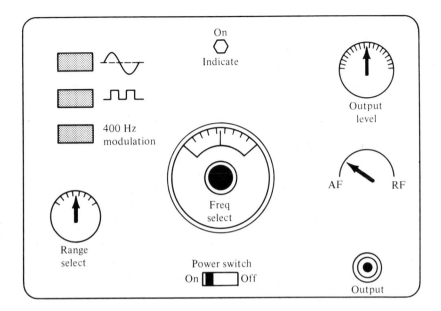

Figure 9–9 Basic Signal Generator Controls

The pulse or square-wave signals that are obtained from the generator can be utilized for determining whether or not harmonic components are attenuated in circuits. Since square waves and pulses consist of a fundamental frequency plus a number of higher harmonics, any loss of the latter will result in a distortion of the signal (see also Sec. 9–10). Where a high degree of frequency stability is required, piezoelectric crystals are incorporated within the generator for precision frequency control. Close-tolerance frequencies are essential during the alignment of IF stages or in the tracking of tuners where the simultaneous tuning of the mixer and oscillator stages of the tuner require a maintenance of the same frequency difference between the two.

Signal generators usually have provisions for modulating the RF signal by an audio signal (often a 400-Hz signal). Such a modulated signal output is useful for testing detector stages or when a visual display of the modulated signal is useful for test purposes. The single-signal generator is also useful to provide a marker for sweep generators (see Sec. 9–9).

9–9. SWEEP GENERATORS

In frequency-modulated communication systems a useful instrument is a signal generator having the ability to vary the frequency of the output signal. By increasing and decreasing the frequency above and below a given value, a fixed rate of signal-frequency sweep is available. Such sweep generators come in a variety of models designed for specific applications. Typical controls and basic layout of the front panel are shown in Figure 9–10(A). The sweep generator is useful for producing on an oscilloscope a visual display of the bandpass of IF or tuner stages. If the generator applies a sweep signal to the initial stages of an intermediate-frequency section, the oscilloscope pattern would appear as shown in Figure 9–10(B).

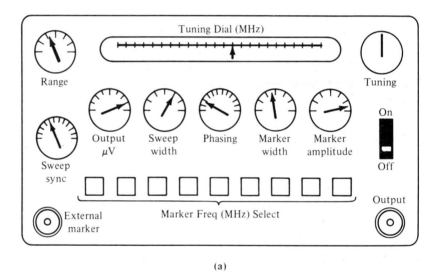

(a)

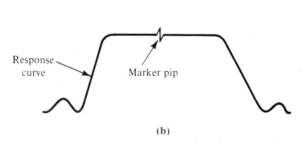

(b)

Figure 9–10　Sweep Generator and Marker Pip

The sweep generator function displays the bandpass characteristics because at any instant it displays the relative gain of the amplifier at the frequency prevailing at that instant. As the sweeping signal frequency encompasses regions below and above resonance the gain is low, while through the resonant frequency the gain rises sharply. For a constant gain over the resonant span, a substantially flat top prevails for the resonant curve. The marker pip is generated by an independent single-signal generator, incorporated either within the sweep generator housing or by an external generator. The single-frequency output signal imposes the marker pip on the response curve at the precise frequency generated. Thus, the marker pip can be moved along the response curve by manually varying the frequency of the single-signal generator. Thus, the marker pip location can determine the frequency span of the bandpass.

9–10. OSCILLOSCOPES

The oscilloscope is a visual-display instrument utilizing a cathode-ray tube. It has the ability to display the waveshape and amplitude of various signals utilized in electronic circuitry. The visual indication is a valuable means for evaluating signal waveforms, for ascertaining the presence of distortion, and for the measurement of amplitudes and phase between different signals. It also provides for a display of bandpass characteristics of IF and RF amplifier stages in various communication circuitry. There are numerous types of oscilloscopes available from various manufacturers. Some types are basic units with fundamental display characteristics only, whereas others provide for dual displays and triggered sweep functions, as discussed later in this section.

A typical front-panel system is shown in Figure 9–11. The signal to be displayed is generally applied to the vertical input terminals (V input) shown and hence reaches a vertical amplifying system. Ultimately, the amplified signal appears across the vertical deflection plates of the cathode-ray tube. The signal causes the internal beam of the tube to move up and down at a rate corresponding to the frequency of the input signal. The amplitude of the display as well as its position are set by the controls. Within the oscilloscope is a sawtooth-signal generator that produces a sweep signal for application to the horizontal deflection plates of the display tube. The sawtooth waveshape sweeps the beam across the face of the tube at a rapid rate until the sawtooth amplitude drops

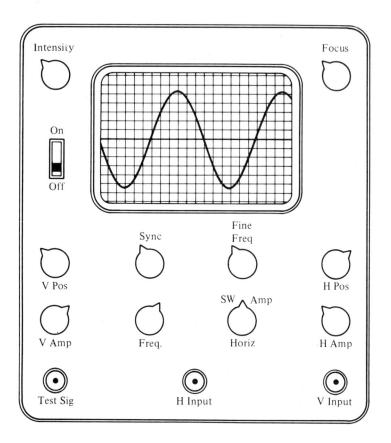

Figure 9–11 Scope Panel—Basic Controls

abruptly, at which time the beam retraces very rapidly to the left. Thus, if a sine-wave signal is applied to the vertical input, and the horizontal sweep frequency pulls the beam across the tube face once for each cycle of the input signal, a single cycle of the sine wave would be displayed. For displaying several cycles, the horizontal sweep would be at a slower rate.

The controls shown in Figure 9–11 permit total adjustment of the displayed image. (The location of the controls shown would, of course, vary for different instruments.) The intensity control varies the bias between the control grid and cathode of the cathode-ray tube to alter the brightness of the display signal. The focus control adjusts voltages on the anode portion of the display tube to adjust the pinpointing of the beam's trace. The switch marked *SW. AMP* maintains horizontal sweep when in the SW position. When placed in the AMP position, an external sweep signal can be utilized and will be amplified when applied to the horizontal input terminals. Variable controls are available for synchronization purposes including a fine-tuning control for precise adjustment of the sweep frequency after an approximate setting by the frequency control.

Vertical and horizontal positioning controls permit shifting the display image either vertically or horizontally for proper placement. The vertical and horizontal amplifier control permits expansion or contraction of the displayed signal as required. The phase and frequency of two sine-wave signals can be determined by switching off the internal horizontal sweep signal and applying one signal to the horizontal input and the other to the vertical input. One of these signals can be obtained from a calibrated signal generator for precise evaluation. With both the vertical and horizontal input signals applied and the scope controls adjusted for equal amplitudes, pattern changes occur when phase differences exist between the two input signals. The sequence of patterns for a phase difference between zero and 180° is shown in Figure 9–12. These phase displays are termed *Lissajous* patterns after the French scientist who first observed them experimentally.

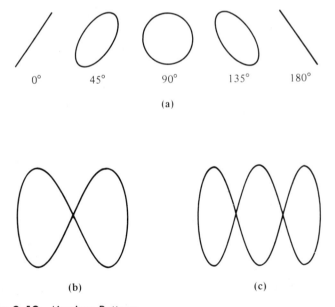

Figure 9–12 Lissajous Patterns

If both input signals are locked in a specific frequency the particular phase display will also be locked into a stationary pattern. If either signal (or both) drift in frequency the patterns shown in Figure 9–12(A) will be progressively displayed in sequence. A difference in amplitude between the applied signals causes an elongation of the display. When one input signal is twice the frequency of the other, the display is a figure-8 type of pattern, as shown in Figure 9–12(B). Thus, one signal could be 200 kHz and the other 400 kHz. A three-to-one frequency ratio of the signals produces the pattern shown in Figure 9–12(C).

By shutting off the scope's horizontal sweep, the resultant single vertical line can be utilized to measure for peak-to-peak voltages as shown in Figure 9–13. Here a sine wave has a peak-to-peak value of 10 V and hence the scope pattern display is calibrated to represent 10 V. Consequently, a decline in the length of the vertical line would permit the reading of successively smaller amplitudes. Peak-to-peak values are often indicated in the schematics of many electronic devices and systems.

Dual-trace oscilloscopes permit the display of two different signals simultaneously, as shown in Figure 9–14. Here one signal consists of square waves and the other sine waves. Some distortion appears in the square waves, indicating higher harmonic signal losses. In such oscilloscopes, dual-channel amplifiers and synchronizing systems are used to process the individual signals for display on a single cathode-ray tube. The dual trace is useful for signal comparison purposes. It can be utilized to observe the individual outputs from a stereo system for testing purposes. With a single signal applied simultaneously to both inputs, the

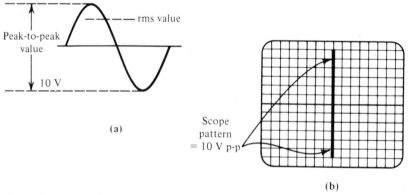

Figure 9–13 Peak-to-Peak Measurements

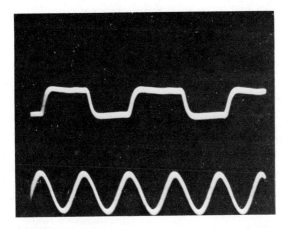

Figure 9–14 Dual-Trace Signals

output signals from the stereo system should be equal in amplitude and waveshape, and any deviation can be ascertained by the display. The dual-trace instrument is also useful for observation of phase differences between signals.

Besides dual trace, other features available include memory, where an observed waveform can be put into storage. Upon retrieval, repeated scan of the signal from memory presents a stationary pattern on the screen. Another feature is the *triggered sweep*, which permits improved stability of sweep synchronization by using the input signal to initiate the trigger for the horizontal sweep. Such synchronization is a precision system and far superior to the basic sweep system that uses a free-running oscillator that must be tuned manually for synchronization.

The recurrent sweep is less advantageous than the triggered sweep because the recurrent mode requires sync readjustment for changes in amplitude or frequency of the vertical input signal being viewed. When triggered sweep is used, the synchronization latches on automatically because the input signal initiates the trigger that controls the horizontal sweep mode. In scopes using triggered sweep, provisions are usually available for selecting either the free-running mode for recurrent sweep operation or the triggered mode. For the latter, the horizontal sweep is replaced by the triggered mode in coincidence with the application of an input signal.

9–11. CROSSHATCH AND BAR GENERATORS

An instrument particularly applicable for adjusting television systems is shown in Figure 9–15. This is a generator of complex waveforms that can produce vertical or horizontal bars on a television screen as well as a crosshatch pattern. Also available are dot patterns and color-bar patterns for adjustments of color receivers. The vertical and horizontal lines as well as the crosshatch patterns are obtained by depressing switches A, B, and C in the generator illustrated in Figure 9–15. For the vertical pat-

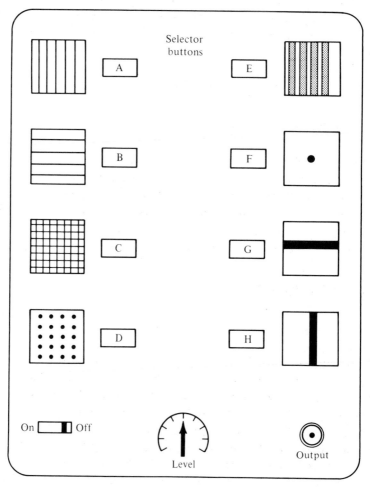

Figure 9–15   Crosshatch and Bar Generator

tern illustrated in (A) adjustments are made to the horizontal sweep linearity of the television receiver until the vertical bars are equally spaced across the screen. Similarly, the horizontal bars produced with pushbutton B permit adjustments of vertical linearity. A typical pattern of this type is illustrated in Figure 9–16. Here, the linearity at the bottom of the screen requires adjustment since the horizontal lines are thicker and farther apart than those at the top of the screen. With the crosshatch pattern obtained by pushbutton C, simultaneous adjustments can be made to correct both the vertical and horizontal linearity.

On occasion a single line (either horizontal or vertical) is useful and is available by pushbuttons G and H. On some instruments these single bars can be positioned to either side for testing linearity distortion (where curvature would occur). The vertical and horizontal linearity adjustments apply to either black-and-white or color receivers, while the other patterns available (the dot patterns and the color bar patterns) are utilized for color receivers exclusively.

In color television systems a televised scene undergoes a special process that filters the images into three primary colors (additive color principle) of red, blue, and green. In the color television receiver, the three-color significant signals initiate electron beams which impinge on phosphor dots of red, blue, and green. For perfect color rendition as well as for the production of a pure white segment of a scene, the electron beams must converge precisely on the respective phosphor dots. Adjustments or corrections are made by utilizing the dot pattern obtained by

Figure 9–16 Bar Pattern

depressing pushbutton D in Figure 9–15. When alignment and convergence is satisfactory all dots appear white. For any visible color fringing, convergence controls are adjusted to correct the convergence errors. As with the crossbars, a single pattern is available utilizing pushbutton F. Again, the single dot can be moved around the screen to check for convergence differences.

Vertical bars of color are obtainable on the screen by depressing pushbutton E for the generator shown in Figure 9–15. These fixed color bars permit testing the phase relationship between the several color signals and also facilitate adjustments of signal amplitude. The color bars are produced in the generator by shifting the phase of the color subcarrier (3.579545 MHz) with respect to the burst signal. When the phase of the subcarrier signal is continuously changed through 360° for a time interval equal to one horizontal line sweep, and repeated for successive horizontal lines, color-bar patterns are produced on the television screen. Sometimes an instrument producing such color bars is called a *rainbow generator*.

9–12. VECTORSCOPES

In Sec. 9–10 reference was made to the types of signals obtained for differences in phase and frequency between vertical and horizontal input signals. The Lissajous pattern production principle is also utilized in the *vectorscope*, another test instrument for color television receivers. Essentially, this instrument embodies the oscilloscope principle but utilizes a special display-tube faceplate that produces a petal-shaped diagram with 10 extensions corresponding to the 10 color bars produced by the rainbow generator. This system is shown in Figure 9–17 and is utilized in conjunction with a color-bar generator. Some commercial units include the rainbow generator within the vectorscope system. As shown in Figure 9–17, the R-Y color signal output from the color detectors is applied to the vertical input of the vectorscope, with the B-Y signal applied to the horizontal input for sweep purposes. The keyed color-bar generator is applied to the television receiver tuner as shown. An ideal representation of the petal formation is illustrated in Figure 9–18. The phase relationships of the signals are shown in (A), while the vectorscope faceplate pattern is illustrated in (B). Such a perfect petal formation does not appear because of circuit factors, and that shown in Figure 9–17 is more representative. The vectorgram display facilitates adjustments and main-

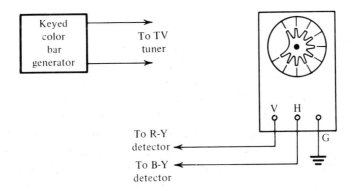

Figure 9–17 Vectorscope Applications

tenance procedures since color problems are displayed by the petal formation. Nonlinear distortion appears as uneven amplitudes of petals.
When petal tops appear flattened instead of rounded, circuit overloading
in the receiver is indicated. Other checks are also possible for the
vectorscope for localization of defective circuits, maladjusted sections in
the color system as well as inoperative stages. Thus, loss of the B-Y sig-

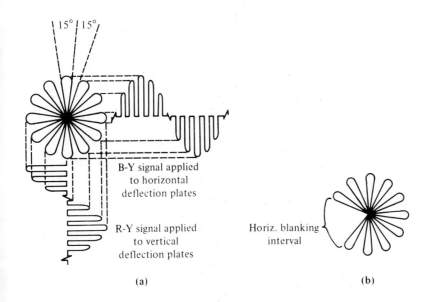

Figure 9–18 Vectorgram Petals (Formation)

nals causes a collapse of the petal formation and only a vertical line is visible.

9–13. TRANSISTOR TESTERS

Transistor checking instruments are available in a variety of models, with the higher-priced units having extended facilities. The basic types provide for general readings, indicating good or defective transistor indication ranges as shown in Figure 9–19. One scale indicates the gain capabilities of the transistor and another scale provides for measurement of resistive leakages between elements.

For the junction transistors the forward-current transfer ratio involves the ratio of a change in collector current (I_c) to base current (I_b). This characteristic is known as beta (β), as indicated by Eq. 9–8. This beta range involves the upper gain scale of the dial shown in Figure 9–19 and is calibrated in micro units.

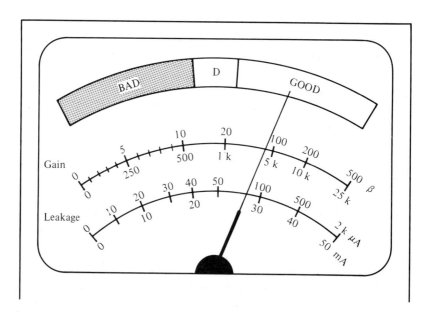

Figure 9–19   Representative Transistor Test Meter Dial

$$\beta = \frac{dI_c}{dI_b} \tag{9-8}$$

The second gain scale is for measurement of field-effect transistors. The transconductance measurement, also in micro units, is of value and indicates the following relationship:

$$q_m = \frac{dI_d}{dE_g} \tag{9-9}$$

where dI_d is the small change in drain current
dE_g is the small change in gate voltage

The better-quality transistor testers include features such as testing transistors without removing them from the circuit, identifying transistor leads automatically, and indicating whether the junction transistor is an *npn* or *pnp* type as well as showing whether the FET is an *n*-channel or *p*-channel unit. Such testers also identify the anode terminal of diodes and reads the front-to-back current ratio.

9-14. CLAMP-AROUND AC METERS

When it is necessary to read current values in electric systems it is inconvenient to open the circuit for insertion of a current-reading meter. When the meter must be placed in series with the load, connections must be firm and adequate to carry currents involved. Hence, the clamp-around type ac meter has been widely used since it permits current readings without disturbing the circuit. As shown in Figure 9-20, the meter structure utilizes a curved metal section with a swival joint. This curved loop section thus can be opened, placed around a single conductor, and closed for obtaining a reading. Current flow through the conductor creates magnetic lines of force which are intercepted by the curved loop of the meter. Thus, the magnetic fields induce a voltage in the single-turn metal loop. This loop forms the primary of a transformer, with the secondary winding connected to the meter. Since induced voltage is proportional to current flow in the conductor, current readings are indicated on the calibrated meter scale. A rotary switch is provided for selecting the

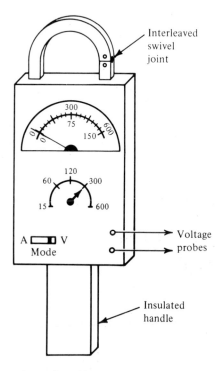

Figure 9–20 Clamp-Around ac Meter

desired meter scale range. Two terminals are also available on the meter for taking voltage measurements.

9–15. WATT-HOUR AND POWER-FACTOR METERS

The *kilowatt hour* refers to the practical unit of electric energy where electric power consumption is related to elapsed time. Thus, the product of elapsed time and power is a measurement of electric energy with respect to *watt hours*. A common-type watt-hour meter extensively utilized in residential installations is shown in Figure 9–21(A). This meter gives a continuous indication of the amplitude of power consumed in relation to elapsed time. As shown, four dial faces are utilized to register the kilowatt hours of the electric energy used. Such meters are read periodically by power company employees for billing purposes.

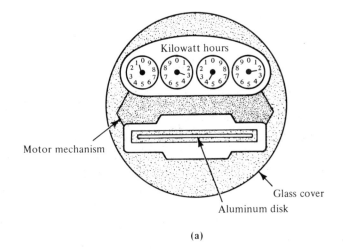

Kilowatt hours

Motor mechanism

Glass cover

Aluminum disk

(a)

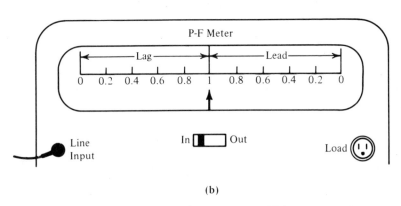

P-F Meter

Lag — Lead

0   0.2   0.4   0.6   0.8   1   0.8   0.6   0.4   0.2   0

Line
Input

In ▮ Out

Load

(b)

Figure 9–21   Watt-Hour Meter and Power-Factor Dial

The watt-hour meter utilizes an induction-type unit in which current is induced into an aluminum disk. The latter obtains torque because of the energy induced by two electromagnets. One of the latter is constructed of heavy wire in series with the line and provides for an in-phase flux condition. The second electromagnet is made up of fine wire and connected across the line with an additional coil for obtaining a 90° phase shift (current lag). The two coils in combination provide the rotating magnetic field for turning the disk. Basically, the assembly is similar to a motor with the torque in the rotating disk proportional to the power. Permanent magnets are mounted in close proximity to the rotating disk. When the magnetic fields are picked up by the disk, eddy currents are produced within the disk and hence create a torque opposed to the disk rotation.

The retarding torque produced by the magnetic currents is directly proportional to the speed of the rotating disk. Hence, the speed of the rotation is proportional to the power consumed by the load. The dials are thus calibrated to provide for kilowatt-hour readings. The amount of power consumed by the load is indicated by the difference in meter readings taken over a fixed period of elapsed time.

The dial face of a power-factor (PF) meter is shown in Figure 9–21(B). Such a meter is useful in testing industrial electrical installations for deviations in *power factor*. When the power factor is less than 1 it should be corrected to reduce excessive currents. When the power-consuming load (such as a motor) is not purely resistive, phase-angle changes occur between voltage and current. An inductive effect, for instance, causes additional current to circulate even though there is no increase in power. (Pure inductors or capacitors have reactance but do not consume electric energy.) The increased current circulating through reactors is returned to the generator, but the generator must still provide for the additional currents. In addition, larger conductors are necessary to carry the additional current (see Sec. 1–1 and Eq. 1–5).

The meter shown in Figure 9–21(B) is placed in series with the line and the load. The degree of lag or lead is then read directly on the dial. A switch is provided for bypassing the meter movement and applying the line input directly to the load. In many meters a dial pointer remains at a given reading until another measurement is made. The lack of spring return for the dial pointer provides for a fixed reading, even when the switch is in the off position for the meter movement. Thus, power-factor corrections can be compared to previous readings.

9–16. FUNCTION GENERATORS

We with other instruments, function generators are available in a variety of models. These generators are useful in design and test applications because they furnish precisely formed signals that can be strictly controlled in frequency and time. The signals available include sine waves, square waves, and triangle waveforms. Depending on the capabilities of the instrument, various degrees of signal modification are provided. A substantially flat response is present, often ranging to 3 MHz with less than 0.5-dB variation. The frequency range for some instruments extends from 0.003 Hz through 3 MHz, with adjustments permitted throughout. The square-wave signals have a high harmonic content, permitting a waveshape that has a rise and fall time of less than 75 ns. Distortion for the sine-wave signals is often substantially less than 1%. The triangle waveform may have a linearity that does not deviate more than 1% beyond 300 kHz for many instruments. Such instruments often provide a 50-dB switch-type attenuator that is variable between ranges with an adjustable waveshape symmetry from a few percentage points to a value below 100.

9–17. DISTORTION METERS

Distortion meters are sometimes referred to as distortion analyzers and are useful for measuring the percentage of distortion present in waveforms. Some instruments measure total harmonic distortion values of less than 0.5% within a range up to 100 kHz. Some instruments of this type are also designed to test for intermodulation distortion (see Table 12–4).

9–18. FREQUENCY COUNTERS

The frequency counter devices provide for an accurate reading of the frequency signals by displaying them in digital form. Some instruments have a range extending between a low of 15 Hz to well over 200 MHz. Most have provisions for a direct connection to sample the signals to be measured as well as having optional connection for an antenna for interception of a broadcast signal. Such frequency counters utilize a crystal-controlled time base to provide for measurement accuracy and circuit stability. Accuracy can be established to have a variation of less than 1 or 2 Hz around the range of 200 MHz.

Portable hand-held frequency counters are also available. With over a half-dozen LED display digits present and automatic decimal placement built in, extreme accuracy is available. Such portable units operate on a few low-voltage batteries, and some have rechargable battery provisions.

10 Graphic Symbols of Basic Components

10-1. BASIC DIODE TYPES

Solid-state sections termed *zones* are fabricated into negative (n) and positive (p) units which can be formed into junctions creating diodes and transistors (see also Sec. 10-5). A *p-n* junction has a low-resistance conducting path for current flow in one direction but a high-resistance barrier in the opposite direction. Thus, these devices are useful for rectification purposes (see Sec. 2-35) and for the detection of modulated signals (see Sec. 2-42).

A typical diode symbol is shown in Figure 10-1(A). An alternative symbol is that shown in (B) using a circle. As shown in (A), the triangular section of the symbol represents the *anode* (conforming to the solid-state *p zone*) and the straight-line section identifies the cathode (conforming to the *n zone*). When the applied voltage connects the positive battery terminal to the anode and the negative to the cathode as at (C), the term *forward bias* is used to identify the coincidence of connecting the positive battery terminal to the *p* zone and negative battery terminal to the *n* zone. Under this condition current flows to the degree established by electric pressure and the amount of circuit resistance. If the battery polarity is reversed as shown in (D), the term *reverse bias* is used to indicate a negative battery polarity to the *p* zone and a positive battery polarity to the *n* zone. For this circuit there is little or no current flow, depending on the design factors of the *p-n* junction.

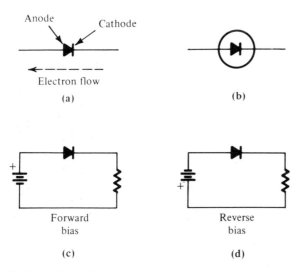

Figure 10–1 Basic Diode Factors

10–2. PHOTODIODES

Photodiode and light-emitting diode symbols are shown in Figure 10–2(A) and (B). The symbol shown in (A) utilizes the arrows that point toward the diode as representative of light input. Such a photodiode converts light energy into electric signals by utilization of a *p-n* junction designed for sensitivity to light photons impinging on the junction. When the output terminals of the photodiode are connected to a closed

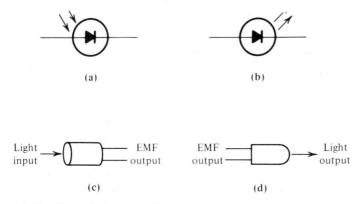

Figure 10–2 Photodiodes and LEDs

circuit the light energy is converted to electron flow. The physical structure may appear as shown at (C) and these diodes are utilized for alarm systems, industrial control, and counting systems based on the interruption of light reaching the photodiode.

The light-emitting diode (LED) is shown in (B). In this device the application of forward bias to the *p-n* junction structure converts electric energy to light. The latter is produced with a minimum of heat generation. The LED units are useful for indicator lights, backlight for electronic watches, readout devices for test instruments, and other similar functions.

10–3. SWITCHING DIODES

A number of diodes are utilized for gating and switching purposes in digital circuits, combining circuits and power supplies that need be turned on only at specific times. The tunnel diode symbol shown in Figure 10–3(A) has negative-resistance characteristics that permit it to be used for special gating and switching functions. Switching is more rapid than junction transistors by a ratio of over 100 to 1. Also, the tunnel diodes are less sensitive to temperature changes than average transistors and thus more stable in many applications where temperature changes prevail. The tunnel diodes also have greater immunity to the adverse effects of nuclear radiation and hence are useful for gating applications in this area.

The tunnel diode is so named because of the *tunnel effect* prevailing at the *p-n* junction because of the presence of an extremely narrow potential barrier. In essence, electric particles reaching the potential barrier between the *p-n* junction disappear and reappear almost instantly at the other side, as though they tunneled under the barrier instead of penetrating it. The electron particle transfer at the speed of light constitutes the rapidity of the switching mode.

The symbol for a Schottky diode is shown in Figure 10–3(B). This diode is far superior to the conventional junction diode in the speed by which it can be switched on or off. It has a lower voltage drop across it than the junction diodes and hence less power loss. It has been extensively utilized for digital functions in integrated circuitry (also see Figure 4–8). Once current flow is initiated in the Schottky diode the conductivity is limited only by the unit's very low internal resistance.

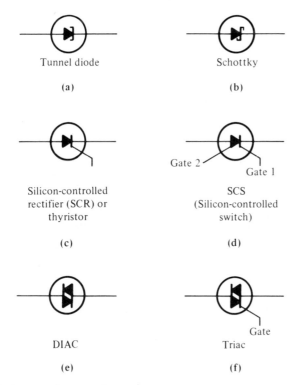

Tunnel diode

(a)

Schottky

(b)

Silicon-controlled
rectifier (SCR) or
thyristor

(c)

Gate 2

Gate 1

SCS
(Silicon-controlled
switch)

(d)

DIAC

(e)

Gate

Triac

(f)

Figure 10–3 Switching Diodes

Within the solid-state structure of the Schottky diode a positive-charge hole flow is inhibited; hence, the diode is a majority-carrier unit utilizing only electron flow. Consequently, recovery time is limited only by the internal capacitance. Since the *junction* diode has a recovery time related to the minority-carrier (hole) charge storage, it has a lower recovery time. The Schottky is superior by a ratio of over 100 to 1.

The silicon-controlled rectifier (SCR) symbol is shown in Figure 10–3(C). This unit has conductive characteristics similar to the *p-n* diode described in Sec. 10–1. As a switching and gating unit it permits the control of high electric power by a small potential of negligible power. With an applied potential of dc, the diode presents an open circuit. When a trigger voltage is applied between the gate and cathode terminals, the unit conducts fully. Once the unit is switched into conduction the removal of the gate potential has no effect on current reduction. Thus, when the SCR has latched on when triggered by a gating pulse, conduction can only be stopped by removal of the anode voltage or by reversing the polarity of the voltage between anode and cathode (see Sec. 2–41).

A silicon-controlled switch (SCS) is illustrated in Figure 10–3(D). This unit has an additional gate element and can be triggered into conduction by either a positive- or a negative-polarity pulse. Unlike the SCR, the SCS can be turned off by gate control (see Sec. 2–41).

The dual-diode unit termed the Diac is shown in Figure 10–3(E). The two diodes are joined in opposite-polarity configuration so that special gating characteristics can be achieved. The Diac remains in a nonconducting state until a specific breakdown voltage is applied. At that time conduction occurs and the unit can pass current in either direction. Such devices are rated at specific breakover (gating) potentials. If the Diac is identified as a 6-V type, the application of any lower voltage does not cause conduction and the Diac maintains a high resistance with virtually no current flow. When the 6-V breakover potential is applied, both diodes have the ability to conduct (depending on the bias polarity).

The Diac shown in (E) can be designed with a gate terminal to form a Triac as shown in Figure 10–3(F). Thus, the three-terminal unit becomes an electronic switch similar in characteristics to the silicon-controlled rectifier except that the Triac can conduct in both directions. Thus, the Triac can process ac signals without rectification.

10-4. REGULATING AND REACTIVE DIODES

The diode that has voltage-regulating characteristics is shown in symbol form in Figure 10–4(A). This diode is termed a *zener* and is used in power supplies for maintaining a fairly constant voltage level during current-drain variations on the power supply. This diode, a silicon type, conducts current when it is forward biased as with the basic diodes. The zener region, however, exists for a specific range of reverse-bias potentials. For a low reverse-bias voltage the internal resistance is high and remains so until the reverse-bias potential is raised to the critical point (called the zener region). During the latter the internal resistance drops sharply and conductivity occurs. Once the zener region is achieved the voltage drop across the unit remains constant within specified limits for

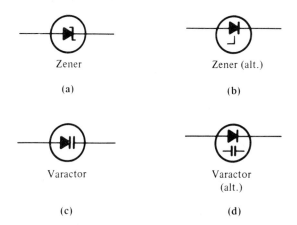

Zener

(a)

Zener (alt.)

(b)

Varactor

(c)

Varactor
(alt.)

(d)

Figure 10–4 Regulating and Reactive Diodes

regulation purposes, as described more fully in Sec. 2–40. An alternative symbol for the zener diode is shown in (B).

A diode having reactive characteristics that can be altered for tuning purposes is illustrated in Figure 10–4(C). An alternative symbol is illustrated in (D). This unit is termed a *varactor diode* and exhibits capacitance characteristics proportional to the applied reverse-bias potentials. Thus, the varactor diode can be placed across an inductor to form a parallel resonant circuit, or in series to form a series-resonant circuit. The resonant frequency can be altered for tuning purposes by regulating the amount of reverse-bias potential applied to the diode, as discussed in Sec. 2–32 and illustrated in Figure 2–24(C).

10–5. JUNCTION TRANSISTORS

Various junction transistor symbols are shown in Figure 10–5. In (A) the *pnp* type is illustrated with the emitter arrow pointing *inward* to designate the *pnp* design. For these transistors the elements are the *base*, the *collector*, and the *emitter*. On occasion the transistor symbol is shown without the circle as in (B). For the *pnp* transistor the forward bias applied at the input would be a positive polarity at the emitter with respect to a negative base. On the output side reverse bias would place a negative polarity at the collector with respect to a positive emitter. Bias con-

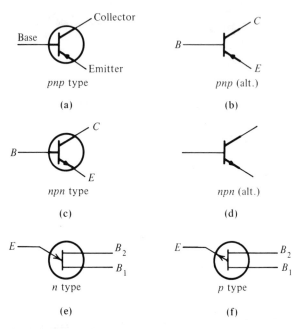

Figure 10–5 Junction Transistors

siderations depend on circuit configurations and reference should be made to Secs. 2–2, 2–4, and 2–6, where circuit applications are illustrated and discussed.

The *npn* transistor is shown in Figure 10–5(C) with the alternate in (D). The unijunction transistor is shown in (E) and (F). These preceded the field-effect transistors and were also formed of *n-p* junctions as with transistors. The *n* type is shown in (E) and the *p* type in (F). Two base terminals plus an emitter are illustrated for these types.

10–6. JUNCTION FIELD-EFFECT TYPES

Symbols for the junction field-effect transistors (JFET) are shown in Figure 10–6. For the FET units the terms *gate, drain,* and *source* are substituted for the base, collector, and emitter designations for the junction transistor. The *n*-channel type is shown in Figure 10–6(A) with the gate arrow pointing inward. The *p*-channel shown in (B) has the gate arrow pointing outward. Dual-gate types are also widely used and are use-

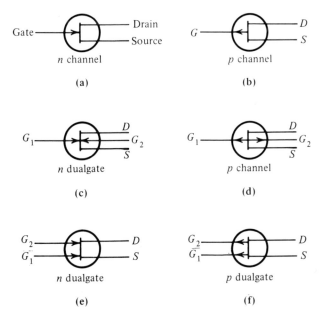

Figure 10–6 Junction Field-Effect Transistors

ful in switching systems. For the dual-gate type shown in (C) the gate terminal (G_1) at the left is retained and another gate terminal (G_2) is shown on the drain–source elements side. When the arrows point inward the n type is indicated. For the p-channel type shown in (D), the gate arrows point outward.

Dual-gate FET units are also shown in (E) and (F), with the gate inputs both at the left. For the n-channel type the gate arrows again point inward, as for the dual-gate type shown in (C). For the p-channel type, the gate arrows point outward, as for the unit in (D). Circuits and applications for the FET units are covered in Secs. 2–2, 2–5, and 2–7 (see also Figure 2–11).

10–7. METAL-OXIDE FIELD-EFFECT TYPES

Symbols for the metal-oxide field-effect transistors (MOSFETS) are shown in Figure 10–7. Terminal depletion types are illustrated in (A) through (D), with both the n and p types depicted. The element indicat-

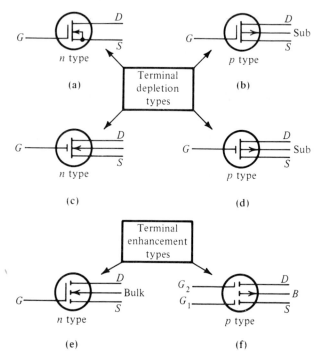

Figure 10–7 MOSFET Types

ed as *Sub* refers to the substrate, the foundation slab for the FET construction. The terminal enhancement types are shown in (E) and (F) and are characterized by broken-line segments also associated with the insulated-gate characteristics of the MOSFET. For this reason this transistor is also known as the insulated-gate field-effect transistor (IGFET) as discussed in Sec. 2–3 (see also Secs. 2–5 and 2–7).

10–8. SIGNAL WAVESHAPE SYMBOLS

Symbols for basic signal waveforms are shown in Figure 10–8. Several cycles of a pure sine wave are shown in (A). This is a fundamental-frequency waveform containing no harmonic signals. The pure sine wave is characterized by a succession of positive and negative alternations, with each alternation having the same amplitude as the others, each having a gradual incline and decline, and all having identical widths (also see Fig-

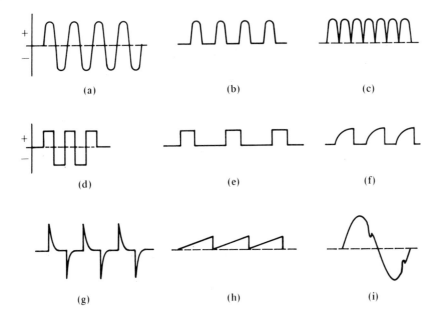

Figure 10–8 Waveshape Symbols

ure 9–11). When a sine-wave signal is processed by a half-wave power supply (Sec. 2–35) the result is a succession of single-polarity alternations as shown in Figure 10–8(B). Here, the negative alternations have been eliminated by the rectification process. For full-wave rectification (Sec. 2–36) the unipolarity alternations have no gaps between them, as shown in Figure 10–8(C).

The symbols for square waves are shown in Figure 10–8(D). Here the waveform has positive and negative alternations as with the sine wave shown in (A), but the waveform alternations have flat tops as shown. Square waves of this type are made up of the fundamental frequency plus a succession of even and odd harmonics of decreasing amplitude for the higher-order harmonics. Pulse waveforms are shown in Figure 10–8(E) and these are of single polarity and can be either a train of positive pulses or a train of negative pulses. Unlike the square wave shown at (D), the pulses at (E) can have different spaces between them. Thus, the pulses could be half as narrow as shown for the same spacing or they could be of any duration and any interval between successive pulses. Pulses are made up of the fundamental signal plus successive odd harmonics of descending amplitude.

The waveforms shown in Figure 10–8(F) are integrated pulses. Thus, lower-frequency signal components predominate as discussed in Sec. 3–1. For the integration of negative pulses the waveform shown in (F) would be inverted. The spiked pulses illustrated in Figure 10–8 represent the differentiation of a pulse train. Thus, high-frequency signals predominate, as discussed in Sec. 3–2.

The waveform shown in Figure 10–8(H) are sawtooth signals, formed as discussed in Sec. 3–6. The gradual rise and abrupt decline make this waveform useful for sweeping electron beams across the inner faceplate of display tubes. Similar sawtooth signals can, of course, have a negative polarity. As with all waveforms other than a pure sine wave, the sawtooth has ascending harmonic components in addition to the fundamental frequency.

Complex waveforms are generated by musical instruments, voice, and other sound sources and consist of a mixture of numerous signal frequencies. The signal shown in Figure 10–8(I) illustrates the initial effect of a harmonic on a fundamental frequency. This waveform represents the fundamental frequency plus a second harmonic component.

10–9. CONDUCTORS AND RESISTORS

Circuit conduction paths are represented by straight lines that interconnect components. When lines cross as shown in Figure 10–9(A) there is no connection between the two and hence no path for electric conduction. When separate lines are connected the intersection is emphasized by a dot, as shown in Figure 10–9(B). When an electric conductor is housed within a shield it is represented as shown in (C) (here the external metal shield is placed at ground potential). A two-conductor twin-lead type transmission line is represented by the symbol shown in (D).

The symbol shown in (E) represents a conductive path only if the potential present exceeds a given value and has sufficient electromotive force to bridge the gap. Such spark gaps have been widely used in television receivers and other high-voltage optical scan systems for providing a discharge path when potentials exceed a desired amplitude.

Illustrations in part (F) represent a fixed resistor and the symbol for a variable resistor is shown in (G). A two-terminal variable resistor connection is shown in (H). For the symbol shown in (I), a thermister is represented. This is a resistor that alters the amount of resistance for a

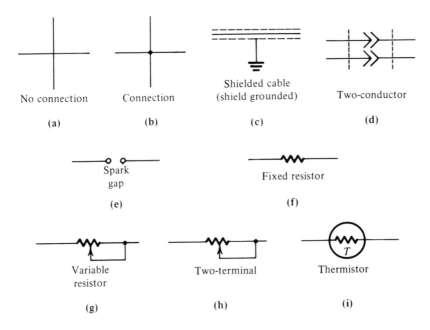

No connection

(a)

Connection

(b)

Shielded cable
(shield grounded)

(c)

Two-conductor

(d)

Spark
gap

(e)

Fixed resistor

(f)

Variable
resistor

(g)

Two-terminal

(h)

Thermistor

(i)

Figure 10-9 Conductor and Resistor Symbols

change in temperature. It is useful in minimizing voltage surges when the equipment is first turned on. In such applications the resistance decreases sufficiently after warm-up to pass the desired amount of current. Thermisters are also available that undergo a resistance *increase* for a rise in temperature.

10-10. INDUCTORS AND TRANSFORMERS

Various inductor symbols are shown in Figure 10-10. In part (A) the single inductors are illustrated with the air core representing the simplest coil. A metallic core inductor is represented by one or two straight lines running parallel with the coil as shown. Variable cores are represented by arrows (see also Sec. 1-3). Transformers are shown in (B). Usually the primary (P) is shown at the left of the secondary (S), as indicated by the air core type illustrated. A fixed iron-core transformer has one or two straight lines between the windings, as also shown. For the tuned

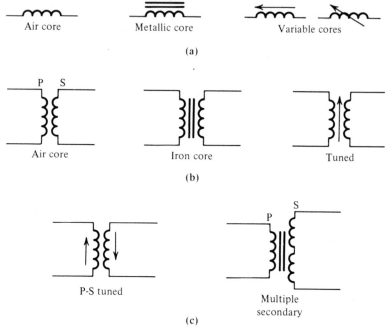

Figure 10–10   Inductor Symbols

transformer an arrow is shown. When both the primary and secondary windings are tuned, individual arrows are used, as shown in (C). Usually, an arrow pointing upward indicates that tuning adjustments can be made from the top of the chassis; a downward-pointing arrow indicates underchassis tuning. Multiple secondaries can also be depicted, as shown in (C) (see also Sec. 1–10).

10–11. CAPACITOR SYMBOLS

Basic capacitor symbols are illustrated in Figure 10–11. In part (A) the standard symbol for a fixed capacitor is shown as well as the variable capacitor and the split stator. The latter is a dual capacitor unit with a fixed stator section and dual rotor sections that are turned by a single shaft (see also Sec. 1–4). The split-stator capacitor is widely used in push-pull RF amplification. When individual capacitors serving separate

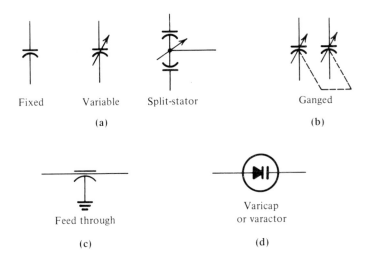

Fixed   Variable   Split-stator   Ganged

(a)   (b)

Feed through   Varicap
                        or varactor

(c)   (d)

Figure 10–11   Capacitor Symbols

circuits are linked together so that the rotors can be turned by a common shaft, they are termed *ganged capacitors*, as shown in (B). These are employed in radio tuners, where they are part of the resonant circuits in RF amplifiers, mixers, and oscillators.

The feed-through type of capacitor is shown in (C). This is a three-terminal unit utilized at high frequencies for bypass purposes (see also Sec. 7–19). The variable-capacitor diode is shown in (D). This device has a reactance change for applied voltage (see Secs. 2–32 and 10–4).

10–12. TRANSDUCERS

Various transducer symbols are shown in Figure 10–12. The standard symbol for a microphone is shown in (A) and a phonograph pickup in (B). A tape recorder head is often represented as in (C), or as in (D), where the alternate symbol is shown. The double-headed arrow indicates the dual function of record and playback. An arrow pointing inward only indicates the record function, while an arrow pointing outward only indicates playback.

A speaker symbol is shown in (E) and a picture tube in (F). The oscilloscope display tube is usually pictured as shown in (G).

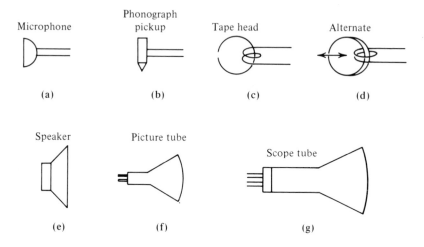

Figure 10–12 Transducer Symbols

10–13. SWITCHES AND RELAYS

Various switch and relay symbols are shown in Figure 10–13. The most basic switch, the single-pole single-throw (SPST) type, is shown in part (A). In (B) the double-pole single-throw (DPST) switch is shown. A single-pole double-throw (SPDT) unit is shown in (C). Here the arrows represent fixed segments, in contrast to those in (A) and (B). The single-pole single-throw switch with a double-break function is shown in (D). In contrast to the SPST in (A), the switch in (D) has the movable section completely disengaged from either side. This switch represents a normally open design. The symbol for the normally closed SPST switch is shown in (E).

A normally closed double-pole single-throw switch is shown in (F). Again, for this symbol the movable arms are the straight-line sections and not the arrows, in contrast to the switch shown in (B). A double-pole double-throw switch is shown in (G), and a single-pole double-throw unit is shown in (H).

Relays contain a coil that is magnetically activated by a potential either to close or to open a switching circuit. A typical single-pole single-throw relay is shown in (I). This is a normally closed type and when current flows through the coil the straight arm is pulled upward away

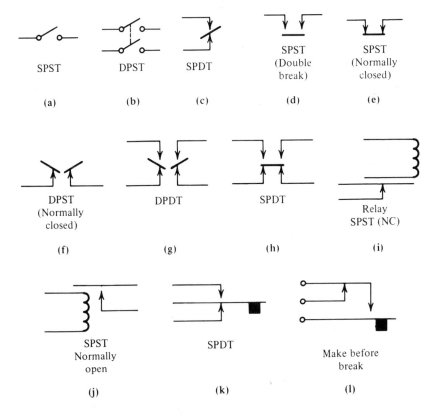

Figure 10-13 Switch and Relay Symbols

from the arrow head to open the circuit. The normally open single-pole single-throw relay is shown in (J). Here the magnetic fields pull the movable arm down to touch the arrowhead line for closing the switch. A telephone-type single-pole double-throw relay is shown in (K), and a make-before-break relay is shown in (L).

10-14. MISCELLANEOUS GRAPHIC SYMBOLS

Miscellaneous symbols are shown in Figure 10-14. Included is the triangle widely used for amplifier representation. Here, the line at the left (at right angles to the parallel line of the triangle) indicates the input. The

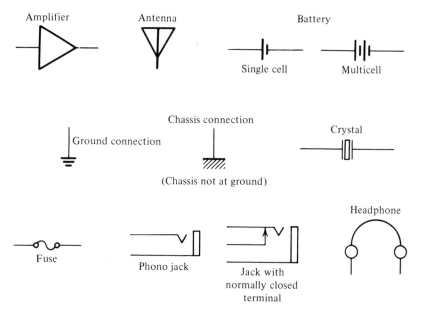

Figure 10-14 Miscellaneous Graphic Symbols

output is usually shown leaving the triangle point. The two commonly used ground connections are also shown and with most manufacturers the chassis ground utilizes the distinctive symbol shown. The remaining symbols include the crystal representation, the fuse, phono (or earphone) jacks, and the headphone.

11 | Complete System Block Diagrams

11-1. AM TRANSMISSION–RECEPTION

The basic amplitude-modulation process is shown in block diagram form in Figure 11–1(A). A crystal-controlled oscillator is used for maintaining a stable frequency for the generated carrier signal. The RF output is fed to successive buffer amplifiers to bring the signal to the level required for driving the final carrier power amplifiers. The carrier modulation process uses low-frequency amplifiers as shown. When an audio signal is involved for modulation, the input is from a microphone, phonograph, or other source, such as recording tape. For television signals, the input consists of the video signal plus synchronization and blanking signals. The modulation signal is in series with the power supply to the final RF amplifier, and hence the modulation process is performed as detailed in Secs. 8–1 and 8–2. Reference should also be made to Figures 8–1 and 8–2, which show the output circuitry as well as the sideband components.

A block diagram of the basic circuits comprising the receiver for AM signals is shown in Figure 11–1(B). The circuit sequence and functions constitute the *superheterodyne* principle commonly utilized in most receiving systems. As shown, the signal from an antenna is applied to an RF amplifier, although in the less expensive receivers the RF stage may be omitted and the antenna fed directly to the mixer circuit. In either case the incoming AM signal is mixed with the signal generated by the oscillator and the heterodyning process that occurs produces an intermediate-frequency signal. Subsequent IF amplifiers reject original signals

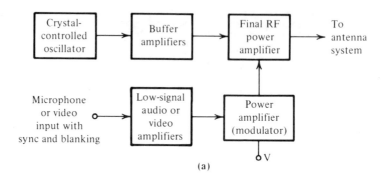

(a)

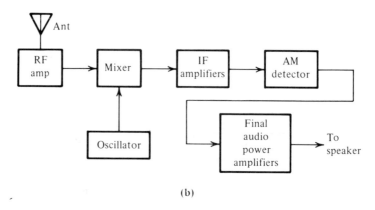

(b)

Figure 11–1 AM Transmission-Reception System

and pass only the intermediate-frequency signal. Thus, the amplitude of such signals is raised as described in Secs. 2–14 and 2–15. The tuning of the RF amplifier, the mixer, and oscillator is performed simultaneously so that the same *difference frequency* is obtained by the heterodyning process. Thus, the IF amplifiers receive only a single-frequency signal at resonance, with sufficient bandwidth to accommodate the sidebands. For public-entertainment reception practices the intermediate frequency is 455 kHz.

The intermediate-frequency signal is applied to a detector system and processed as described in Sec. 2–42 and illustrated in Figure 2–31. The resultant audio signal is then applied to several amplifier circuits to increase signal amplitude to that required for loudspeakers.

11–2. FM (MONO) TRANSMITTER

The frequency-modulation process is more complex than the amplitude-modulation process described in Sec. 11–1. For frequency modulation, there are several methods that can be employed. A basic system is described in Sec. 8–3 and illustrated in Figure 8–3. In that system a phase-locked loop is utilized to assure stability to a variable-frequency oscillator modulated by a reactance-control system to which audio signals are applied. Sideband factors are discussed in Sec. 8–4. Another system is the *indirect frequency modulation* process illustrated in Figure 11–2. In this system advantage is taken of the fact that some significant similarities prevail between AM and FM for low levels of frequency modulation. For the latter, very small carrier deviations (where the carrier change is less than approximately 30°) result in the production of *only two* significant sidebands, as in AM. The only difference is that the two sidebands obtained for low levels of FM are displaced 90° in relation to the carrier. (In AM the two sidebands are in phase with the carrier.) The frequency-modulation process illustrated in Figure 11–2 is based on similarities described in the preceding paragraph. Essentially, amplitude modulation is converted to frequency modulation by displacing the two sidebands 90° and recombining them with a carrier. In shifting the phase of the side-

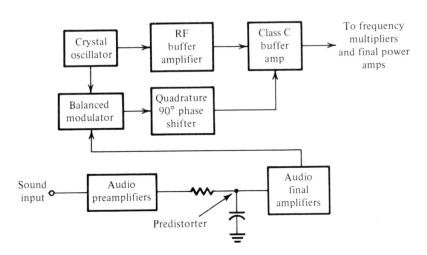

Figure 11–2 FM (Mono) Transmitter

band signals in this manner, *phase modulation* occurs. A *predistorter* is utilized for correction purposes as described later in this section.

As shown in Figure 11–2, a crystal oscillator is utilized and its signal is amplified and multiplied in frequency to that required for the final carrier signal. The audio signal from the final audio amplifier is applied to a balanced modulator in conjunction with a signal from the crystal oscillator as shown (see Sec. 3–15). In this special modulator, the audio signal causes the carrier signal to be amplitude modulated and hence two sideband signals are created. The latter are applied to a quadrature circuit and shifted in phase by 90°, and then combined with the carrier signal, producing frequency modulation. As described in Sec. 3–15, the balanced modulator suppresses a carrier signal so that the output consists only of the sideband signals.

As mentioned earlier in this section, the phase-shift process produces phase modulation wherein the deviation of the carrier is related to the *frequency* of the audio-modulating signal multiplied by the maximum phase shift utilized. Consequently, the higher-frequency audio signals produce a greater carrier frequency deviation than do lower-frequency audio signals. This must be corrected because in frequency modulation only the *amplitude* of the audio signals determines the amount of carrier frequency deviation. The predistorter circuit shown in Figure 11–2 is the correction circuit that produces the required frequency modulation. The series resistor has a high ohmic value compared to the ohmic value of the reactance of the shunt capacitor (for the full range of audio-signal frequencies). Consequently, no appreciable phase change results for any audio signals appearing across the predistorter. However, since the output to the audio final amplifier is obtained only *from across* the shunt capacitor, the amplitude of the audio signals differs for various frequencies. As the frequencies of the signals rise, capacitive reactance decreases and hence there is an increasing shunting effect. The result is a decrease in the amplitude of the audio signals as they rise in frequency. Since the phase-modulation process increases carrier deviation for higher-frequency signals, the predistorter opposes this process and hence nullifies the characteristics of phase modulation. Thus, the process is equivalent to that of pure frequency modulation.

11–3. FM (MONO) RECEIVER

A frequency-modulation receiver (mono) is illustrated in block diagram form in Figure 11–3. The superheterodyne principle is utilized in similar

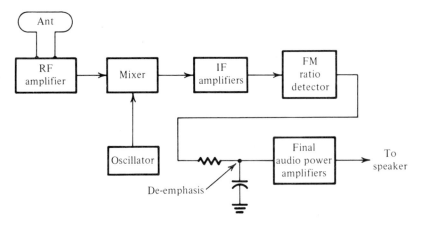

Figure 11–3 FM (Mono) Receiver

fashion to the AM receiver discussed in Sec. 11–1. For public-entertainment FM receivers, the intermediate frequency is usually 10.7 MHz. The output from the IF amplifiers is fed to a detector sensitive to frequency modulation. Although several types are available, the ratio-detector circuit is the most commonly used (see Sec. 2–43 and Figure 2–32). The output from the ratio detector is applied to a series resistor/shunt capacitor combination for deemphasis. The latter process restores the proper amplitude to the audio signals which had been altered during the preemphasis process of frequency modulation transmission (see Sec. 8–3). As with the AM receiver, final audio power amplifiers raise the signal to the level required for application to loudspeakers.

11–4. FM (STEREO) TRANSMITTER

The basic sections of a stereo FM transmission system are shown in Figure 11–4. Audio signals picked up by microphones are applied to a right-channel input as well as a left-channel input, as shown. The system is more complex than would be the case if two separate carriers were modulated to produce left- and right-channel signals. To conserve spectrum space the stereo transmission must be compatible so that a mono receiver can process the stereo signals as it would a mono signal. At the same time a stereo receiver must be capable of processing mono reception. Thus, left- and right-channel signals undergo special mixing and are

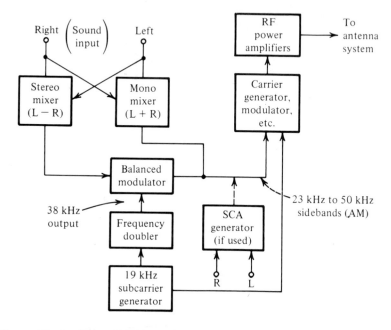

Figure 11–4 Stereo FM Transmitter

applied to balanced modulators for carrier suppression, as shown in Figure 11–4 (see also Sec. 3–15).

For FM transmission, 100% modulation is defined as a carrier deviation of 75 kHz each side of the carrier resting frequency. In multiplex systems such as stereo the imposed limits may not be exceeded; hence, the various modulating signals encountered in stereo transmission must utilize a modulation process confined to the existing limits imposed. The nominal audio frequency range is from at least 50 Hz to 15 kHz with a 75-μs preemphasis for each channel. Modulating-signal frequencies can thus extend beyond 15 kHz to perform the multiplex process. This is possible because the higher-frequency modulating signals increase the *rate* of carrier deviation. (The *extent* of carrier-signal deviation on each side of the center frequency is still determined by the amplitude of a modulating signal.)

As shown in Figure 11–4, compatibility is maintained because a mono signal is transmitted by adding the two signals received from the right- and left-channel sources. The mono mixer signal (L + R) is applied to the modulating section of the primary FM transmitter and the process creates the *main channel*. The spectrum frequencies are illustrated in Figure 11–5. As shown, the mono modulating signal occupies the lower-frequency section of the total modulating-signal spectrum utilized for the multiplexing process. To form the separate left and right channels of stereo, an additional signal is utilized and multiplexed. For the latter process, a *difference* signal is formed by subtracting the right-channel signal from the left-channel signal (a process wherein the L and R signals are applied to a mixer with the right signal 180° out of phase with the left). Such a *difference* signal modulates an additional carrier (subcarrier) and the amplitude-modulating process forms sidebands which share in modulating the transmitted FM carrier as shown in Figure 11–4. The subcarrier is suppressed and hence must be re-formed and reinstated at the stereo receiver.

The frequency of the subcarrier is 38 kHz and this frequency is obtained by doubling a 19-kHz signal produced by the subcarrier generator. This 19-kHz signal modulates the carrier for synchronization purposes during stereo detection at the receiver. The 19-kHz signal is referred to as the *pilot subcarrier* and is held to $+2$ Hz of assigned frequency. The 19-kHz signal modulates the transmitted FM carrier by only 10% (an adequate amount that enables the receiver to derive this signal and double its frequency to form the 38-kHz subcarrier signal for recombination with the stereo sidebands (see also Sec. 11–5).

As shown in Figure 11–5, the sidebands generated by the modulation of the 38-kHz subcarrier with the L − R signals are located above

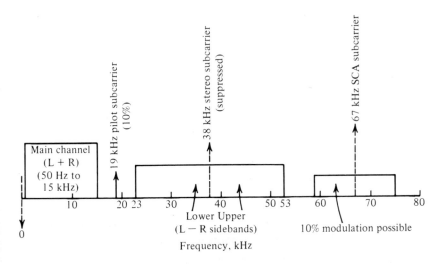

Figure 11–5 Stereo Multiplex FM Spectrum

the mono modulating signals. Such sidebands occupy the region between 23 and 53 kHz. As with the mono signal, audio-signal frequency response extends from approximately 50 Hz to 15 kHz. Hence, the complete multiplex modulating signal consists of a mono (L + R) signal in the audio range, a supersonic 19-kHz pilot subcarrier signal, plus a L − R supersonic signal with suppressed 38-kHz carrier.

The 19-kHz pilot signal for public-entertainment transmission is granted a 10% injection as mentioned earlier, thus providing a carrier frequency deviation of 7.5 kHz on each side of center frequency. With no SCA transmission (discussed later in this section) there is a 90% modulation possibility for the other signals during multiplex transmission. This 90% capability is divided between the mono and stereo channels. This 90%-modulation possibility is shared by the L + R and L − R signals. Hence both cannot simultaneously modulate the transmission by 90%. The L + R can modulate the main channel by 90% during mono broadcasting, at which time the stereo sidebands would not modulate the FM carrier. The L − R sidebands are capable of only 45% modulation as a maximum. If stereo sidebands are modulating at the 45% level, the L + R modulating maximum is 45%.

When the SCA (*Subsidiary Communications Authority*) system is utilized, it connects to the modulator section as shown in Figure 11–4. This permits an FM station to broadcast on another channel in addition to the standard FM. The SCA transmission is for private subscribers who pay a fee for background music in public places. The block for the SCA section shown in Figure 11–4 represents a complete low-power transmitter (compared to the main transmitter) with a center subcarrier frequency of 67 kHz (the latter frequency has been generally adopted as a standard for stereo–SCA combination stations). The spectrum space for the SCA signal is also illustrated in Figure 11–5. With stereo, the SCA injection is held to 10% and hence causes a carrier deviation of only 7.5 kHz on each side of center frequency. This 10% injection for SCA added to the 10% for the pilot subcarrier reduces the remaining modulation capability to 80%.

11–5. FM (STEREO) RECEIVER

A block diagram of an FM stereo receiver system is illustrated in Figure 11–6. Note that the initial stages following the antenna constitute a complete *mono FM receiver* (RF, mixer, oscillator, IF amplifiers, and detector). The output from this section is applied to a composite signal

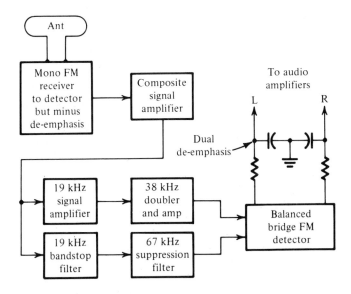

Figure 11–6 Stereo FM Receiver System

amplifier as shown and then applied to both a 19-kHz signal amplifier and a band-stop filter. After the signal has been amplified by the 19-kHz amplifier, it is applied to a frequency-doubler circuit, where the signal is raised to 38 kHz.

The composite signal appearing at the input of the 19-kHz band-stop filter encounters resonant circuits that pass all signals except the 19-kHz pilot carrier. Thus, the output from the band-stop filter consists of the 50-Hz to 15-kHz demodulated L + R signals, the 23- to 53-kHz sideband signals (L − R), and the 67-kHz SCA carrier signal if the latter is being transmitted. The SCA signals are removed by the suppression filter and the remaining signals are then fed to a balanced bridge demodulator circuit. Individual deemphasis circuitry is utilized as shown for the left and right channels and the resultant signals are applied to the stereo audio amplifier system.

11–6. TELEVISION (BLACK-AND-WHITE) TRANSMITTER

In public entertainment the picture (video) signal is used to amplitude-modulate the picture carrier in a fashion similar to that of the AM transmitter shown in Figure 11–1(A). The video signal not only contains the picture details but must also contains appropriate blanking and synchronization pulses for proper horizontal and vertical scanning purposes at both the transmitter and receiver (see also Sec. 8–5). The signal timing and other details for black-and-white as well as color TV are given in Sec. 11–8. The audio signals accompanying the video are frequency modulated (mono) similar to the system shown in Figure 11–2 and described in Sec. 11–2. In the United States the bandwidth allocation per television station as well as the specific frequency apply equally to black-and-white and color receivers. Tables 7–23 and 7–24 show allocation frequencies for both VHF and UHF stations.

11–7. COLOR SIGNAL SYNTHESIS

For television color signal transmission, it is necessary to utilize a camera designed so that it derives individual red, blue, and green signal information contained in the scene being televised. The initial process is discussed in Sec. 8–6 and illustrated in Figure 8–5. For conservation of space and in the interest of compatibility the signals are processed to produce a luminence signal with symbol Y, and in-phase color signal with symbol I, and an out-of-phase quadrature color signal identified as Q, as shown in Figure 8–5. These signals are then applied to filter circuits as shown in Figure 11–7, the block diagram of the basic circuits utilized in television color modulation, and discussed in Sec. 11–8. As mentioned in Sec. 11–6, the frequency allocations for television stations apply equally to black-and-white and color (see Tables 7–23 and 7–24).

11–8. TELEVISION (COLOR) TRANSMITTER

The basic circuitry for a television color modulation system is illustrated in block diagram form in Figure 11–7. As with black-and-white transmission discussed in Sec. 11–6, amplitude modulation is employed. A crystal carrier oscillator is utilized as shown to generate the carrier signal. Frequency multiplication is utilized to raise the frequency of the carrier to that required for final transmission. Class C buffer amplifiers raise the signal energy to the level needed to drive the final Class C modulated RF amplifiers. The modulated video signal is applied to a diplexer antenna system in conjunction with the FM sound signal so that both picture and sound may be transmitted by a single antenna system.

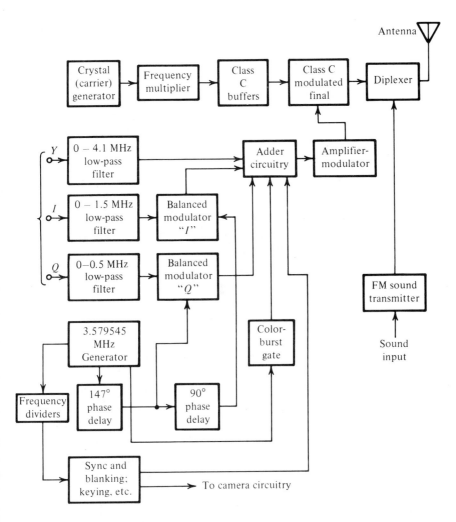

Figure 11–7 TV Color Modulation (AM)

The output signals obtained from the camera section (see Figure 8–5) are applied to appropriate filter circuits as shown in Figure 11–7. To minimize interference during color reception, the I signal is transmitted with one sideband extending to 1.48 MHz and the Q as a double-sideband signal each of which is 0.5 MHz distant from the frequency used for the subcarrier, but which is suppressed at the transmitter. The I and Q signals are applied to balanced modulators (see Sec. 3–15). These I

and Q signals modulate two subcarriers each of 3.579545 MHz but separated by a 90° phase difference, with the I signal phase leading the Q signal phase. The subcarrier signals, plus the I and Q signals, are suppressed and only the sideband components are attained at the output (see also Table 7–30).

A 3.58-MHz oscillator is utilized to inject a minimum of eight cycles on the horizontal blanking level for synchronization purposes at the receiver. The phase of the burst signal is 58° ahead of the I signal, as shown in Figure 11–7, with the I leading Q by 90°. All signals are combined in an adder circuit, including the synchronization and blanking pulses. All such signals are then amplified and utilized to amplitude-modulate the Class C amplifier as shown. A separate FM transmitter is audio-modulated and the carrier plus sideband signals are applied to a diplexer antenna system that uses a common antenna to propagate both video and sound signals.

11–9. TELEVISION RECEIVER SYSTEM

The television receiver system for either black-and-white or color reception is based on the superheterodyne principle (see Sec. 11–1). In contrast to the radio receiver, where only a single incoming carrier signal is heterodyned with the oscillator signal, the television receiver must heterodyne two incoming carrier signals with the oscillator signal. Thus, for any station tuned in, the tuner section oscillator signal is mixed with both the modulated video carrier (AM) and the modulated sound carrier (FM). Consequently, two intermediate-frequency signals are obtained, necessitating both an AM detector and an FM detector. In addition, the vertical and horizontal scanning signals must be synchronized at the receiver, and if the latter is color, additional circuitry is necessary. A block diagram of the basic circuits of a color television receiver is shown in Figure 11–8. The color receiver uses the identical circuits found in the black-and-white set but must supplement them with the additional circuits to process the color signals. In Figure 11–8 each block that contains a triangle is a circuit present only in a color receiver.

The video signals at the output of the tuner have a wide bandpass (about 4.2 MHz for the video); hence, a wide bandpass is also necessary in the IF amplifier stages. As shown, the output from the IF amplifier is applied to individual detectors. The video detector extracts the picture information (plus sync and blanking signals) and applies it to the video

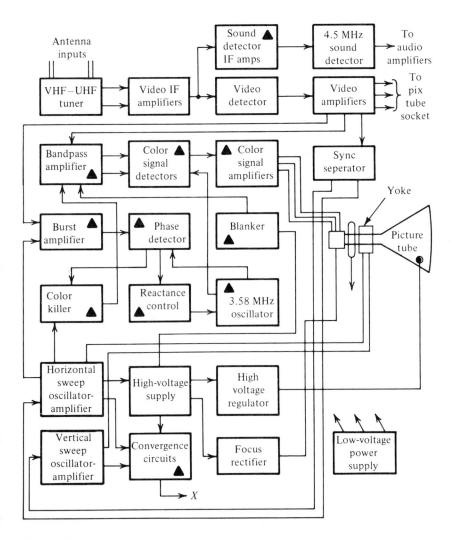

Figure 11–8   Television Receiver

amplifier stages. The sound signals are attenuated so that they do not cause interference on the picture tube screen. For the sound detector, the incoming video and sound signals are heterodyned and produce the final sound IF of 4.5 MHz, the same frequency as in black-and-white receivers. This new IF signal is applied to IF amplifiers and the final sound detector. The resultant demodulated signal is then applied to standard audio amplifiers for loudspeaker drive. Generally, the picture IF is 45.75

MHz in the United States, with a sound IF of 41.25. Since these frequencies are maintained for any station tuned in, the heterodyning of the two always produces 4.5 MHz. (The oscillator circuit in the tuner changes resonant frequencies for each station to maintain the same IF signal.)

For a black-and-white receiver the output from the final video amplifier is applied to either the control grid or the cathode of the picture tube. For the color receiver shown, however, the luminance (Y) signals are applied to the cathode elements and the color signals to grid elements. Additional outputs from the video amplifiers feed the color signal circuits, the color synchronization section (burst), and the sync separator stage. The latter, also found in black-and-white receivers, applies the transmitted synchronizing signals to the horizontal- and vertical-sweep oscillators. The sweep signals are then amplified and applied to the yoke (inductors combined in a single housing and utilized for sweeping the electron beam vertically and horizontally). In addition, the horizontal signals are stepped up in a high-voltage transformer for generating the 25 kV or more needed for the second anode of the picture tube. The high voltage is applied to an inner conductive coating, and the electrostatic field generated increases the velocity of the electron beam. A lower amplitude potential (approximately 5 kV) is utilized for controlling picture-tube focus. Conversion circuits correct improper scanning linearity in three-gun color picture-tube circuitry so that the respective electron beams representing red, blue, and green merge properly for proper color rendition.

The color signals from the video amplifier are applied to a bandpass amplifier and then to color signal demodulators. The I and Q color signals have minus quantities of green in relation to the Y (luminance) signal, and matrix units composed of resistive networks mix the I and Q signals in proper proportions for obtaining the original red, blue, and green video signals. However, since the color subcarrier was suppressed at the transmitter, it is necessary to generate such a carrier in the receiver so that it can be mixed with the color signals to obtain the composite modulated waveform. The color signal detection process can then be accomplished and the color signals (G-Y, B-Y, and R-Y) applied to the individual control grids of the picture tube. The subcarrier oscillator is held in synchronization by a transmitted eight-cycle burst of a 3.58-MHz signal mounted on the horizontal blanking pulse. This burst signal is obtained from the video amplifier and applied to a burst amplifier. It is then utilized in a phase-locked loop (PLL) composed of a phase detector, a reactance control, and the 3.58-MHz oscillator. The

3.58-MHz oscillator is crystal controlled and the frequency is compared to the burst signal in the phase detector. For any deviation of the oscillator frequency, a reactance control compensates for the deviation and corrects the frequency. The color-killer circuit disables the color circuitry during reception of black-and-white transmission to minimize interference if such circuits are left operative (see also Secs. 2–9, 2–10, 2–23 through 2–25, 2–30 through 2–32, 2–45, and 2–46 and Table 7–30).

11–10. CALCULATOR AND COMPUTER SYSTEMS

The vast array of interconnected circuits that can be fabricated into an integrated-circuit chip was a significant breakthrough in the production of hand-held calculators and desk-top computer systems. The versatility of an integrated circuit that permits the structuring of both linear and digital sections has enabled manufacturers to produce calculators having capabilities boardering and overlapping some of those that were formerly attributes of the computer alone. One of the prime capabilities of the computer is its ability to branch to another procedure when necessary. However, some calculators now have such decision-like capabilities, although restricted to terms of storage capacity when compared to a computer. (A decision command involves a statement such as: If the sum exceeds 500, follow procedure A; if the sum is at or below 500, follow procedure B.) The A and B procedures are also spelled out in the commands to the computer.

The basic sections and linkages of a computer system are illustrated in Figure 11–9. The term *peripheral equipment* refers to external adjuncts utilized with a computer, such as input keyboards or tape readers, output printers, or plotters, as well as external storage devices. The central processor unit (CPU) consists of the internal storage system made up of both random-access memory (RAM) and read-only memory (ROM) units. The random-access types are for input and output data flow as needed during computation. The read-only memory system contains specific routines and other information which is permanently stored and utilized as needed, without erasure possibilities by the operator. A control section containing logic gates and routing capability channels the information along specified paths as indicated during initiation of the calculating processes. Logic decoders and encoders convert input data to binary values and convert the latter into decimal or alphanumeric out-

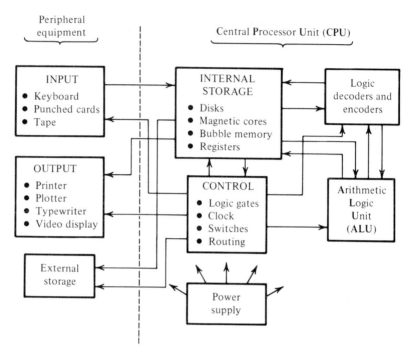

Figure 11–9 Computer Sections and Linkages

puts as needed. An arithmetic logic unit contains registers and logic circuitry that not only perform the basic functions of add, subtract,
multiply, and divide, but in association with ROM units can perform
square roots, cube roots, or other equations selected by the designer.

The more common calculators require that all data be punched in
by pressing appropriate keys in the sequence involved in the arithmetic
process. The more expensive hand-held calculators are capable of reading
a prepared program from card strips inserted as needed. For a computer,
the input data system is much more complex because the set of instructions must spell out in detail the precise steps and procedures required.
The set of instructions that comprise a specific progress of computations
is termed a *program*. Computers generally are of the stored-program
type. Thus, the complete program is entered into the computer's storage
facilities and the computer is instructed to read and execute the program
in sequence. Some computers are general-purpose types, whereas others
may be specifically oriented by their permanently stored routines. Thus,
a mathematically oriented unit has many common equation routines per-

manently stored for recall as needed. A business-oriented computer utilizes data-processing procedures involving bookkeeping practices, inventory control, statistical data listings, and so on. When internal storage is insufficient for retaining all the data required, external units are linked to the computer as needed, such units consisting of floppy disk memory, magnetic tape, or similar devices. The access time of data retrieval is slower than that for internal storage.

Since the logic circuitry of a computer operates in the binary system, programs are encoded into the binary machine language by special units (see Chap. 5). The basic computer-oriented language is one wherein alphabetical abbreviations are used, such as MPY for multiply and DIV for divide. Such usage is sometimes termed *mnemonic* coding (aid to memory) or *symbolic* program language. This coding, in turn, is translated into machine language by an assembler that converts the data into equivalent binary numbers. The conversion is from a *source* code into the binary language (*object* code). Storage locations are addressed by symbolic terms rather than by binary numbers, and the assembly language maintains a one-to-one relationship with the machine language. The term *macro assembly language* applies to a language that utilizes the basic concepts of mnemonic instructions and addresses but permits the inclusion of additional mnemonic instructions.

The term *high-level language* refers to a language designed for convenience of use in a specific area such as business, scientific, or general purpose. Such languages are symbolic types and include COBOL, BASIC, FORTRAN, ALGOL, PL/1, and others. All these terms are acronyms made up by using the first letters or portions of words that describe the system. COBOL, for instance, is derived from *Common Business-Oriented Language*. FORTRAN stems from the phrase *Formula Translator*. PL/1 is derived from *Program Language* 1, and BASIC is obtained from *Beginners' All-Purpose Symbolic Instruction Code*. ALGOL is from the phrase *Algebraic-Oriented Language*. For additional data on these computer languages, see Chap. 12.

The conversion of high-level (source) languages into the binary (object) machine language is more complex than converting assembly language to binary. For high-level languages a program termed a *compiler* performs the conversion process. These high-level languages are convenient because they permit the preparation of a program in mathematical or data-processing sequences similar to the actual calculation or data retriever involved. For each high-level language, however, specific rules and phrases must be utilized for proper programming preparation.

11-11. ELECTRONIC GAMES

Because an integrated-circuit chip can contain thousands of transistors and associated components it has been possible to design numerous electronic games in compact form. Some of these are portable self-contained types utilizing light-emitting diodes or liquid-crystal diode matrix display areas. Storage facilities are provided utilizing read-only memories for game play progression and random-access memories for storing data plus scores as games progress. The portable units contain sound amplification and speaker units, thus providing for audio as well as visual output signals. Some portable games are designed for one or more players and are capable of keeping a running score for each.

The more complex games (such as backgammon and chess) contain sophisticated microprocessors that have the ability to search through game variations and progressions to provide a strong opponent when the computerized game plays against a live adversary. Numerous games are available with a level of play ranging from child to adult. The more sophisticated games utilize random play so that no two games will be played in identical fashion.

A number of games have also been designed for use with television receivers. The screen is utilized to display the game field and the television speaker produces the accompanying sound effects. Many such television games have provisions for plug-in cartridges to extend the number of games that can be played. All such television games utilize the same basic units as shown in block diagram form in Figure 11-10. Here, storage facilities are again provided as mentioned for the portable game. The read-only memories (ROM) have been preprogrammed to contain the rules of the game, the proper progression, and the data displays. The random-access memory (RAM) displays the running score and stores the game progression of the players. All these units are contained within the IC chip as shown, and connections are made to the remote-control units as well as to the required power source (batteries or ac line).

Most television game units provide for a color display when used with a color receiver. They can, however, be played on a black-and-white receiver and would function in an identical fashion except for the lack of color. As shown in Figure 11-10, additional circuits are required, including a VHF modulator plus the associated color and sync generator sections. The output signals from the VHF modulating unit are applied to the antenna input terminal of the television receiver.

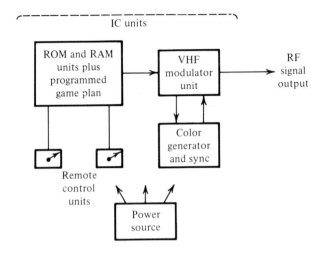

Figure 11–10   Basic Sections of Electronic Game Systems

11–12. SPEECH SYNTHESIS

Many electronic games, language translators (see Sec. 11–13), and some computer peripheral equipment have facilities for speech output. The methodology for speech production differs from that obtained with phonograph records, recorded tape, or other prerecorded devices. Instead, the speech utilized in electronic devices is synthesized and all the circuitry necessary is present within an IC that contains analog-to-digital conversion, storage, synthesizer sections, and signal filter units. Any one of several different procedures can be utilized in the speech synthesis process. Two representative examples are shown in Figure 11–11. In part (A) is shown the circuit sequence for utilizing the stored speech components to synthesize words. Here, consonants and vowels are fed to a microphone. An analog-to-digital converter produces a digitized signal that is pulse-code-modulated, compressed, and stored as more fully described later in this section. When a particular word is to be synthesized the sound combinations needed are retrieved from storage and linked together in series (concatenation) as required. With adequate storage of segments of speech sounds, the proper selection can produce male or female voices and the timbre can be established so that the speech sounds like that of an adult or child.

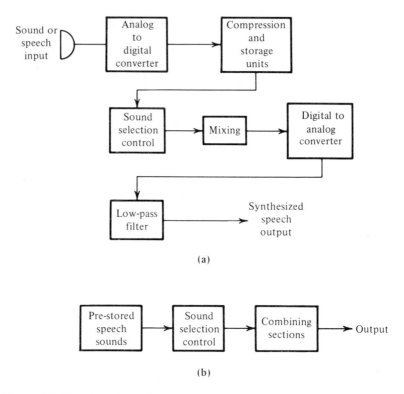

(a)

(b)

Figure 11–11 Speech-Synthesis Systems

Complete phrases or words can be stored as shown in (B) and the appropriate one selected as needed. Although this procedure is simpler than that shown in (A), the storage requirements are much greater because of the numerous words and phrases that must be stored. In contrast, the system in (A) requires a much smaller storage since there are a limited number of vowels and consonants that are needed in speech formation. Although more circuitry is involved, the ability of the IC to contain thousands of solid-state components minimizes the circuit problem. Thus, this system uses pulse-code modulation (see Sec. 8–11). The sound selection control selects the proper vowels or consonants from the storage, mixes them as needed in proper sequence, and reconverts the digital signal to analog. A low-pass filter provides the synthesized speech output.

The compression section shown in Figure 11–11(A) decreases the quantity of data required for digital speech storage and results in the storage of amplitude changes of signal sections that are considerably below the absolute amplitude values. Consequently, the data rate is less than that which prevails for pure pulse-code modulation. This compression, plus pulse-code modulation, is also referred to as *delta* modulation because a fixed step of change (delta) is involved in the sampling of the original speech waveform. The digitized waveform method of speech synthesis samples the waveform at a rate double that of the highest frequency prevailing. The latter is termed the *Nyquist rate* (see Table 12–3).

11–13. SYSTEM MINIATURIZATION

The integrated-circuit chip has been of great value in the miniaturization of many devices, such as calculators, computers, and digital timepieces. Some of the miniaturized games would have been impossible to produce in the size now available without the IC. Another typical example is the hand-held language translator. These units utilize liquid-crystal displays and provide for a miniature keyboard. The word to be translated is punched on the keyboard and the translation appears on the LCD display. The units are usually available with module plug-in capabilities for selection of a particular language to be translated. Some units utilize speech synthesizers (Sec. 11–12) and thus produce a spoken word during the translation process. At the same time, the word is spelled out on the display screen.

In all electronic systems, signals are processed and amplified and finally appear on a screen in alphanumeric form or are converted to synthesized speech. Since the initial process can be done on extremely low amplitude signals, all the initial circuitry can be contained within a single IC. The latter can develop sufficient voltage amplitudes for audible or visual displays, although if a high-volume output is needed, external transistor circuitry is required. Thus, the miniaturization qualities of the IC have been utilized to produce extremely small portable equipment. Typical are the stereo radio and tape players for earphone use only.

The cassette tape players for earphone operation alone accept standard-sized cassettes. Miniature earphones are utilized that provide exceptional tonal characteristics. Powerful magnets are formed by cobalt and rare-earth magnetic elements such as samarium. The latter, combined with precision-mounted thin Mylar diaphrams, produce the full audio spectrum with a minimum of distortion at levels in the earphones that reach maximum tolerable amplitudes. The tape units have many of the features present in the larger models, such as fast forward or reverse, automatic stop, tone and volume controls, and so on. Some units have provisions for recording as well as playback, and many units measure approximately 4 cm $\times$ 10 cm $\times$ 15 cm. The portable stereo radios are smaller units since they do not require the space for the cassettes. Some cassette players have a plug-in module shaped like a cassette but converting the tape player into a stereo radio unit.

Cassette tape players utilize electronic speed control of tape movement instead of a heavy mechanical flywheel, thus reducing space and weight. Circuits within the IC sense variations in tape speed and correct for deviation before it would be noticeable by the listener.

12 Letter Symbols, Acronyms, and Definitions

12-1. INTRODUCTION

In electronic techology, letter symbols are widely used to expedite written or oral descriptions and discussions of circuits and systems. It is, of course, much more convenient to use the symbol MOSFET than to refer to the unit as a *metal-oxide semiconductor field-effect transistor.* Similarly, the letter symbol EAROM is certainly preferable to the phrase *electrically alterable read-only memory.* Since, however, there are so many such alphabetical symbols, as well as alphanumerical types (such as I^2L), it becomes difficult to recall the definitions of each encountered unless we have a constant working familiarity with them. Thus, the lists in Tables 12-1 and 12-2 contain the most common types currently in use at the time of publication of this text.

Acronyms, which are essentially also alphabetical or alphanumerical symbols, differ from the common letter symbols because the chosen letters form a word. Thus, COBOL is derived from the initial letters of each word in the phrase *common business-oriented language* and refers to one of the several high-level computer languages used for data entry. Similarly, the acronym BASIC is derived from the first letters of the phrase *beginners' all-purpose symbolic instruction code.* Some of the memory designations of electronic computers can be considered as acronyms, since their constant usage in speech can be considered as expressing a word, such as EARPROM for electrical erasable programmable read-only memory, and FET for field-effect transistor, and so on. Hence, such acronyms are found in Tables 12-1 and 12-4.

TABLE 12–1. Miscellaneous Letter Symbols and Abbreviations

α	(alpha) current gain in transistors
A	ampere, amplifications
ac	alternating current
ACC	automatic color control
a-d	analog to digital
ADC	analog to digital converter
AF	audio frequency
AFC	audio frequency control
AGC	automatic gain control
ALU	arithmetic and logic unit
ASR	automated send/receive
ATC	automatic tint control
ATE	automated test equipment
ATM	automatic teller machine
AVC	automatic volume control
β	bel (ratio of powers, voltages, currents), susceptance (beta) feedback voltage, transistor current gain
BCD	binary-coded decimal
BFL	buffered field-effect-transistor logic
BFO	beat-frequency oscillator
BIFET	bipolar field-effect transistor
bit	binary digit
BMC	bubble memory controller
C	capacitance, capacitor
$^\circ$C	degrees Celsius
CAD	computer-aided design
CAM	computer-aided manufacturing (also content-addressable memory)
CCD	charge-coupled device
CCSL	compatible current-sinking logic
CDI	collector-diffusion isolation
CED	capacitance electronic disc (video)
Cerdip	ceramic dual in-line package
cgs	centimeter-gram-second system
C_i	input capacitance
CKT	circuit
CML	current-mode logic
C-MOS	complementary metal-oxide semiconductor
CODEC	coder-decoder
CPU	central processing unit

TABLE 12–1. *continued*

CRO	cathode-ray oscilloscope
CROM	control read-only memory
CRT	cathode-ray tube
CSL	current-steering logic
CTL	complementary transistor logic
CW	continuous wave
d-a	digital to analog
DAC	digital to analog converter
DAD	digital audio disc
dB	decibel (commonly used term; equal to one-tenth of a bel)
DBTR	digital bit-timing recovery
dc	direct current
DCFL	direct-coupled field-effect-transistor logic
DCL	direct-coupled logic
DCTL	direct-coupled transistor logic
DES	data encryption standard
DI	de-ionized water
D_{IN}	data input
DIP	dual in-line package
DMA	direct memory access
DMM	digital multimeter
D-MOS	diffused metal-oxide semiconductor
D_O	data output
DOTS	digital-optical technology system
DSW	direct step-on wafer
dt	change in time
DTL	diode-transistor logic
DUF	diffusion under epitaxial film
DUV	data under voice
EAROM	electrically alterable read-only memory (same as EE-PROM)
EBCDIC	extended binary-coded decimal interchange code
E beam	electron beam
ECD	electrochromic displays
ECL	emitter-coupled logic
ECM	electronic countermeasures
EFL	emitter-follower logic
emf	electromotive force
emi	electromagnetic interference
EMR	electromechanical relay

TABLE 12–1. *continued*

epi	epitaxial
ϵ	(epsilon) natural base log (2.7183)
E-PROM	erasable programmable read-only memory
EE-PROM	electrically erasable programmable read-only memory (also E^2 PROM)
ERP	effective radiated power
ESS	electronic switching system
EXOR	exclusive-or (gate)
F	farad of capacitance
˚F	degrees Fahrenheit
f_{oo}	frequency of infinite attenuation
Famos	floating-gate avalanche-injection metal-oxide semiconductor
f_c	cutoff frequency
fdm	frequency-division multiplex
FET	field-effect transistor
FFT	fast Fourier transform
FIFO	first in, first out
FLOTOX	floating gate tunnel oxide
FM	frequency modulation
FPLA	field-programmable logic array
FPLF	field-programmable logic family
FPLS	field programmable logic switch
F-PROM	field-programmable read-only memory
f_r	resonant frequency
FSA	formater/sense amplifier
G	conductance, giga as in gigahertz (GHz)
g_m	mutual conductance (transconductance) of tubes and field-effect transistors
Ge	germanium
GPIB	general-purpose interface bus
H	henry (magnetizing flux)
HCMOS	high-density complementary metal-oxide semiconductor
HIC	hybrid integrated circuit
HiNIL	high-noise-immunity logic
HMOS	high-performance metal-oxide semiconductor
HTL	high-threshold logic
HV	high voltage
Hz	hertz (frequency in cycles per s)

TABLE 12–1. *continued*

I	current
I_c	capacitive current
i_c	instantaneous capacitive current
IC	integrated circuit
ICD	iridium-crystal display
ICE	in-circuit emulator
ICW	interrupted continuous waves
IEC	infused emitter coupling
IF	intermediate frequency
IGFET	insulated-gate field-effect transistor
IHF	institute of high fidelity
I_L	inductive current
i_L	instantaneous inductive current
I^2L	integrated injection logic
I_m	maximum current
I/O	input/output
I_p	plate current (primary I)
I_R	current through resistance
IR	infrared
i_R	instantaneous resistive current
I_s	secondary current
I_t	total current
j	imaginary-number operator in rectangular notation
J	joule (work, energy, etc.)
JFET	junction field-effect transistor
JI	junction isolation
k	coefficient of coupling, dielectric constant
˚K	degrees Kelvin
kHz	kilohertz (frequency in thousands of cycles per second)
λ	(lambda) wavelength
L	inductance, inductor
LAPUT	light-activated programmable unijunction transistor
LASCR	light-activated silicon controlled rectifier
LC	inductance-capacitance
LCD	liquid-crystal display
LCR	inductance-capacitance-resistance
LDR	light-dependent resistor
LED	light-emitting diode

TABLE 12–1. *continued*

LIC	linear integrated circuit
LIFO	last in, first out
LOCMOS	local-oxidation complementary metal-oxide semiconductor
LPC	linear predictive coding
LSB	least significant bit
LSI	large-scale integration
LS (TTL)	low-power Schottky (transistor-transistor logic)
L_t	total inductance
LVI	low-voltage inverter (logic)
LVR	longitudinal video recorder
m	a constant used in filter design, also milli
M	mutual inductance
M_b	megabit
MBE	molecular-beam epitaxy
MBM	megabit bubble memory
MCU	microprocessor control unit
MCW	modulated continuous wave
MD-MOS	multi-drain metal-oxide semiconductor
MDS	microprocessor development system
mH	millihenry
MHz	megahertz (frequency in millions of cycles per second)
MIS	metal insulator silicon
mks	meter-kilogram-second system
MLA	microprocessor language assembler
MLE	microprocessor language editor
MNOS	metal-nitride-oxide semiconductor
modem	modulator/demodulator
MOS	metal -oxide semiconductor
MOSFET	metal-oxide semiconductor field-effect transistor
MPU	microprocessor unit
MPX (or MUX)	multiplex
MCR	multiple register counter
MSB	most significant bit
MSI	medium-scale integration
MSW	magneto static wave
MTL	merged-transistor logic (same as I^2L)
MUX (or MPX)	multiplex
μ	(mu) micro (as in μF), also amplification factor

TABLE 12–1. *continued*

NDRO	nondestructive readout
NMOS	n-channel metal-oxide semiconductor
N_p	number of turns in primary
NRZ	non-return to zero
NRZI	non-return to zero inverted
N_s	number of turns in secondary
ω	(omega) angular velocity (6.28f)
Ω	(omega) ohms
OCR	optical character recognition
OEM	original-equipment manufacturer
OVD	optical video disc (laser)
π	(pi) 3.1416
p	pico, as in picofarads (pF)
P	power
PAL	programmable-array logic
PAM	pulse amplitude modulation
P_{ap}	apparent power
PAR	program-aid routine
P_{av}	average power
pc	printed circuit
pcb	printed-circuit board
PCM	pulse-code modulation
p^2D-MOS	double polysilicon complementary metal-oxide semiconductor
PDM	pulse duration modulation
P_{eff}	percentage of efficiency
PIA	peripheral interface adapter
PIU	peripheral interface unit
PIV	peak inverse voltage
PLA	programmable logic array
PLL	phase-locked loop
PMOS	p-channel metal-oxide semiconductor
POS	point-of-sale terminal
PPM	pulse position modulation
PRACL	page-replacement algorithm and control logic
PROM	programmable read-only memory
PSK	phase-shift key (modulator)
PSKM	phase-shift keyed modulation
PUT	programmable unijunction transistor

TABLE 12–1. *continued*

Q	charge, quality, coulomb
QTAT	quick turn-around time
R	resistor, resistance
RALU	register (and) arithmetic logic unit
RAM	random-access memory
RCTL	resistor-capacitor-transistor logic
R & D	research and development
RF	radio frequency
RFC	radio-frequency choke
RFI	radio-frequency interference
RIM	read-in mode
R_L	load resistance or load resistor
RMM	read-mostly mode
rms	root mean square
ROM	read-only memory
rpm	revolutions per minute
RTL	resistor-transistor logic
R/W	read/write
SAW	surface-acoustic wave (devices)
SBS	silicon bilateral switch
SCA	subsidiary communications authority
SCR	silicon controlled rectifier
SDFL	Schottky-diode field-effect-transistor logic
SDLC	synchronous data-link control
SHF	super-high frequency
Si	silicon
SIP	single in-line package
SLIC	subscriber-loop interface circuit
S/N	signal-to-noise ratio
SOS	silicon on sapphire
S/R-D	synchro/resolver-to-digital (converter)
SSB	single sideband
SSI	small-scale integration
SSR	solid-state relay
STT	studio-to-transmitter
SUS	silicon unilateral switch
SW	short wave, switch
SWR	standing-wave ratio

TABLE 12–1. *continued*

τ	(tau) time constant
t	time
TDM	time duration (or time division) modulation
THD	total harmonic distortion
T²L	transistor-transistor logic
T-MOS	(see D-MOS)
TRL	transistor-resistor logic
TTL	transistor-transistor logic
TTY	teletypewriter
TV	television
θ	(theta) phase angle
UART	universal asynchronous receiver/transmitter
UHF	ultra high frequency
URCLK	universal receiver clock
USART	universal synchronous/asynchronous receiver/transmitter
USRT	universal synchronous receiver/transmitter
UTCLK	universal transmitter clock
V	volt, voltage
VCO	voltage-controlled oscillator
VCR	video cassette recorder
VDG	video display generator
VHD	video high-density disc
VHF	very high frequency
VHSIC	very high-speed integrated circuit
VLSI	very large-scale integration
V/m	volt per meter (field strength)
V-MOS	V-groove metal-oxide semiconductor
V_p	pinch-off voltage (or V_{po})
VSWR	voltage standing-wave ratio
VTL	variable-threshold logic
VU	volume unit
W	watt, power
WSI	wafer-scale integration
X	reactance
X_c	capacitive reactance
X_L	inductive reactance
XMOS	high-speed metal-oxide semiconductor

TABLE 12–1. *continued*

Y	admittance
Z	impedance
ZIF	zero-insertion force
Z_L	load impedance
Z-MOS	(see D-MOS)
Z_o	characteristic impedance (surge impedance)
Z_p	primary impedance
Z_t	total impedance
Z_s	secondary impedance

TABLE 12–2. Transistor Parameter and Miscellaneous Symbols

Note: Generally, in the following the subscript letters that are capitalized indicate dc or static conditions; for example, h_{FE} and h_{FB}. (On occasion, the first letter may appear as an uppercase one, as H_{FE}. Lower case subscripts refer to ac signal-current ratios (h_{fe}, h_{fb}, etc.).)

h_{fe}	Common emitter	Small-signal forward current transfer ratio
h_{fb}	Common base	
h_{fc}	Common collector	
h_{FE}	Common emitter dc forward-current transfer ratio	
h_{FB}	Common base dc forward-current transfer ratio	
h_{ie}	Common emitter	Small-signal input impedance
h_{ib}	Common base	
h_{ic}	Common collector	
h_{oe}	Common emitter	Output admittance
h_{ob}	Common base	
h_{oc}	Common collector	
h_{re}	Common emitter	Small-signal reverse voltage transfer ratio
h_{rb}	Common base	
h_{rc}	Common collector	
I_c	Collector current (rms)	
i_c	Collector current (instantaneous)	
I_b	Base current (rms)	
i_b	Base current (instantaneous)	
I_e	Emitter current (rms)	
i_e	Emitter current (instantaneous)	
BV	Breakdown voltage	
V_{EB}	Emitter-base voltage	

TABLE 12–2. *continued*

V_{CE}	Collector-emitter voltage
V_{CB}	Collector-base voltage
V_{gs}	Gate-to-source voltage

TABLE 12–3. FET Parameter and Miscellaneous Symbols

V_{DD}	Drain voltage (high)	Most positive voltage applied to unit, such as $+9V$
V_{SS}	Source voltage	Most negative supply potential applied and used as reference for other voltages (generally indicative of ground reference)
V_{IH}	Input voltage (high)	High-logic level range of input V
V_{IL}	Input voltage (low)	Low-logic level range of input V
$V_{IH}(\text{min})$	Minimum input voltage (high)	Minimum permitted input high-logic level
$V_{IL}(\text{max})$	Maximum input voltage (low)	Maximum permitted input low-logic level
V_{OH}	Output voltage (high)	Range of voltages at output terminal with specified output load and given supply potential (Inputs conditioned for high-logic level at output)
V_{OL}	Output voltage (low)	Range of voltages at output terminal with specified output load and a given value of supply potential (Unit inputs are set for low-logic level at output)
I_{IN}	Input current	Current flow into unit at a given input voltage and V_{DD}
I_{OH}	Output current (high)	Drive flow out of unit at given output voltage (logic high) and V_{DD}
I_{OL}	Output current (low)	Drive current flow into unit at given output E (logic low) and V_{DD}

TABLE 12–3. *continued*

I_{DD}	Quiescent value of supply source I	Current flow into drain terminal at given input signal and established V_{DD} values
t_{TLH}	Transition time, low to high	Time between two specified reference points (usually given between 10 and 90 percent) on a waveform change from low to high
t_{THL}	Transition time, high to low	Time between two specified reference points (usually 90 and 10 percent) on a waveform changing from high to low
Y_{is}	Common source	
Y_{ig}	Common gate	Small-signal FET input admittance
Y_{id}	Common drain	
Y_{os}	Common source	
Y_{og}	Common gate	FET output admittance
Y_{od}	Common drain	
Y_{fs}	Common source	
Y_{fg}	Common gate	FET forward-transfer admittance
Y_{fd}	Common drain	
Y_{rs}	Common source	
Y_{rg}	Common gate	FET reverse transfer admittance
Y_{rd}	Common drain	

Some program language titles are *eponyms* rather than acronyms. Eponyms are the names of persons. Thus, the *Pascal* computer programming language is an eponym since it uses the name of the famous French mathematician Blaise Pascal (1623–1662), an early pioneer in mathematical logic.

In addition to the acronyms, Table 12–4 is essentially a listing of common definitions of electronic terms. While complete coverage would entail a dictionary-type text, the definitions contained herein comprise many that need to be referenced on occasion because of their common and wide usage. If more information is needed than that provided by the listings in the tables in this chapter, reference should be made to the index for the exact page number that provides detailed data.

TABLE 12–4. Definitions of Commonly Used Words and Phrases

ADA   A special computer-programming language containing some structured design from the Pascal computer language plus aspects that considerably widen its application possibilities. The word Ada is an eponym for Augusta Ada Byron, who programmed one of the first computers (Charles Babbage's "difference engine").

Addend   A number to be added. In setting one number above the other the addend is usually the upper one.

Admittance   The reciprocal of impedance is admittance (symbol Y). (*See* Sec. 1–12.)

Air Gap   The air space between segments of inductor cores. The gap between special electrodes for the discharge of excessive-amplitude potentials.

ALGOL   An acronym derived from the first letters of the phrase *algebraic-oriented language*. It is a computer-programming process.

Algorithm   In computer operations, the methodology used for setting up a mathematical equation.

Allophone   A variation of a phenome, such as the aspirated *p* of *pill* or the unaspirated *p* of spill.

Amplifier   In electronics, a circuit that increases the amplitude of an input signal. (*See* Chap. 2.)

Amplitude Modulation   The earliest type of modulation system commonly employed for radio broadcasting (public entertainment). It is also used for picture-information broadcasting in television. The carrier signal is modulated by the low-frequency signals so that the composite waveform produced has an amplitude that varies above and below the normal carrier amplitude level at a rate and amplitude change corresponding to the modulating signal.

Analog Meter   A test instrument providing a display by physical movement of an indicator device as opposed to the digital display meters. (*See* Sec. 9–1.)

and **Circuit**   *See* **Coincidence Gate**

Angstrom Unit   In the measurement of a wavelength of light, one angstrom $= 10^{-8}$ cm.

Angular Velocity   A term identifying the expression $2\pi f$ (6.28f). The symbol is ω. (*See* Sec. 1–16.)

Anode   That element of a solid-state diode (or tube) that forms one of the conducting elements. The anode potential must be positive with respect to the cathode element for current conduction.

TABLE 12–4. *continued*

Antiskate A term relating to the balancing out of the lateral force applied to a phonograph needle (and hence the phonograph cartridge and tone arm) as the record grooves apply pressure to the needle during playback. The antiskate assembly is a mechanical arrangement producing a counterforce that is adjustable for the particular tracking force used. Hence the device minimizes skating (sliding) of the needle over the record's surface (assuming the turntable level for width and depth is properly adjusted).

APL Language A computer programming process. APL is derived from the first letters of A Programming Language. Alphanumeric designations and special symbols are utilized.

Apparent Power The electric ac power represented by EI without considering any possible phase difference between voltage and current. (*See* Sec. 1–1.)

Armstrong Oscillator An oscillator utilizing a pick-up inductor coupled from the output resonant circuit to the input terminal of the transistor. The feedback loop forms a continuous energy interchange between output and input systems to sustain oscillations. (*See* Sec. 2–26.)

Assembler A program for translating a mnemonic program into machine (computer) language.

Attenuator A circuit composed of resistors and/or other components for diminishing the amplitude of signals. (*See* Sec. 3–8.)

Augend A number to be added. In setting one number above the other the augend is usually the lower one.

Auto Transformer A transformer having a single coil to which the primary ac is applied and having taps to furnish the secondary potentials.

Automatic Gain Control (AGC) A circuit which obtains a voltage from the detector system for gain control purposes. The signal is filtered to produce a dc level proportional to the amplitude of the incoming RF signal and uses this dc as a corrective bias for the IF amplifier stages. The system minimizes gain variations for stations of different signal strength. If a stronger station is tuned in, the AGC bias reduces the gain of the IF stages and corrects for an increase above the level preset by the viewer.

Automatic Volume Control (AGC) A circuit which obtains a voltage

TABLE 12–4. *continued*

from the detector system for volume-control purposes. The system operates in the same manner as the AGC described above.

Average Value That value of ac obtained when signal alternations are divided into a number of ordinates and the amplitudes averaged out. (*See* Sec. 1–13.)

Back EMF Back electromotive force (counter *emf*) is the potential generated in an inductor during alternating-current flow through it. The back *emf* opposes the source voltage and current change.

Balanced Modulator A symmetrical circuit utilized to modulate a carrier, generate sidebands and suppress the original carrier plus the modulating signal. (*See* Sec. 3–15.)

Bandpass Amplifier A circuit utilized in color television receivers for increasing the signal gain of the color video signals while at the same time preventing passage of synchronization and blanking signals that would cause interference if applied to the picture tube circuitry. (*See* Sec. 2–23.)

Bar Code A code consisting of parallel heavy and light lines of varying spacing representing coded characters that are read by an electronic scanning device.

Bar Generator *See* **Crosshatch Generator**.

Base Terminal That element of a transistor commonly used for signal-input purposes.

BASIC An acronym derived from the first letters of the phrase *beginners' all-purpose symbolic instruction code*. It is a computer-programming language.

Batch Processing The handling in sequence of a number of stored programs in a computer.

Baud The number of times per second that the computer line condition changes. For a line condition representative of 1 or 0 the presence or absence of a bit indicates that the signaling speed in bauds is identical to the bits per second rate.

Beat Frequency The frequency of the signal generated as the result of mixing (heterodyning) two signals of different frequencies.

Bel The unit value representing the difference between two powers, voltages, or currents. One-tenth of a bel is the commonly used expression decibel.

TABLE 12–4. *continued*

Bessel Functions A mathematical process utilized to indicate the number of significant sidebands in FM. (*See* Sec. 7–7.)

Beta (B) Current gain in a common-emitter transistor amplifier.

Bias The potential applied between elements of a semiconductor (or tube) to establish a predetermined operating level.

Binary-coded Decimal A term relating to the method whereby each decimal number is coded in terms of its binary equivalent. (*See* Sec. 5–2.)

Binary Notation The base-2 arithmetic system where only 0 and 1 is utilized. (*See* Sec. 5–1.)

Biquinary A coding system wherein dual groups of binary bits are used to reduce the number of computer counter circuits required for decimal-coded binary. (*See* Sec. 5–7.)

Bit In binary notation a bit is either a 1 or a 0.

Block Oriented Refers to a random-access memory that can be sequentially read out or data inserted in sequential form.

Blocking Oscillator A signal generator of the nonresonant type establishing frequency by circuit resistance and inductance and/or capacitance. (*See* Sec. 2–34.)

Bridge Circuits A circuit utilizing components in a symmetrical formation for measurement purposes or for production of full wave rectification. (*See* Secs. 2–39 and 9–7.)

BSAL An acronym derived from the phrase *block structured assembly language.* It is a computer programming process specifically designed for microprocessors.

Bubble Storage Computer memory device using magnetic bubbles on moving magnetic domains.

Buffer Stage A circuit between amplifier stages for isolation of specific signals or transients.

Burst-Gate Circuit A circuit utilized in color television receivers for gating the 3.58-MHz synchronizing burst signal at time intervals required.

Burst Signal A short-duration signal utilized primarily as a synchronizing signal. In color television an eight-cycle signal having a frequency of 3.58 MHz is utilized to synchronize the subcarrier oscillator of the receiver.

Byte A specific number of digital bits handled as a group in computer data processing. Usually 8 bits comprise one byte or word.

TABLE 12–4. *continued*

C Language A computer programming language designed and formulated by Bell Laboratories. It is a structured language retaining a number of assembly-language features.

Candela The unit of luminous intensity in the International System of Units. (*See* Sec. 7–21.)

Capacitance The quantity of electric charge that can be created in a capacitor for a given applied potential.

Capacitive Reactance The opposition created by a capacitor to the flow of alternating current having a given signal frequency.

Capacitor A device capable of storing an electrostatic charge between two conducting surfaces.

Capture Ratio The term refers to the ability of a receiver's tuner to pull in (*capture*) one station while rejecting another of nearly the same frequency. A 1.5-dB capture ratio rating indicates the tuner will not pass a station signal if it is 1.5 dB lower in signal strength than the one to which the receiver is tuned. (A lower capture ratio dB rating is the preferred.)

Cascade In electronics, the sequential linkages of circuits by coupling the output of one stage to the input of the next.

Cassette A tape cartridge used for recording and playback purposes.

Cathode That element of a solid-state diode which has opposing electrical characteristics to the anode. Also that element within a vacuum or gas tube which emits electrons.

Celsius (Formerly *centigrade*.) A temperature reference related to Fahrenheit by $°C = {}^5/_9 (°F - 32)$.

***cgs* Unit System** An earlier measurement standard known as the centimeter-gram-second system. (*See* Sec. 7–20.)

Characteristic In mathematics, the whole-number portion of the logarithm.

Characteristic Impedance A term referring to the impedance of a transmission line having series inductor and resistive components, plus shunt capacitance. (*See* Sec. 1–14.)

Charge Coupled Device A device that stores minority current carriers in a potentially charged area and transfers such carriers from beneath one electrode area to an area beneath an adjacent electrode.

Chroma Signals The signals utilized in color television systems for conveying the color information.

TABLE 12–4. *continued*

Clamper   A circuit that locks in and holds to a predetermined level the dc component of a signal waveform.

Class A Amplifier   For Class A amplifier operation the bias is such that operation is on the linear portion of the characteristic curve of the transistor. The input signal does not have an amplitude that drives the transistor to cutoff or to saturation. Class A provides for a minimum of harmonic distortion compared to other classes. Conversion of dc power to signal power (efficiency) is relatively low and may range between 10 and 15%.

Class AB_1 Amplifier   This type amplifier has a larger signal-input characteristic than Class A and is used when a higher signal power output is needed. Bias for Class AB_1 is usually set so that the zero-signal idling current permits the input signal to swing the collector (or drain) current to the cutoff point in one direction and to the saturation level in the opposite direction. Class AB_1 has been extensively used in audio-power output amplifiers. Distortion is higher than Class A though it can be minimized by push-pull or complementary-symmetry operation. Efficiency runs between 20 and 35% depending on bias, supply potentials, and transistors used. The subscript 1 denotes that the input signal's amplitude is held to a level below where saturation occurs at one extreme and cutoff at the other.

Class AB_2 Amplifier   For this amplifier classification the input signal has sufficient amplitude to drive the transistors output current into the cutoff as well as the saturation region. Though output power and efficiency are superior to the Class AB_1 type, distortion is higher because of operation on the nonlinear portion of the transistor's curve. The high amplitude of the input signal also causes some signal clipping which adds to distortion. Push-pull or complementary-symmetry operation is needed to keep distortion at low levels. Efficiency ranges from 35 to 50% depending on potentials and transistors utilized.

Class B Amplifier   This type amplifier can be used as a single-ended type for either audio or RF signals, though for audio the push-pull or complementary-symmetry systems must be used if distortion is to be kept at a minimum. Bias is set at approximately cutoff, though often the projected cutoff point is used. The latter is the point where the linear portion of the curve is projected downward

TABLE 12–4. *continued*

to meet the horizontal line of the graph of characteristic curves. The latter point provides better performance and less distortion than would otherwise be the case. Efficiency is between 60 and 70%. For RF signals the distortion is lower because of the resonant circuitry.

Class C Amplifier The bias for this circuit is set beyond the transistor's cutoff point and collector (or drain) current flows for only a portion of the applied input signal. Since some portions of the input waveform are lost, this amplifier is not suitable for processing audio signals, and is used exclusively for RF signals. With a well-designed Class C stage, efficiency may exceed 90%. The flywheel effect of the resonant circuit reestablishes the pure sinewave signal even though an input sinewave signal undergoes clipping.

Class D Amplifier This amplifier system is a special high-efficiency type employing pulses in modulated form. For pulse modulating purposes, several systems may be utilized and typical is the case where pulses are given amplitude changes corresponding to the amplitude changes of the modulating signal. For audio such type amplification achieves a high degree of efficiency and signals can be driven into higher peak-current amplitudes than is possible with amplifiers of the Class A, AB and B varieties. (*See* Sec. 8–9.)

Clipper A circuit that eliminates peak portions of signal waveforms for purposes of amplitude reduction, overshoot elimination, or suppression of noise and transients. (*See* Secs. 3–4 and 3–5.)

Clock Pulses In digital systems the precisely-timed pulse signals generated by the fundamental signal source. (*See* Sec. 6–17.)

COBOL An acronym derived from the first letters of the phrase *common business oriented language.* It is a computer-programming method.

CODEC This word is derived from coder-decoder. A typical example is a device for converting analog signals to digital data.

Coefficient of Coupling (k) A term relating to the percentage of coil interaction when inductors are coupled. (*See* Sec. 1–3.)

Coincidence Gate A digital logic circuit necessitating input-signal coincidence to obtain an output. (*See* Sec. 6–3.)

Collector Terminal That terminal of a bipolar junction transistor that often forms part of the output circuit.

Cologarithm The logarithm of the reciprocal of a given number.

TABLE 12–4. *continued*

Colpitts Oscillator An oscillator wherein the resonant circuit capacitance is formed by dual capacitors having a common stator shaft placed at signal ground. Thus, the resonant circuit is effectively split into two sections that couple output signals back to the input for sustained oscillations. (*See* Sec. 2–28.)

Combining Circuits A circuit for inserting at precise time intervals a new group of signals within a given signal train. (*See* Sec. 3–14.)

Common Base Circuit A circuit wherein the base terminal of the transistor is placed at signal ground. The input signal is applied between the emitter and base and the output obtained from the collector section. There is no phase reversal between input and output signals. Another term for this system is the *grounded base* circuit.

Common Collector Circuit A circuit wherein the collector terminal of the transistor is placed at signal ground. The input signal is applied between base and emitter. The output signal is obtained from across the emitter resistor. This circuit is also known as the *emitter-follower* circuit because the output phase of the signal *follows* that of the input signal.

Common-Drain Circuit A circuit wherein the drain terminal of a transistor is placed at signal ground. The input signal is applied between gate and source terminals. The output signal is obtained from across the source resistor. This circuit is also known as the *source follower* circuit because the output phase of the signal *follows* that of the input signal.

Common-Emitter Circuit A circuit wherein the emitter terminal of the transistor is placed at signal ground. The input signal is applied between base and emitter and the output obtained from the collector section. There is a 180° phase reversal between input and output signals. Another term for this system is the *grounded emitter* circuit.

Common-Gate Circuit A circuit wherein the gate terminal of an FET is placed at signal ground. The input signal is applied between the source and gate terminals and the output obtained from the drain section. There is no phase reversal between input and output signals. Another term for this system is the *grounded gate* circuit.

Common-Source Circuit A circuit wherein the source terminal of an FET is placed at signal ground. The input signal is applied be-

TABLE 12–4. *continued*

tween gate and source and the output obtained from the drain section. There is a 180° phase reversal between input and output signals. Another term for this system is the *grounded source* circuit.

Compander An electronic circuit that compresses the dynamic audio range to accommodate the extremes of loud and soft audio within a given medium. (*See also* **Expander.**)

Compiler A program designed to translate a high-level computer programming language into machine (computer) language.

Complement Number In digital logic systems the complement is an inverse representation such as binary 0101 for 1010, or in the decimal system 3194 for 6805. For the latter the representation is in nine's complement, while the former is one's complement.

Complementary-symmetry A term usually applied to an audio amplifier utilizing complementary transistors (*npn* and *pnp*) in a symmetrical circuit for increasing audio power output and reducing signal distortion.

Compliance The inherent mobility of a phonograph needle and cartridge assembly during record playback. Compliance is the ability of a phonograph needle to *comply* with the variations within the record grooves that produce the sound. Greater compliance provides for improved reproduction of a broad frequency span of signals. A cartridge rating of 35×10^{-6} represents excellent compliance and is somewhat superior to another having a rating of 15×10^{-6}.

Compression In audio the limiting of amplitude excursions of soft and loud sounds. In speech synthesis the process of compacting a group of signals into a shorter time span.

Concatenation In speech synthesis, the linking or connecting in series of certain sounds.

Conductance The symbol G is used for conductance. The latter is the reciprocal of resistance. (*See* Sec. 1–12.)

Conductivity The ability of a conductor to pass current.

Contact Potential A term identifying the voltage established by placing into contact two dissimilar metals.

Continuous Wave The term applied to a continuous-amplitude unmodulated RF waveform. The term is also applied to the transmission of such a signal in Morse code form.

Control Grid That element in a gas or vacuum tube to which the input signal is usually applied. The grid is adjacent to the cathode and

TABLE 12–4. *continued*

the amplitude and polarity of the potential applied to the grid controls electron flow.

Cosine   In a right triangle the ratio of the adjacent side over the hypotenuse.

Coulomb   The unit for the quantity of electric charge. It represents that quantity of electrons representing one ampere of current flow past a given point in one second.

Coupling   The linkage formed between circuits or systems.

Critical Coupling   In resonant circuits, that degree of coupling producing the maximum peak of energy transfer at the resonant frequency of the applied signal.

Cross Neutralization   The type of neutralization typical in dual-transistor push-pull RF amplifiers that couples a portion of the output signal of each transistor to the input circuit of the other.

Crosshatch Generator   A signal generator producing vertical and horizontal display lines on a television screen for test purposes. (*See* Sec. 9–11.)

Crossover Frequency   That frequency, in a multiple-speaker audio system, where equal signal amplitude prevails at both the high- and low-frequency sections.

Crystal Oscillator   An oscillator having a quartz crystal as part of the frequency-determining circuit for improved operating stability. (*See* Sec. 2–29.)

Current Feedback   A system where the feedback signal voltage is proportional to the amount of signal current.

Cutoff Frequency   The signal frequency in a special circuit or filter beyond which point all signals are abruptly diminished or eliminated in amplitude.

CW Transmission   The type of transmission known as *continuous wave* consisting of short and long duration signals having a continuous and constant amplitude and unmodulated by audio tones. (*See* Sec. 8–7.)

Cycle   Any two successive signal alternations (of opposing polarity) in alternating current.

Damping Factor   A term relating to the ability of an amplifier-speaker assembly to suppress in rapid fashion the cone motion once the actuating signal has dropped to zero. A factor of 45 is superior to a lower value such as 20. A high damping factor reduces the sound

TABLE 12–4. *continued*

hangover (wherein tones tend to fade out slowly or *hang* over beyond the cessation point of the initiating signal).

Darlington Amplifier   A dual-transistor assembly with an emitter follower circuit of the first transistor feeding the base input of the second. It features exceptionally high gain and has an impedance stepdown characteristic. It is an efficient driver with low supply potentials. (*See* Sec. 2–20.)

dc Amplifier   Direct-current amplifier.

De Morgan's Theorem   The duality condition established by the negation of some logic expressions. (*See* Sec. 6–11.)

Decibel (dB)   The decibel is a unit of difference in levels of electronic quantities. It is not a unit of measurement but rather compares high and low levels of power, voltage, or current. The unit *bel* is not used. Instead, one-tenth of a bel, the *decibel* is commonly used. (*See* Secs. 1–7 and 7–1.)

Decoupling Circuit   A network usually composed of a resistor and capacitor combination placed in a voltage feed line to isolate signal components from the power supply. By preventing the power supply from acting as a common coupler, interaction among stages is avoided and undue signal attenuation or regeneration is avoided. The decoupling network provides a short return path for signal energy back to the transistor. (*See* Sec. 2–8.)

De-emphasis   In public entertainment FM radio reception the reduction of the excessive levels of high-frequency signals created at the transmitter during *pre-emphasis*. The system raises the signal to noise ratio. (*See* Sec. 3–9.)

Degeneration   The attenuation of signal amplitude caused by inverse feedback or other signal-diminishing factors.

Delay System   A circuit used for delaying a signal for a specific time interval compared to its normal mode. (*See* Sec. 3–13.)

Demodulator   A circuit for extracting the original modulating signal from the composite modulated carrier. (*See* Secs. 2–42 to 2–45.)

Denominator   The quantity below the division line of a fraction, hence that quantity by which the numerator is divided.

Detector   *See* **Demodulator**.

Deviation Ratio   In frequency modulation the ratio of the maximum frequency deviation of the carrier to the highest frequency of modulation signal. (*See* Sec. 8–4.)

TABLE 12–4. *continued*

Diac A dual diode unit used for power switching. Conduction occurs when a predetermined voltage amplitude is reached, and either ac or dc can be gated. (*See* Sec. 2–41.)

Dielectric Constant (k) A reference of the characteristics of dielectric material referenced in relation to air which has a k of 1, and all other material having a higher constant. (*See* Table 7–12.)

Difference Frequency A signal obtained during the heterodyning of two signals wherein the new signal has a frequency equal to the difference between the two original signals.

Differential Amplifier A dual-transistor direct-coupled circuitry section with a common emitter system. The differential amplifier has an excellent signal bandpass, exceptional circuit stability, and a wide range of application possibilities. It utilizes no capacitors or inductors and is useful in forming amplifiers, mixers, limiters, modulators, and signal frequency multipliers. (*See* Sec. 2–22).

Differentiation In electronics, the signal-modification circuit composed of a series capacitor and a shunt resistor having a short time constant in relation to the duration of input-pulse signals. The differentiator circuit attenuates to a greater degree progressively lower-frequency components. (*See* Sec. 3–2.)

Diffusion In IC fabrication a process utilizing high temperatures and a shifting of specific densities of n-type or p-type impurity atoms into the silicon slab for establishing specific electrical characteristics.

DIN Dual input.

Direct Coupling The linkage of two circuits or systems without intervening series components such as capacitors, inductors, or resistors.

Discharge Circuit A circuit utilizing the charge and discharge characteristics of a capacitor to form a sawtooth signal. There is a slow rise time compared to the abrupt decline of the amplitude. (*See* Sec. 3–6.)

Discriminator *See* **Phase Discriminator**.

Distributed Capacitance That capacitance created between the turns and layers of wire in an inductor.

Dolby System A patented noise-reduction system widely used in public-entertainment electronic devices. It employs a dual process: the increase in level in a group of high frequency signals during record-

TABLE 12–4. *continued*

ing (or transmission) and reversing the process during reception by a matching decoder. (*See* Sec. 3–9.)

Drain Terminal   The element (of a field-effect transistor) often utilized for the output section of the circuit.

Dyne   The unit of force in the centimeter-gram-second (*cgs*) system (*see* Sec. 7–20). Dyne is that force required to produce, in a 1-gram weight mass, an acceleration of 1 centimeter per second for every second that the force is present.

Edison Effect   The production of current flow between two vacuum-tube elements. Electronics from a heated cathode of negative potential, are attracted and flow to a positive-potential anode structure.

Effective Value   That value of ac capable of performing the same work as an identical dc value. The effective value is ascertained by squaring instantaneous value, adding the latter, and finding the average. The square root of the latter is the effective value. (*See* Sec. 1–13.)

Electret   A device made up of a material that retains an electric charge permanently.

Electron Gun   A term applied to the cylindrical electrode assembly that forms and focuses the electron beam within a cathode-ray tube.

Emitter-Follower Circuit   *See* **Common-Collector Circuit.**

Emitter Terminal   One of the electrodes of the bipolar junction transistor often used in conjunction with the collector for the output system.

Encoder Disc   A device used for the conversion of an analog function into a digital representation. (*See* Sec. 5–11.)

Epitaxial   In IC technology a multilayer structure.

Error-detection Codes   Special codes so designed that they identify errors in digital systems. (*See* Sec. 5–9.)

Etching   A term used in the fabrication of integrated circuits that involves applications of gas plasmas or acids to etch away undesired materials from the surface of a semiconductor wafer.

Even-parity Code   An error detecting code wherein all digits in the binary representation (including the parity digit) produce an even number of 1's. (*See* Sec. 5–9.)

Excess-Three Code   A mathematical system wherein each number is

TABLE 12–4. *continued*

raised in value by three in relation to the decimal equivalent. (*See* Sec. 5–6.)

***Exclusive-or* Gate**   A logic circuit such as one that produces an output for an A or B input but no output when both A and B inputs prevail. (*See* Sec. 6–12.)

Expander   An electronic circuit that expands to the normal level the dynamic audio range that had been compressed by a compander.

Exponent   A number, letter, or other symbol placed at the upper right of a number, letter, etc. to indicate the number of times the number (or symbol) is to be taken as a factor.

Fahrenheit   A temperature measurement related to Celsius by $°F = (\frac{9}{5} \times °C) + 32$.

Farad   The unit of capacitance. (In practical electronics only fractional values are utilized.)

FDM Transmission   A term relating to frequency-division multiplexing wherein several bands are used for the transmission of differing modulations. (*See* Sec. 8–12.)

Ferrite   A brittle compound of ferromagnetic materials used for high-Q core materials for inductors.

Ferro-Magnetic Materials   Those magnetic materials having a high degree of permeability.

Fiber Optics   The system of using special light-wave carrying fibers for the propagation of data.

Field-effect Transistor   A transistor formed by the metal-oxide semiconductor process.

Fifty-dB Quieting   A term referring to the standard generally accepted for indicating the degree of noise suppression necessary for high-fidelity performance. Stereo reception requires more signal strength than mono to achieve 50-dB quieting.

Filament   In a gas or vacuum tube that electrode which is heated to produce electron emission directly, or indirectly by heating a separate cathode. (The filament is also termed a *heater*.)

Flip-flop Circuit   A symmetrical circuit that produces an output signal only when its bistable state is changed by an input signal. (*See* Sec. 6–15.)

Floating-Gate Transistor   A transistor designed primarily for computer-storage systems.

TABLE 12–4. *continued*

Floppy Disc A flexible circular disc similar to phonograph records used for data storage in computer systems. A disc slightly larger than five inches can store well over 100 k-bytes of data.

Flywheel Effect A term describing the continuous interchange of electric energy between the storage capabilities of a capacitor and inductor in a parallel-resonant circuit.

Formant In speech synthesis, any one of a group of frequency bands of signal amplitudes that combine to form the particular characteristics of a vocal sound.

FORTH A computer-programming language developed by Forth Inc. It permits the user to customize the system by adding and defining new commands.

FORTRAN An acronym derived from the first letters of the phrase *for*mula *tran*slator. FORTRAN is a computer-programming language.

Forward Bias A bias potential applied to semiconductor elements in such a manner that the bias polarity coincides with that of the *p-n* zones.

Forward-Current Transfer Ratio The ratio of the signal-current gain of a transistor circuit taken between the input and output circuitry. (*See* **Beta**.)

Frequency-Division Multiplexing (FDM) *See* **Telemetry**.

Frequency Modulation The modification of an RF carrier signal by a low-frequency signal to convey information. The frequency of the carrier is shifted above and below its unmodulated or resting frequency at a rate corresponding to the frequency of the modulating signal. The extent of carrier deviation is determined by the amplitude of the modulating signal. (*See* Sec. 8–3.)

Full-wave Power Supply A power supply circuit for converting the alternating line current to direct current by utilizing successive alternations of the ac input. (*See* Sec. 2–36.)

Function Generator An instrument that produces precisely formed signals controlled with respect to frequency and waveshape. (*See* Sec. 9–16.)

Gate Terminal That terminal in a field-effect transistor usually employed in the signal-input circuitry. The term is also applied to switching devices such as the silicon-controlled rectifier and switching diodes.

TABLE 12–4. *continued*

Gating Circuits   Circuits that insert specific signals into an existing signal train, or circuits that switch power at specific intervals. (*See* Secs. 2–41 and 3–14.)

Gauss   The unit of flux density in the *cgs* system of units. (*See* Sec. 7–20.)

Gilbert   The magnetomotive force in the *cgs* system of units. (*See* Sec. 7–20.)

Glitch   An undesired pulse, transient, or other signal in a digital system.

Gray Code   A special code wherein only one digit changes for each numerical value increase. (*See* Sec. 5–5.)

Grounded-Base Circuit   *See* **Common-Base Circuit**.

Grounded Collector   A circuit wherein the collector element of the transistor is placed at signal ground and the output signal is from the emitter element. (*See* also **Emitter-Follower.**)

Grounded Drain   A circuit using a field-effect transistor in which the drain element is placed at signal ground. (*See* **Common-Source Circuit.**)

Grounded-Emitter Circuit   *See* **Common-Emitter Circuit**.

Grounded-Gate Circuit   *See* **Common-Gate Circuit**.

Grounded-Source Circuit   *See* **Common-Source Circuit**.

Half-wave Power Supply   A circuit for converting the alternating line current to direct current by utilizing every other alternation of the ac input. (*See* Sec. 2–35.)

Hall Effect   A term referring to the voltage developed between the edges of a crystal slab (of indium arsenide, for instance) that is subjected to a magnetic field. This voltage develops when current is passed through the crystal structure and the voltage forms at right angles points to the direction of current flow. The developed voltage is proportional to the product of the magnetic field (H) and the current (I).

Hardware   In computer terminology, the peripheral equipment such as readers, storage devices, etc. as distinguished from *software* such as computer programs.

Harmonic Distortion (HD)   Undesired alterations of a given signal during amplification or routing with a resultant poor-quality signal output. Harmonic distortion relates to spurious signals harmonically related to the original signal. Harmonic distortion is given in

TABLE 12–4. *continued*

percentage related to the total signal amplitude. Such distortion ratings may be given as a percentage for several signal frequencies, or for the total frequency span of the receiver or amplifier. A typical example is 0.2 percent for 20 Hz to 20 kHz. *See also* **Intermodulation Distortion.**

Hartley Oscillator An oscillator wherein the resonant-circuit inductor has a center tap to ground that effectively splits the resonant circuit into two sections. The dual sections couple output signals back to the input for sustained oscillations. (*See* Sec. 2–27.)

Henry The unit of inductance in the International System of Units. (*See* Sec. 7–21.)

Hertz (Hz) A word designating the number of cycles per second in electricity and electronics.

Heterodyne The electronic mixing of two signals having different frequencies in a non-linear circuit. The process produces a third signal having a frequency equaling the difference between the original signals. The new signal is termed the intermediate-frequency (IF) signal.

Hexadecimal Notation A system in arithmetic using base-16 notation. (*See* Sec. 5–3.)

High Fidelity An audio amplifying or processing system that has an output response extending from approximately 20 MHz to 20 kHz, with negligible harmonic distortion.

Hole Flow Current carriers in semiconductor devices. In solid-state electronics, hole flow occurs below the conduction band of the atom and the direction of flow is opposite to that of electron flow.

Hypotenuse The side opposite the right angle in a right triangle.

Hysteresis In magnetic materials the characteristic of the flux density lagging the magnetizing force.

I and Q Signals Two color signal components obtained (in color transmitting circuitry) for eliminating one signal of the red, blue, and green signals needed for color. In addition, the color subcarrier is also suppressed to conserve spectrum space. (*See* Secs. 2–45 and 2–46.)

ICW Transmission The type of transmission known as *interrupted continuous waves* consisting of an amplitude-modulated carrier that is broken up into Morse-code segments. (*See* Sec. 8–7.)

IHF Sensitivity A term referring to the characteristics of a radio re-

---

TABLE 12–4. *continued*

---

ceiver's tuner. The sensitivity indicates the μV required at the tuner's input to obtain an output signal having less than 3 percent distortion and noise. (IHF refers to the Institute of High Fidelity.) The sensitivity for a stereo tuner is below that of a mono tuner. The lower figure ratings are superior: a 1.8-μV sensitivity is better than a 1.9 μV rating.

Image Rejection The ability of a receiver's tuner to reject image-frequency signals. The latter are produced by the heterodyning of the signal produced by the tuner's oscillator with that of an undesired signal picked up by the tuner. The higher the dB rating the better the rejection characteristics. (A rating of 100 dB is superior to one of 90 dB.)

Impedance This unit has for its symbol Z and is the amount of opposition in ohms offered to ac by a combination of reactance and resistance. (*See* Secs. 1–5 and 1–14.)

Inductive Reactance The opposition created by an inductor to the flow of alternating current having a given signal frequency.

Injection-logic Circuit A circuit using two transistors with complementary characteristics, one of which consists of a multiple-emitter input section. The symbol is I^2L.

Integrated Circuit A term referring to a micro-miniaturized electronic circuit system utilizing a semiconductor chip.

Integration In electronics, a signal-modification circuit composed of a series resistor and a shunt capacitor having a long time constant in relation to the duration of input-pulse signals. The integrator circuit attenuates to a greater degree progressively higher-frequency components. (*See* Sec. 3–1.)

Interface In computer technology, the linking of compatible peripheral equipment.

Intermediate Frequency (IF) *See* **Heterodyne**.

Intermodulation Distortion (IM) This term refers to the type distortion caused by the undesired electronic mixing (heterodyning) of two primary signals. Equipment ratings are given in the percentage of IM in relation to the total signal amplitude. *See also* **Harmonic Distortion**.

Inverse Feedback A feedback circuit which samples a portion of the output signals from a system for transfer back to an earlier stage. The feedback is to a point where fed back signals are out of phase

TABLE 12–4. *continued*

with existing signals. The system increases frequency response and stability while reducing harmonic distortion. Amplification is decreased in proportion to the amplitude of the degenerative signal fed back. (*See* Sec. 2–19.)

Ionosphere Ionized layers above the earth's surface that affect high-frequency communications, both reception and transmission, depending on the density and position of the ionized layers. The original term was *Kennelly-Heaviside* layer.

j **Operator** The lower-case letter *j* is used in electronic math as a substitute for i (imaginary number). The symbol *j* indicates an operator used in rectangular notation. (*See* Sec. 1–11.)

J-K Flip-Flop A bistable logic circuit so named because input lines are designated by the letters J and K. (*See* Sec. 6–16.)

Joule The unit of energy, work, or quantity of heat.

Junction Transistor A transistor formed by combining *n* and *p* zones of semiconductor material.

Kelvin An absolute-temperature scale related to the Celsius scale by °K = °C + 273.

Kilohertz A frequency of 1000 cycles per second (kHz).

Latch A circuit switching mode that locks in a predetermined state.

Limiter *See* **Clipper.**

Linear-predictive Coding A speech synthesis technique for generating the natural resonances of human speech by using established characteristics for determining filter coefficients.

Lisp A computer programming language particularly useful in processing lists of data. Also of value in computer-aided design, and research in artificial intelligence technology of computers.

Lissajous Figures Signal patterns showing phase displacement. (*See* Sec. 9–10.)

Logarithm The exponent to which a base is raised to obtain a number is the logarithm of that number.

Logic Gates Switching circuits that gate signals in or out of other circuits or systems in a logical operational process.

Logical Connective In digital logic systems an arithmetic sign used to identify the type logic. The plus sign identifies an *or* gate (A+B) and a multiplication sign identifies an *and* gate (A·B).

Lumen The unit reference in the International System of Units for the flux of light.

TABLE 12–4. *continued*

Luminance Signals In television systems, the signals that are equivalent to the black-and-white picture information.

Lux The unit of illumination in the International System of Units. (*See* Sec. 7–21.)

Magnetometer A device that produces an output signal when a magnetic field is impressed.

Magnetoresistive Effect This term relates to the Hall-effect device wherein the resistive characteristics are altered by the application of a magnetic field.

Magnetostrictive Effect A term relating to the change in length of certain metals when magnetized.

Mainsail A computer programming language designed for specialized applications such as computer-aided design.

Majority Carriers In semiconductor electronics, the term identifying the primary current-movement process. For a *pnp* transistor the chief current carriers are the electronic hole configurations.

Mantissa In mathematics, the *decimal* fraction portion of a logarithm.

Masking A term used in the fabrication of integrated circuits where glass plates or chrome sections are formed that have circuit patterns involving a single layer of the wafer.

Matrix Circuit A circuit utilizing electronic components for mixing quantities of signals to produce a desired output signal. (*See* Sec. 2–46.)

Maxwell The unit of magnetic flux in the cgs system of units. (*See* Sec. 7–20.)

Minuend A number from which another number is to be subtracted.

***mks* Unit System** An earlier measurement standard known as the meter-kilogram-second system. (*See* Sec. 7–20.)

Mnemonic Coding This term applies to a computer symbolic program language designed as an *aid to memory*, such as DIV for divide, and MPY for multiply.

Modulation Index A term used in frequency modulation that relates to the ratio of the frequency deviation of the carrier to the frequency of the modulating signal. (*See* Sec. 8–4.)

Module A printed-circuit board containing ICs and electronic components that combine to make up a section of a complete system.

Monolithic Comprising a single type or layer in IC technology.

Morse Code A system of identifying numerals and the letters of the al-

TABLE 12–4. *continued*

phabet by assigning combinations of dots and dashes. Used in telegraphy. (*See* Table 7–28.)

Multiplexing   The process of utilizing several bands to transmit two or more modulating signals. In addition to a primary RF carrier, several subcarriers are utilized which, in turn, modulate the primary carrier. (*See* Sec. 8–12.)

Multiplicand   That number which is multiplied by another.

Multivibrator   A signal generator of the non-resonant type establishing frequency by circuit resistance and inductance and/or capacitance. (*See* Sec. 2–33.)

Mutual Conductance   That inductance created when two coils are electromagnetically coupled. One henry of mutual inductance is created when one ampere of ac in the primary coil induces one volt of ac across the secondary coil.

Mutual Inductance (M)   A term relating to the additional inductance produced by the coupling of two or more inductors. (*See* Sec. 1–3.)

***nand* Circuit**   A digital logic circuit that inverts the *and*-logic function. (*See* Sec. 6–8.)

Negated Logic   The logic prevailing when a digital signal is inverted. It is identified by an overbar such as $\overline{A+B+C}$.

Negative Feedback   In amplifiers, the feeding back of an out-of-phase signal to a previous stage to improve performance. (*See* Sec. 2–21.)

Nepers   A term used extensively in Europe relating to comparison of unit values. The neper uses the natural base ϵ (2.7182. . . .) to express the same factors as decibels. There is a constant relationship between decibels and nepers and 1 dB = 0.1151 neper, and 1 neper = 8.686 dB. (*See* Sec. 1–8.)

Neutralization   The process by which a feedback loop is utilized between the input and output of an RF amplifier to minimize oscillatory tendencies. *See also* **Unilateralization**.

Newton   The unit of electric force in the International System of Units. (*See* Sec. 7–21.)

Nibble   The least significant (or the most significant) group of four bits of a byte.

Nonlinear Distortion   A distortion of a signal waveform caused by operation in the circuit's non-linear characteristic curves.

***nor* Circuit**   A digital logic circuit that inverts the *or*-logic function. (*See* Sec. 6–6.)

TABLE 12–4. *continued*

Numerator   The quantity above the division line of a fraction.

Nyquist Interval   The maximum separation in time allocated to evenly spaced instantaneous portions of a signal waveform of a bandwidth designated as W to achieve full analysis of the signal waveform. It is equal to $1/2$ Ws.

Nyquist Rate   Sampling a signal waveform in a time domain twice that of the highest frequency of the signal. Hence for a bandwidth of F cycles the rate measured in code elements is not to exceed $2 F$ (the Nyquist rate).

Octal Notation   A notation wherein a binary number is separated into individual groups of three bits each. (*See* Sec. 5–4.)

Odd-parity Code   An error detecting code wherein all digits in the binary representation (including the parity digit) produce an odd number of 1's. (*See* Sec. 5–9.)

Oersted   The unit of magnetic field intensity in the *cgs* system of units. (*See* Sec. 7–20.)

Off Line   Peripheral computer equipment indirectly used in association with a computer but not directly fed into the central processor. (A keypunch machine is an example.)

Ohm   The unit of electric resistance.

Ohm's Law   A mathematical statement of the relationships of current, voltage, and resistance. ($E = IR$.)

Ohms-per-volt   The ohmic value that a meter multiplier resistor must have to increase the meter scale by one volt. It is a measurement of the meter sensitivity.

On Line   Peripheral equipment feeding data directly into the computer.

Operational Amplifier   A direct-coupled amplifier system utilizing a feedback loop. The system has linear amplifying characteristics, a wide-signal frequency response, low distortion, and a gain possibility of over a million. (*See* Sec. 2–21.)

***or* Circuit**   A digital logic circuit that produces an output for one or more input signals. (*See* Sec. 6–2.)

Oscilloscope   An instrument having a cathode-ray tube for visual display of signals. (*See* Sec. 9–10.)

Pads   *See* **Attenuators.**

PAM Transmission   A term referencing pulse-amplitude modulation wherein the waveform of a pulse train is modified in amplitude, width, or position. (*See* Sec. 8–8.)

TABLE 12–4. *continued*

Pascal A computer programming language. It is an eponym for the French mathematician Blaise Pascal.

PCM Transmission A term relating to pulse-code modulation involving the conversion of amplitude variations of the modulating signal to a group of pulses coded in binary form to represent a specific amplitude. (*See* Sec. 8–11.)

PDM Transmission A term referring to pulse-duration modulation wherein the width of each pulse in a pulse train is gradually changed in relation to the changing amplitude of the modulating signal. (*See* Sec. 8–10.)

Peak Inverse Voltage The maximum voltage amplitude present across rectifier elements at the time such voltage has a polarity opposite to that voltage producing conduction.

Peak-to-peak Value The amplitude of a signal measured from its lowest or most negative peak amplitude to its highest or most positive peak amplitude.

Peak Value A term relating to the maximum amplitude reached by a signal waveform having segments of different amplitude. (*See* Sec. 1–13.)

Peaking Coils Inductors utilized in video or other high-frequency amplifier systems for extending the frequency response range and overcoming the effects of shunt capacitances that tend to diminish high-frequency signal levels. (*See* Sec. 2–9.)

Peltier Effect The temperature change phenomenon that occurs when current is passed through the junction of a *pn* semiconductor.

Peripheral Equipment External devices utilized with a computer, such as printers and keyboards.

Permeability The degree by which a material can carry magnetic flux. Air has a permeability of 1 (unity) and all other materials are rated above 1.

Phase Discriminator A circuit that compares the phase difference between two signals and generates a voltage in proportion to such a difference. The circuit is utilized for frequency-correction purposes. (*See* Sec. 2–31.)

Phase Inversion A change of phase for a given signal. Phase inversion circuitry is utilized to obtain two signals having a 180° phase difference for push-pull operation. (*See* Sec. 2–12.)

Phase-locked Loop A continuous circuit loop wherein the phase of one

TABLE 12–4. *continued*

signal is locked into synchronization with a reference signal. (*See* Sec. 7–30.)

Phasor   In a phasor diagram the angle represents a timing difference as opposed to a directional difference for the vector. (*See* Sec. 1–17.)

Phoneme   The part of a word in speech synthesis that is the smallest unit identifying one word from another. The *s* in the word *sit* is a phoneme in the English language.

Photoconductive   *See* **Photoelectric Effect.**

Photoelectric Effect   The effect of incident light on photosensitive materials such as cesium, germanium and certain semiconductor junctions. A photoconductor device undergoes a resistance change for a change of light intensity. A photovoltaic type generates a potential in proportion to the intensity of the light impinging on it.

Photovoltaic   *See* **Photoelectric Effect.**

Piezoelectric Effect   A term relating to crystal structures used as transducers. These generate a voltage between the crystal plates when placed under physical stress (twisted slightly), or they vibrate at a specific frequency upon the application of electric potentials.

Pilot Subcarrier   The 19-kHz signal utilized in the multiplexing process of stereo FM generation.

PL/1   A computer-programming language combining some of the features of FORTRAN and COBOL. PL/1 indicates *program language* 1.

Planck's Constant   This refers to the constant 6.624×10^{-27} that relates energy to the frequency of the initiating signal. In the equation $E = hf$, the amount of E (radiant energy) produced by a signal frequency f multiplied by Planck's constant (h) expresses the difference between two energy levels. Planck's constant thus relates to such phenomena as lasers, masers, fluorescence, and other aspects of quantum physics involving photons.

Planer Process   The formation of components in an IC on a single plane or surface of the foundation slab.

Plasma Etching   In IC fabrications, an etching process utilizing a cloud of ionized gas. *See also* **Etching.**

PL/M   A microcomputer system programming language based on the PL/1 system. Some ALGOL methodology is also employed.

Polar Notation   A method for indicating impedance and phase angles simultaneously. (*See* Sec. 1–11.)

TABLE 12–4. *continued*

Potential Barrier The internal inherent resistance of a transistor in reference to the potential existing between *n-p* junctions.

Power Factor In alternating current the power factor is expressed as the cosine of the phase angle between current and voltage. The power factor is equal to resistance divided by impedance.

Power Output A term usually used to rate the signal power available from an amplifier. Ratings in rms EIA and IHF have been used in the past (Electronic Industries Association and Institute of High Fidelity).

PPM Transmission A term referring to pulse-position modulation or pulse-time modulation because a change in the modulating signal causes a corresponding change in the pulse position in time. (*See* Sec. 8–9.)

Predistorter A circuit utilized in some frequency-modulation processes. The predistorter alters phase-modulation characteristics to produce frequency modulation. (*See* Sec. 11–2.)

Pre-emphasis In public entertainment FM radio transmission the pre-emphasis of increasingly higher frequency signals for noise reduction purposes. A *de-emphasis* circuit is needed at the receiver. (*See* Sec. 3–9.)

Prosody In speech synthesis the accent or tone of a syllable; the sound modulation or pronounciation of the syllable.

Pulse Amplitude Modulation (PAM) In this system the amplitude of a series of pulses is raised or lowered to coincide with amplitude changes of the modulating signal. (*See* Sec. 8–8.)

Pulse-Code Modulation (PCM) In this system the amplitude variations of a modulating signal are converted to a set of pulses. Each set, in binary form, represents a specific amplitude. (*See also* Sec. 8–11.)

Pulse Duration Modulation (PDM) In this system the width of each pulse is progressively altered to conform to the amplitude of the modulating signal. Because the modulated pulse train has a fixed amplitude, noise signals can be minimized by amplitude limiter circuitry. This system is also known as *pulse-width modulation* (PWM). (*See* Sec. 8–10.)

Pulse Position Modulation (PPM) In this system a change in the pulses' position in time is undertaken for changes in the amplitude in the modulating signal. The time change can relate to the time interval between pulses or to the time a pulse occurs in relation to

---

TABLE 12–4. *continued*

---

a fixed marker pulse position. This system has also been referred to as *pulse-time modulation* (PTM). (*See* Sec. 8–9.)

Pulse-Time Modulation (PTM)   *See* **Pulse-Position Modulation.**

Pulse-Width Modulation (PWM)   *See* **Pulse-Duration Modulation.**

Push-Pull Circuit   A signal-amplifier system utilizing two or more transistors in which the signals appearing at each input group at any instant are 180° out of phase. (*See* Secs. 2–13 and 2–17.)

Quadrature Circuit   A circuit so designed that a signal phase displacement of 90° occurs.

Quiescent Operating Point   The zero-signal current or voltage values in electronic circuit.

Quotient   The number resulting from the division process.

Radian   The length of a radius along the circumference of a circle creates an angle for its arc of 57.3° which is termed a radian. (*Sec* Sec. 1–16.)

Rainbow Generator   A signal generator producing vertical bars of color relating to phase relationships with respect to the color subcarrier of television systems. (*See* Sec. 9–11.)

Raster   A rectangular area on a television screen formed by the horizontal and vertical sweep system. (*See* Sec. 2–25.)

Ratio Detector   A dual-diode detector utilized for the demodulation of FM carriers. Frequency deviations are sensed across a resistive network where the ratio of voltages changes for the frequency deviations of a carrier. (*See* Sec. 2–43.)

Reactance   The opposition in ohms offered to ac by either an inductor or capacitor. (*See* Sec. 1–5.)

Reactance Control Circuit   A circuit simulating either a capacitive or inductive reactance, the value of which is determined by the amplitude of the applied potential. Varactor diodes also perform this function. (*See* Sec. 2–32.)

Real Time   Computer operation wherein the computer calculates data and performs program modifications as required (such as in satellite tracking).

Rectangular Notation   *See j* **Operator.**

Regeneration   Utilizing a portion of an amplified output signal for positive feedback to cause and sustain oscillations. (*See* Sec. 2–44.)

Regulation   A term referring to power supplies and indicating in per-

TABLE 12–4. *continued*

centage the degree by which the voltage varies as the current drain by the load changes. (*See* Sec. 2–35.)

Relaxation Oscillator A non-resonant type oscillator establishing the frequency of the generated signal by resistance and circuit inductance and/or capacitance. (*See* Sec. 2–33.)

Relay A switching unit that is initiated by an applied potential.

Reluctance The degree of opposition present in a material to magnetic flux.

Residual Magnetism The flux density that remains in a material after the applied magnetizing force has been removed.

Resistance The amount of opposition in ohms offered to the flow of either direct or alternating current.

Resonance A condition achieved when an electronic system is tuned to a frequency that causes the inductive reactance (X_L) of the circuit to have an identical ohmic value to circuit capacitive reactance (X_C). This results in cancellation of reactive effects and resistance predominates. Resonance permits tuning to a specific signal frequency. (*See* Secs. 1–6 and 7–8.)

Retentivity The degree of magnetic retention of a material.

Reticle In IC fabrication a chrome plate (or glass emulsion) containing a magnified circuit-pattern image.

Reverse Bias A bias potential applied to semiconductor elements in opposite polarity to the *p-n* zones.

Root-mean-square Value of ac *See* **Effective Value.**

Saturation In a transistor (or tube) the point where current amplitudes level off despite an increase in applied potential. For inductors the point at which the flux density levels off despite an increase in magnetizing force.

Sawtooth A term referring to a signal having a gradual amplitude increase to a predetermined height followed by an abrupt decline. Successive waveforms resemble the teeth of a saw, hence the name. (*See* Sec. 3–6.)

Scalar A term defined as a quantity of length, time, temperature, etc. Exactly specified numerically on an appropriate scale. (*See* Sec. 1–17.)

Schmitt Trigger A monostable multivibrator that has its switching sensitivity related to the amplitude of the input pulse. (*See* Sec. 6–20.)

TABLE 12–4. *continued*

Schottky Diode A special-purpose diode characterized by a low-voltage switching mode and high switching rate.

Seebeck Principle A term relating to the production of a voltage when the junction of dissimilar metal wires (such as constantan and iron) are heated.

Selectivity (*Q*) A word describing the ability of a tuning circuit to reject undesired signals having frequencies higher or lower than the desired signal. Thus, selectivity relates to the bandpass characteristics of an electronic circuit. The higher ratings indicate better selectivity. (*See* Sec. 1–6.)

Series Aiding A term referring to the coupling of inductors where the coil terms are wound in identical directions to increase total inductance. (*See* Sec. 1–3.)

Series Opposing The coupling of inductors that are wound in opposing directions causing the fields of one coil to oppose the other. (*See* Sec. 1–3.)

SI Unit System The modernized version of the metric system, known as the International System of Units. This system is an absolute one, utilizing absolute units for simplicity. (*See* Sec. 7–21.)

Sidebands The signals generated during the modulation process and related to the carrier frequency by the characteristics of the modulating signal. (*See* Secs. 8–2 and 8–4.)

Siemens The unit of conductance in the International System of Units. (*See* Sec. 7–21.)

Signal Generator A circuit containing a free-running oscillator that generates a specific type of signal in electronic systems. (*See* Sec. 9–8.)

Signal-to-Noise Ratio (S/N) The degree to which a receiver raises the signal amplitude of the desired station above the general residual noise level. The higher the S/N ratio the better.

Significant Sidebands In frequency-modulation communication systems the sidebands that have sufficient amplitude to be of consequence during transmission and reception.

Silicon-Controlled Rectifier (SCR) A power-switching diode having a special gate. A gate signal causes conduction which continues even after the gate signal is removed. (*See* Sec. 2–41.)

Silicon-Controlled Switch (SCS) A power-switching diode having two gating terminals for controlling conduction. (*See* Sec. 2–41.)

TABLE 12–4. *continued*

Sine In a right triangle, the ratio of the opposite side over the hypotenuse.

Sinewave A signal having a waveform characterized by a succession of positive and negative alternations, each having the same amplitude as the others, each having a gradual incline and decline, and all having identical widths.

Single-shot Multivibrator A circuit producing an output signal of fixed duration for a wide latitude of input-pulse wave shapes. (*See* Sec. 6–19.)

Single-Sideband (SSB) Modulation A type of transmission wherein one sideband is suppressed to conserve spectrum space and minimize interference. (*See* Sec. 8–2.)

Skin Effect A term relating to the tendency for current to flow on the outer surface (*skin*) of a wire at very high-frequency signal operation. The higher frequency of the signals increases the rate of change of the wire's current and magnetic fields, increasing internal inductive reactance.

SMAL An acronym derived from the phrase *structured macro-assembly language*. It is a computer programming process specifically designed for microprocessors.

Software A term designating computer programs and sub-routines as distinguished from computer *hardware* such as peripheral equipment.

Source-Follower Circuit *See* **Common-Source Circuit.**

Source Terminal One of the elements of a field-effect transistor often used in the output section of a circuit.

Spark Gap A gap of pre-determined width established between a chassis component and ground to discharge an accumulated potential after it reaches a certain level. Television receivers use a number of spark gaps for such voltage-discharge purposes. (*See* Sec. 2–10.)

Speech Synthesizer An electronic device (usually an IC) that produces sounds of speech by combining generated vowel and consonant tones.

Split Stator Variable capacitors having the rotor connected to a common shaft and the stators separated (split) into two or more sections. (*See* Sec. 2–16.)

Squarewave A signal having a waveform with a linear and sharp rise in

TABLE 12–4. *continued*

amplitude and a substantially constant level flat-top peak amplitude.

Standing Waves A term describing the condition that occurs along transmission lines at very high signal frequencies. Under certain conditions (see Sec. 1–14) reflections of the signal energy occur resulting in the formation of loops and nodes of voltage and current at specific places along the line.

Steradian A unit of measure relating to solid angles in the International System of Units. (*See* Sec. 7–21.)

Stereo Separation The ability of a stereo receiver, amplifier, phonograph cartridge, or tape head to minimize the signal spillover between stereo channels. Generally a 20-dB rating provides adequate separation. Manufacturer's specifications are usually based on tests performed using a 1-kHz signal with the rating expressed in decibels (dB). The higher the rating the better the separation.

Stereophonic A sound reproduction system containing two separate channels (feeding two separate loudspeakers) for reproduction of output signals spanning the distance between the two speakers.

Stripping An IC fabrication process employing plasmas or acids for removal of certain wafer coatings after the processing steps of exposure, etching, etc.

Subcarrier A second carrier signal independent of the primary carrier. (*See* Sec. 2–30.)

Substrate An extremely thin wafer (such as silicon) utilized as the foundation slab of an integrated-circuit semiconductor.

Subtrahend That number which is subtracted from another.

Superheterodyne A term usually applied to a television or radio receiver system wherein the incoming carrier signal is heterodyned with the signal produced by an oscillator. (*See* Sec. 2–42.)

Surface-acoustic Wave A piezoelectric device utilized as a filter in television and other superheterodyne receivers.

Surge Impedance *See* **Characteristic Impedance.**

Susceptance The reciprocal of reactance is susceptance (symbol B). The symbol may also be expressed as B_L or B_C to indicate inductive or capacitive susceptance. (*See* Sec. 1–12.)

Sweep Generator An oscillator producing an output signal that is varied in frequency by a specific amount. It is useful for testing fre-

TABLE 12–4. *continued*

quency-modulation systems and for bandpass measurements. (*See* Sec. 9–9.)

Synthesis   The formation of a complete unit by the combination of separate elements.

Tangent   In a right triangle the ratio of the opposite side over the adjacent side.

TDM Transmission   A term referring to time-division multiplexing. This process is capable of transmitting two or more signals by allocating each signal a finite time interval. Instantaneous amplitudes of the signals are sampled and transmitted in a given time sequence. (*See* Sec. 8–12.)

Telemetry   The process wherein several special modulating systems are utilized for the transmission of information. Multiplexing is employed and the system thus permits the transmission of various data (including voice transmission). The system is also known as *frequency-division multiplexing* (FDM). (*See* Sec. 8–12.)

Tesla   The unit of magnetic flux density in the International System of Units. (*See* Sec. 7–21.)

Thermistor   A resistor characterized by having a change of resistance for a temperature change.

Time Constant   When a potential is applied to an inductor or capacitor circuit containing resistance the specific interval of time for voltage or current to attain 63% of maximum is known as the time constant. (*See* Secs. 1–9 and 7–4.)

Time-Duration Multiplexing (TDM)   This is a system capable of transmitting two or more signals by allocating each a finite time interval. Instantaneous amplitudes of the various signals are sampled and transmitted in a time sequence. *See also* **Multiplexing**.

Time Sharing   A computer term designating the use of a single central processor unit by a number of users who employ remote-programming devices such as keyboard-entry units.

Total Harmonic Distortion (THD)   A term referring to the total distortion created by unwanted harmonic signal components within an electronic system. *See also* **Harmonic Distortion**.

Tracking Force   The grams of pressure exerted by a phonograph needle on the record during playback. Decreased tracking force causes less record wear; hence a phonograph needle exerting 1 gram of pres-

TABLE 12–4. *continued*

sure is superior to another having a tracking force of 3 grams. The ability of a phonograph assembly to track at low levels requires a free moving arm and a cartridge having good compliance. An antiskate device would also aid in permitting a low tracking force to be achieved.

Transconductance   The conduction characteristics of a field-effect transistor in relation to the applied signal potentials at the circuit input. (The symbol is g_m.)

Transducer   A device for converting one form of energy to another, such as vibratory to electrical (phonograph pickup), or audible sounds to electric signals (microphone), etc.

Transient   A signal or component of a signal having a fractional duration compared to the primary signal.

Transistor   A solid-state semiconductor having characteristics of amplification, signal generation, and switching.

Triac   A dual-diode switching unit similar to the Diac but having a gate electrode for controlling either ac or dc power switching. (*See* Sec. 2–41.)

Triggered Sweep   A term referring to a special sweep system in oscilloscopes where synchronization is initiated by the input signal. (*See* Sec. 9–10.)

True Power   In ac systems, the product of voltage, current, and the cosine of the angle between current and voltage. *See also* **Apparent Power**.

Tunnel Effect   A term relating to the tunnel diode solid-state unit wherein current carriers have the effect of passing through the potential barrier of the semiconductor material at virtually the speed of light; as though they were *tunneling* beneath the barrier to overcome its transfer-delay characteristics.

Turns Ratio   The ratio of the number of turns of wire in the primary of a transformer in relation to the number of turns in the secondary. (*See* Sec. 1–10.)

Unilateralization   A process by which an external feedback loop is used between the input and output sections of an RF amplifier. The loop is tunable and adjusted for cancelling resistive and reactive coupling that may cause oscillations. *See also* **Neutralization**.

Varactor   A solid-state diode having a capacitive characteristic that can be altered by a change of applied potential.

TABLE 12–4. *continued*

Vector A vector quantity is one having both amplitude and direction and essentially represented by a straight-line segment having motion in a particular direction. (*See* Sec. 1–17.)

Vectorscope An instrument utilizing the oscilloscope principle in conjunction with a rainbow generator for television system test purposes. (*See* Sec. 9–12.)

Velocity A word often used in electronics as a synonym for speed, although actually speed is more accurately defined as the time rate of change of position in a given direction. Velocity is the time rate of motional change of position in a specific direction. (*See* Sec. 7–11.)

Vestigial Sideband The portion of a modulated signal that represents the remnant of an attenuated section, such as when the lower sidebands are suppressed almost fully, but a portion (vestigial section) remains.

Voltage Doubler Circuit A power-supply circuit wherein two series capacitors are charged alternately to the peak rectified potential of the input line ac. The output terminals are connected across the two series capacitors to obtain approximately double the line potential. (*See* Sec. 2–37.)

Voltage Tripler Circuit A power-supply circuit wherein capacitors are charged alternately so that the sum of their charges plus the input potential produces approximately triple the input voltage. (*See* Sec. 2–38.)

Volume Unit (VU) A term used in audio testing. It is a decibel-oriented unit wherein a reference level is indicated. With volume units, the zero level is assumed to equal 0.001 W (1 mW) across 600 Ω of Z.

Wafer-scale Integration Formation of an integrated circuit over the face of a wafer.

Watt The unit of electric power in the International System of Units. (*See* Sec. 7–21.)

Watt Hour One watt of electric power dissipation for one hour. It is the unit of electric energy related to time.

Wavelength The span of a signal waveform related to the distance of the propagated wave in relation to a single cycle with a wave velocity of approximately 300,000,000 meters per second. (One cycle = 300,000,000 m.)

TABLE 12–4. *continued*

Weber The unit of magnetic flux in the International System of Units. (*See* Sec. 7–21.)

White Noise A signal containing several discrete frequencies generated for test purposes in electronic systems.

Wiegand Effect A pulse-generating characteristic imparted to ferromagnetic wires.

Winchester Nickname for rigid disk-memory drives.

Word In computer technology, a group of bits (0 or 1) handled as a specific group.

Wow and Flutter A term designating the percentage of speed variations in phonograph turntables. Usually the designations are such as: *less than* 0.03% or *less than* 0.1%. On occasion the degree of phonograph turntable rumble is also given in dB, such as *rumble better than* −60 *dB*.

Yoke As in television, a multiple inductor arrangement around the neck of the picture tube for providing electromagnetic deflection of the beam both vertically and horizontally.

Zener Diode A solid-state diode characterized by achieving a special breakdown region at a specific reverse-bias potention. The breakdown region is known as the *zener region* and, despite the current increase, the voltage drop across the diode remains virtually the same as before the zener region is reached. Thus, the zener diode is useful in voltage-regulation applications.

Index